THE PARAKEET

Espé

THE PARAKEET

graphic mundi

TEETH

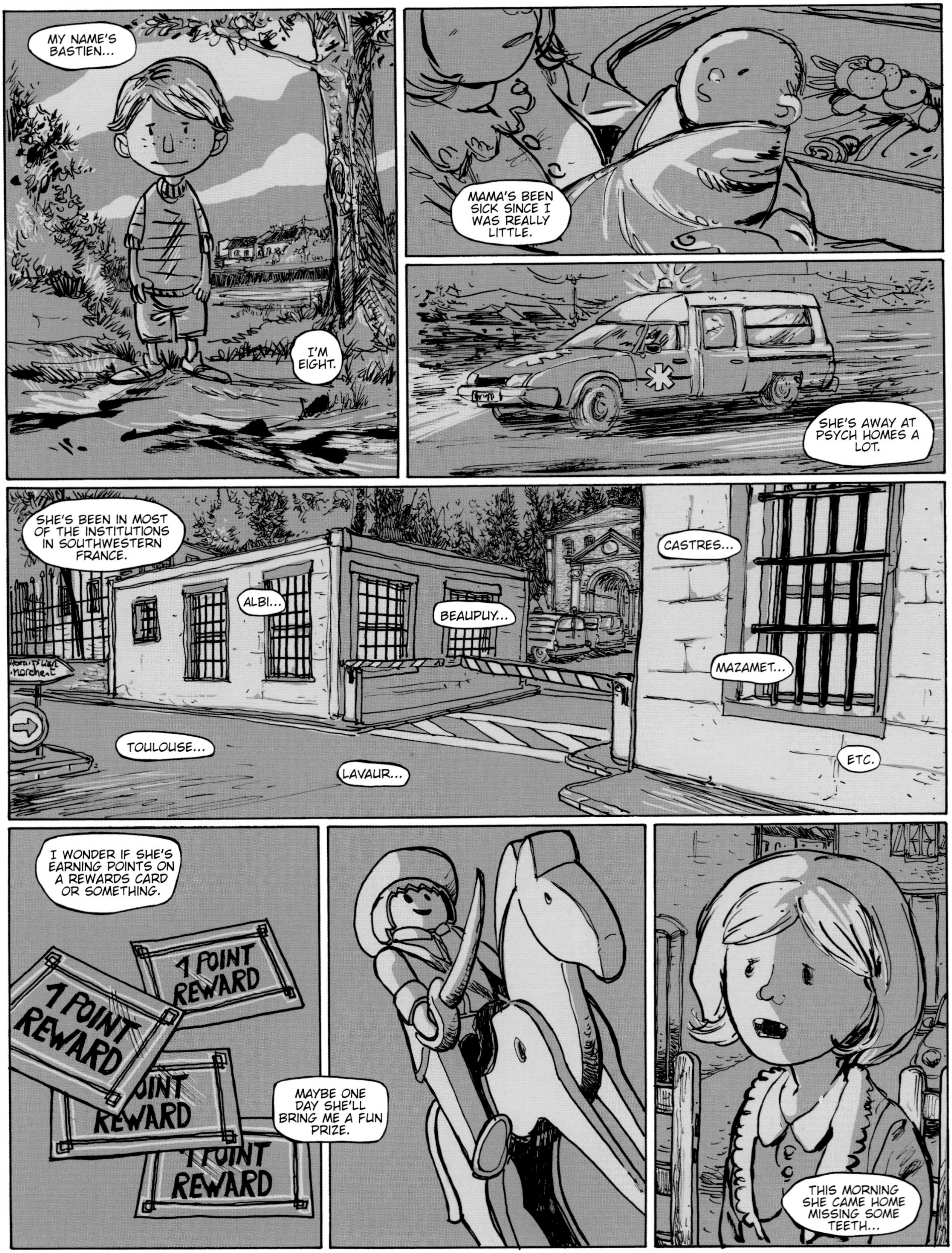
MY NAME'S BASTIEN...
I'M EIGHT.
MAMA'S BEEN SICK SINCE I WAS REALLY LITTLE.
SHE'S AWAY AT PSYCH HOMES A LOT.
SHE'S BEEN IN MOST OF THE INSTITUTIONS IN SOUTHWESTERN FRANCE.
ALBI...
BEAUPUY...
CASTRES...
MAZAMET...
TOULOUSE...
LAVAUR...
ETC.
I WONDER IF SHE'S EARNING POINTS ON A REWARDS CARD OR SOMETHING.
1 POINT REWARD
1 POINT REWARD
POINT REWARD
1 POINT REWARD
MAYBE ONE DAY SHE'LL BRING ME A FUN PRIZE.
THIS MORNING SHE CAME HOME MISSING SOME TEETH...

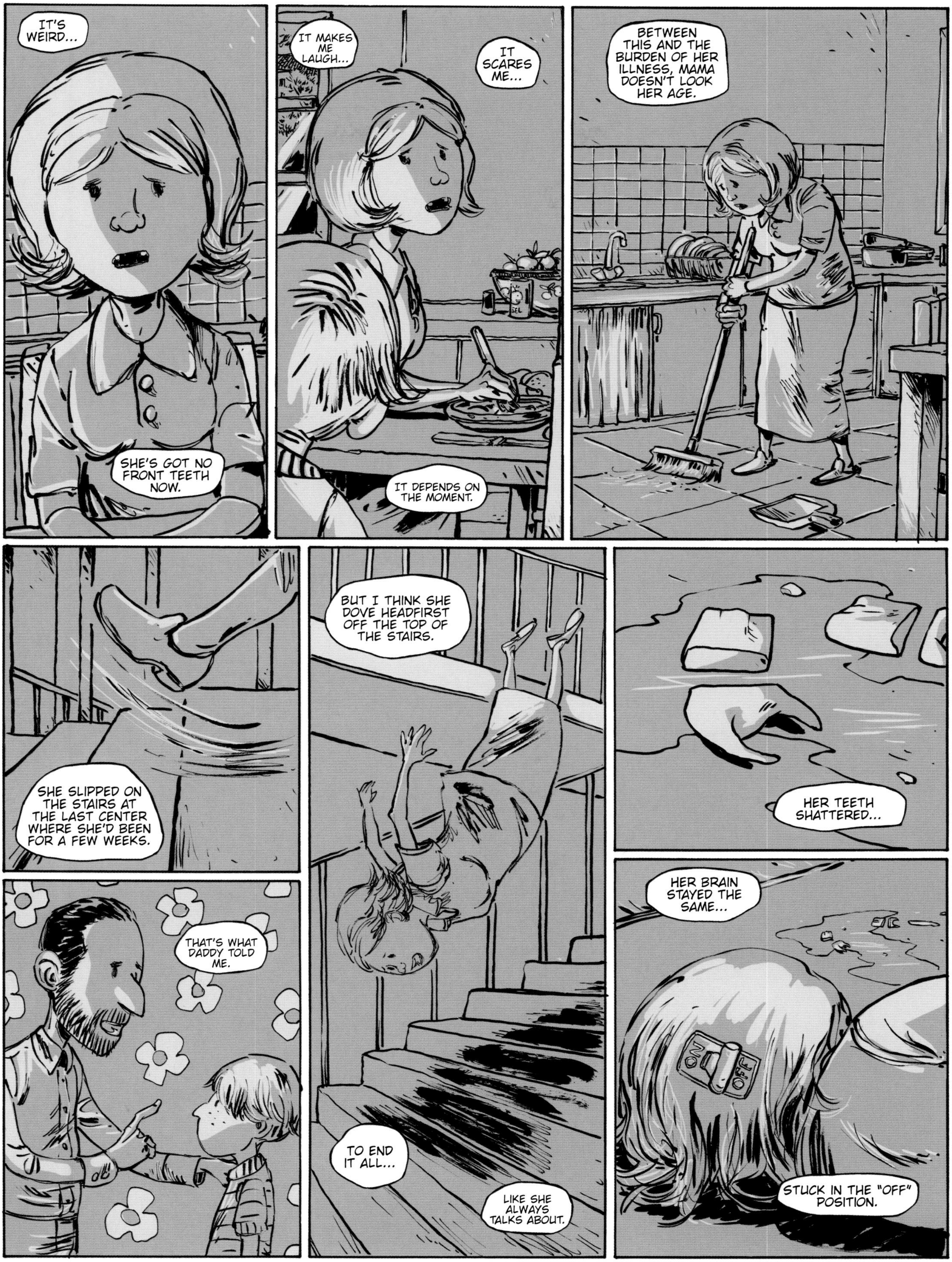
IT'S WEIRD...
SHE'S GOT NO FRONT TEETH NOW.
IT MAKES ME LAUGH...
IT SCARES ME...
IT DEPENDS ON THE MOMENT.
BETWEEN THIS AND THE BURDEN OF HER ILLNESS, MAMA DOESN'T LOOK HER AGE.
SHE SLIPPED ON THE STAIRS AT THE LAST CENTER WHERE SHE'D BEEN FOR A FEW WEEKS.
THAT'S WHAT DADDY TOLD ME.
BUT I THINK SHE DOVE HEADFIRST OFF THE TOP OF THE STAIRS.
TO END IT ALL...
LIKE SHE ALWAYS TALKS ABOUT.
HER TEETH SHATTERED...
HER BRAIN STAYED THE SAME...
ON
OFF
STUCK IN THE "OFF" POSITION.

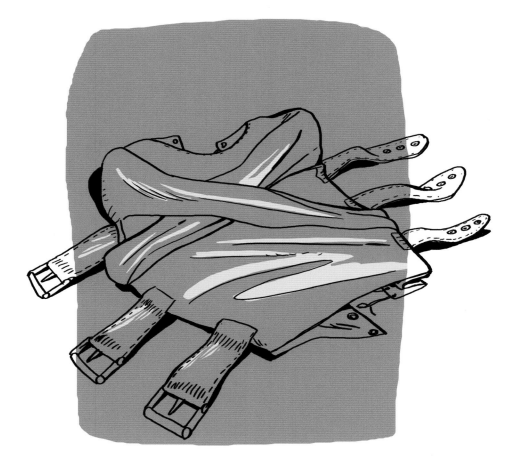

THE SHIRT WITH THE BELTS

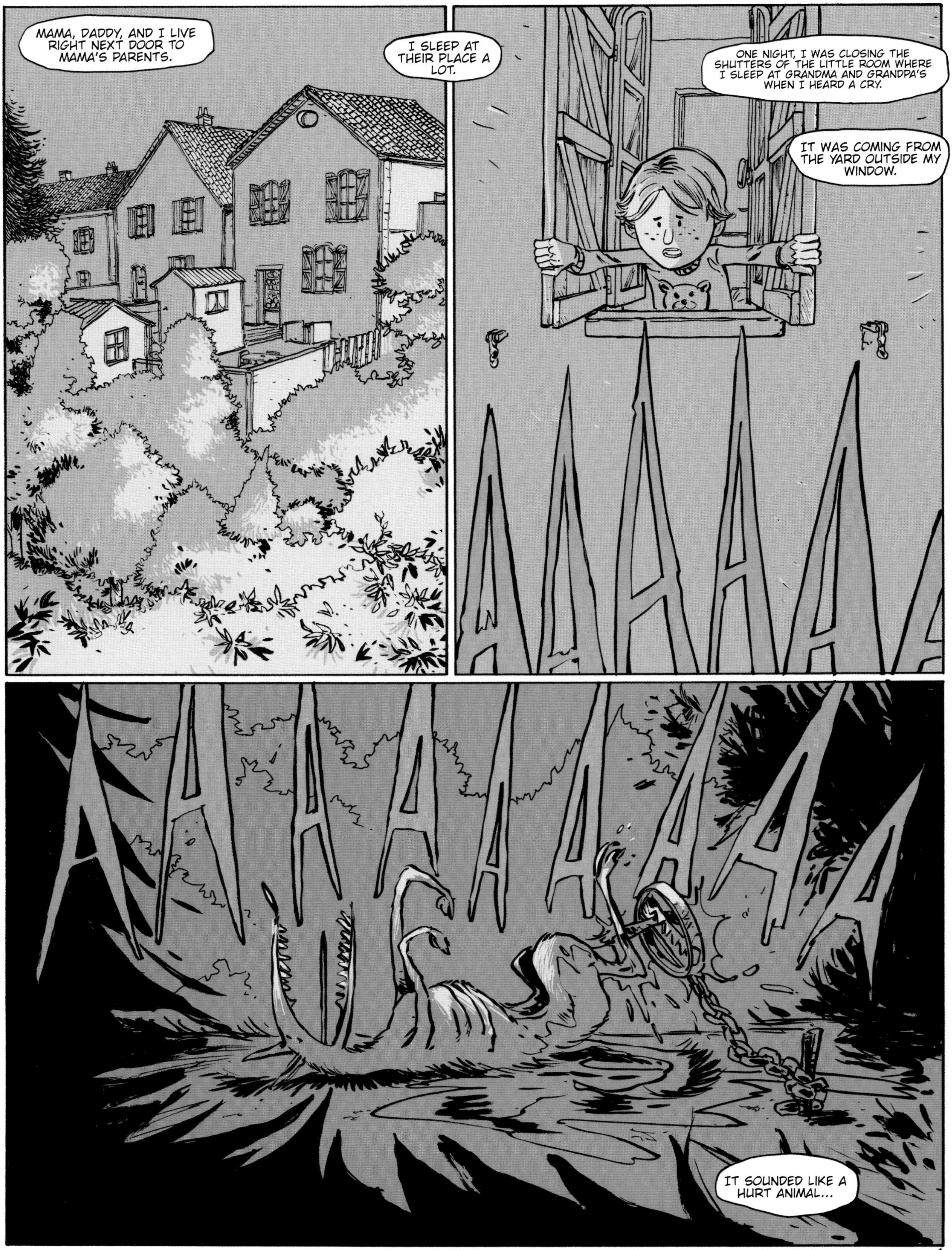
MAMA, DADDY, AND I LIVE RIGHT NEXT DOOR TO MAMA'S PARENTS.
I SLEEP AT THEIR PLACE A LOT.
ONE NIGHT, I WAS CLOSING THE SHUTTERS OF THE LITTLE ROOM WHERE I SLEEP AT GRANDMA AND GRANDPA'S WHEN I HEARD A CRY.
IT WAS COMING FROM THE YARD OUTSIDE MY WINDOW.
AAAAAAA
AAAAAAAAAAA
IT SOUNDED LIKE A HURT ANIMAL...
1.

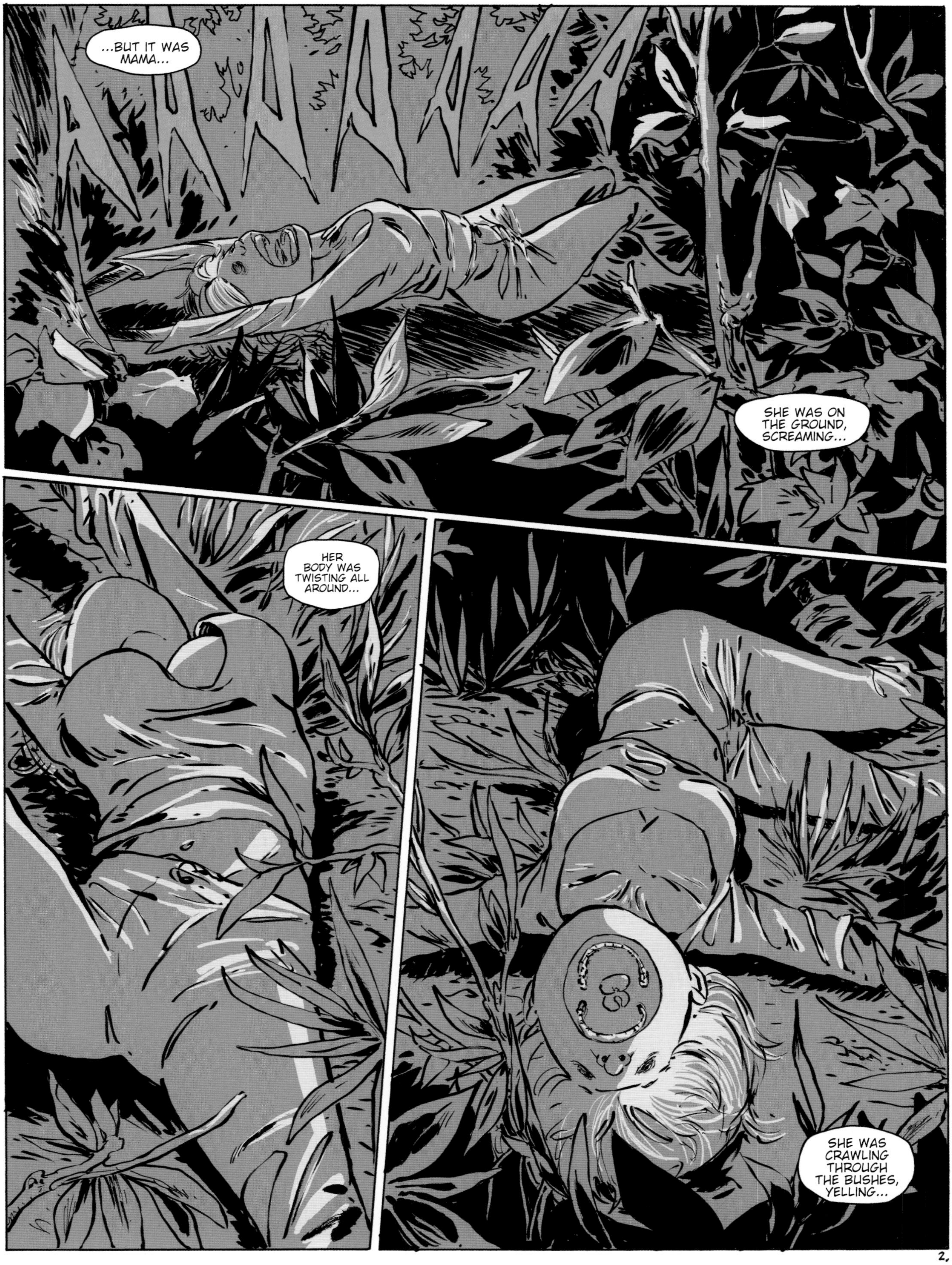
...BUT IT WAS MAMA...
SHE WAS ON THE GROUND, SCREAMING...
HER BODY WAS TWISTING ALL AROUND...
SHE WAS CRAWLING THROUGH THE BUSHES, YELLING...

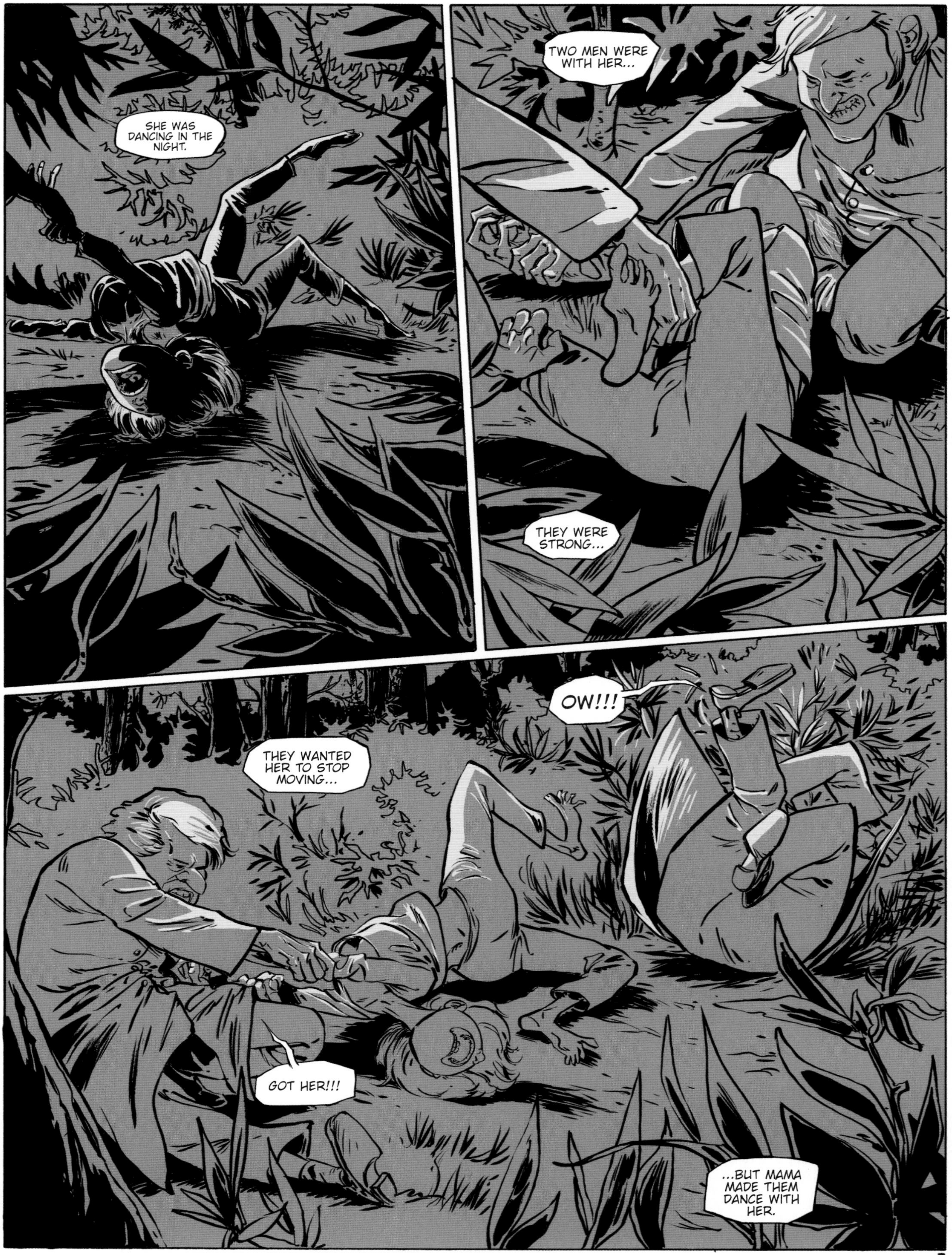
SHE WAS DANCING IN THE NIGHT.
TWO MEN WERE WITH HER...
THEY WERE STRONG...
OW!!!
THEY WANTED HER TO STOP MOVING...
GOT HER!!!
...BUT MAMA MADE THEM DANCE WITH HER.

3.

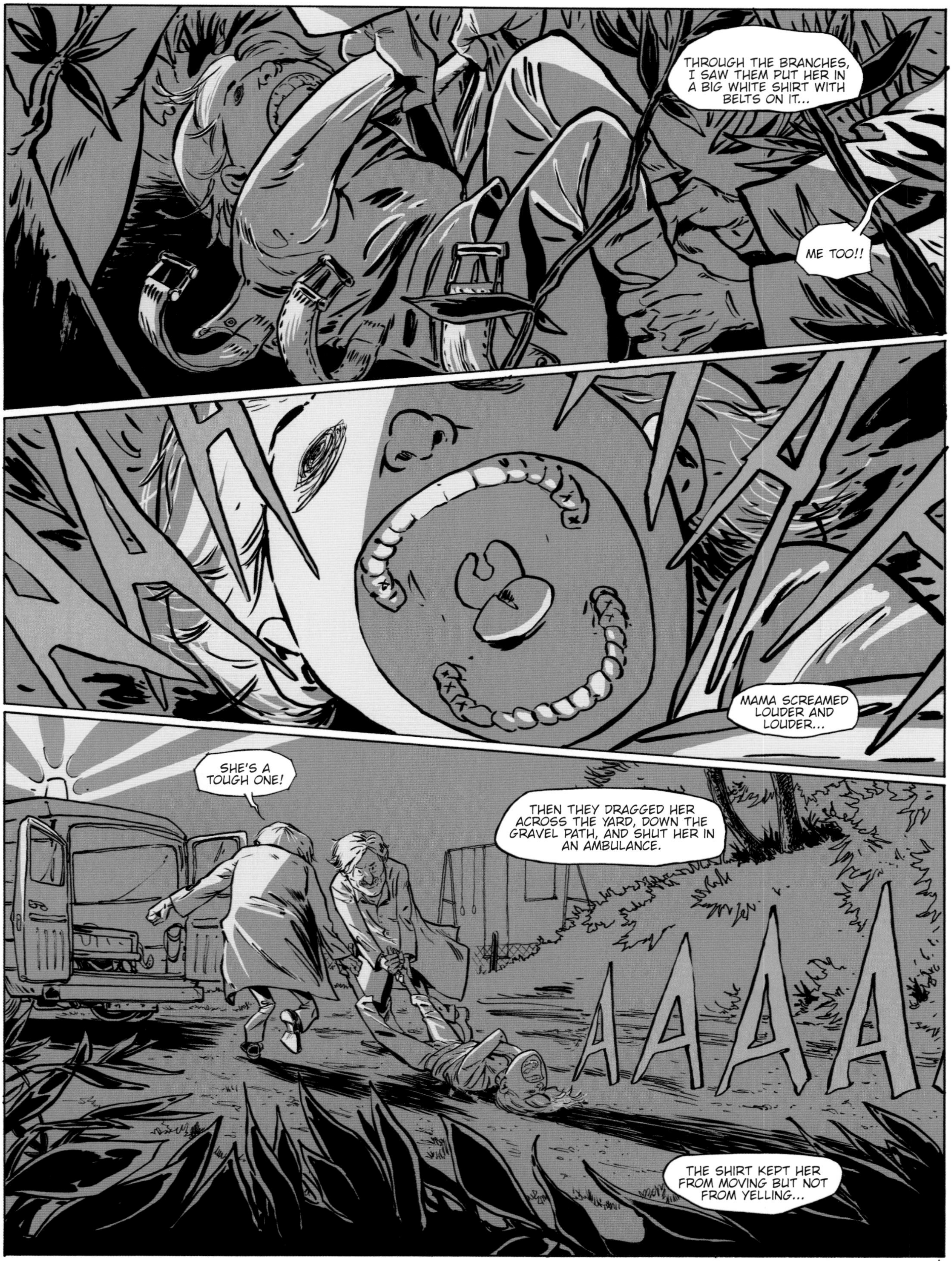
THROUGH THE BRANCHES, I SAW THEM PUT HER IN A BIG WHITE SHIRT WITH BELTS ON IT...
ME TOO!!
MAMA SCREAMED LOUDER AND LOUDER...
SHE'S A TOUGH ONE!
THEN THEY DRAGGED HER ACROSS THE YARD, DOWN THE GRAVEL PATH, AND SHUT HER IN AN AMBULANCE.
AAAA
THE SHIRT KEPT HER FROM MOVING BUT NOT FROM YELLING...

4.

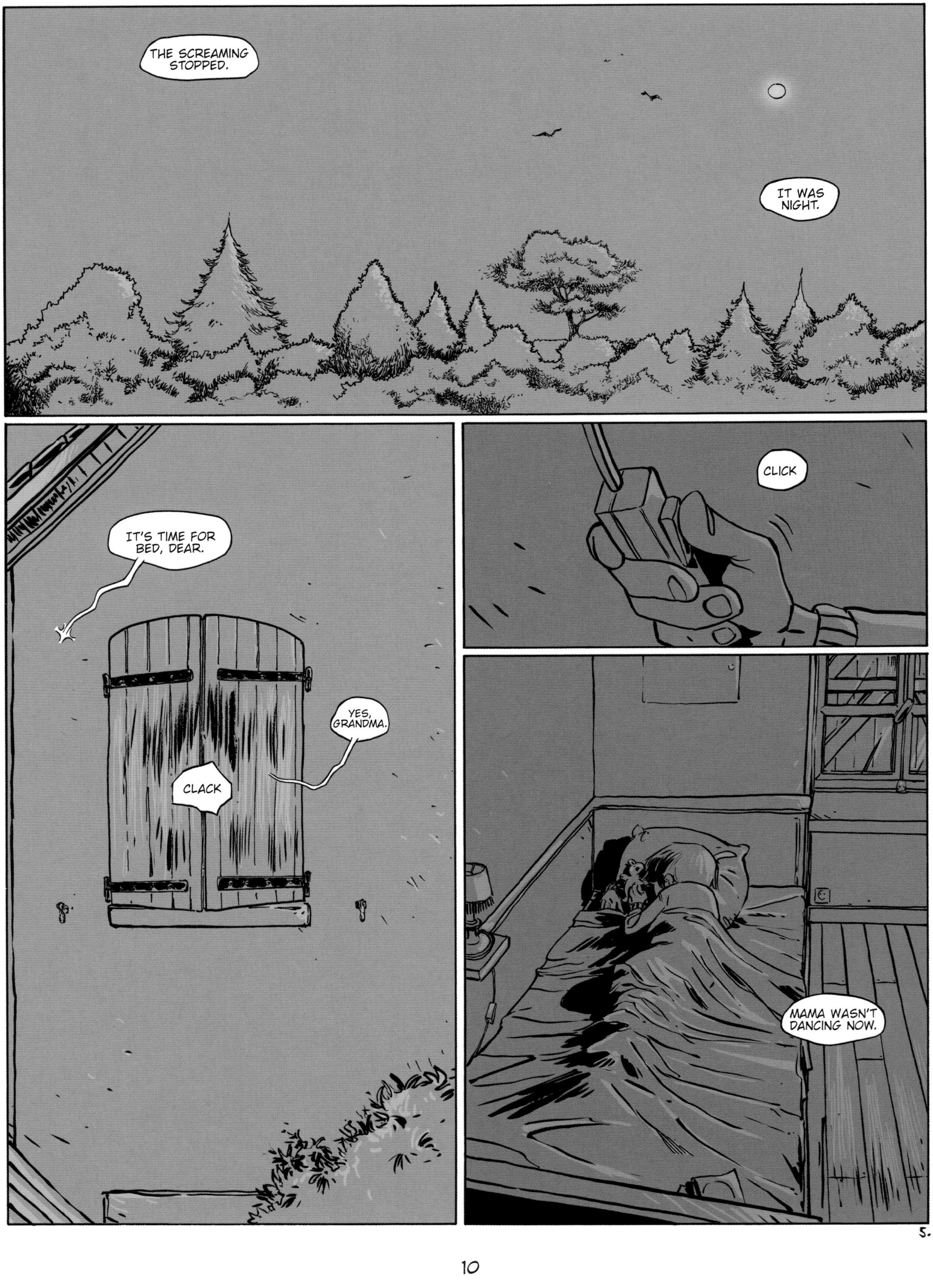
THE SCREAMING STOPPED.
IT WAS NIGHT.
IT'S TIME FOR BED, DEAR.
YES, GRANDMA.
CLACK
CLICK
MAMA WASN'T DANCING NOW.
5.

GRANDPA

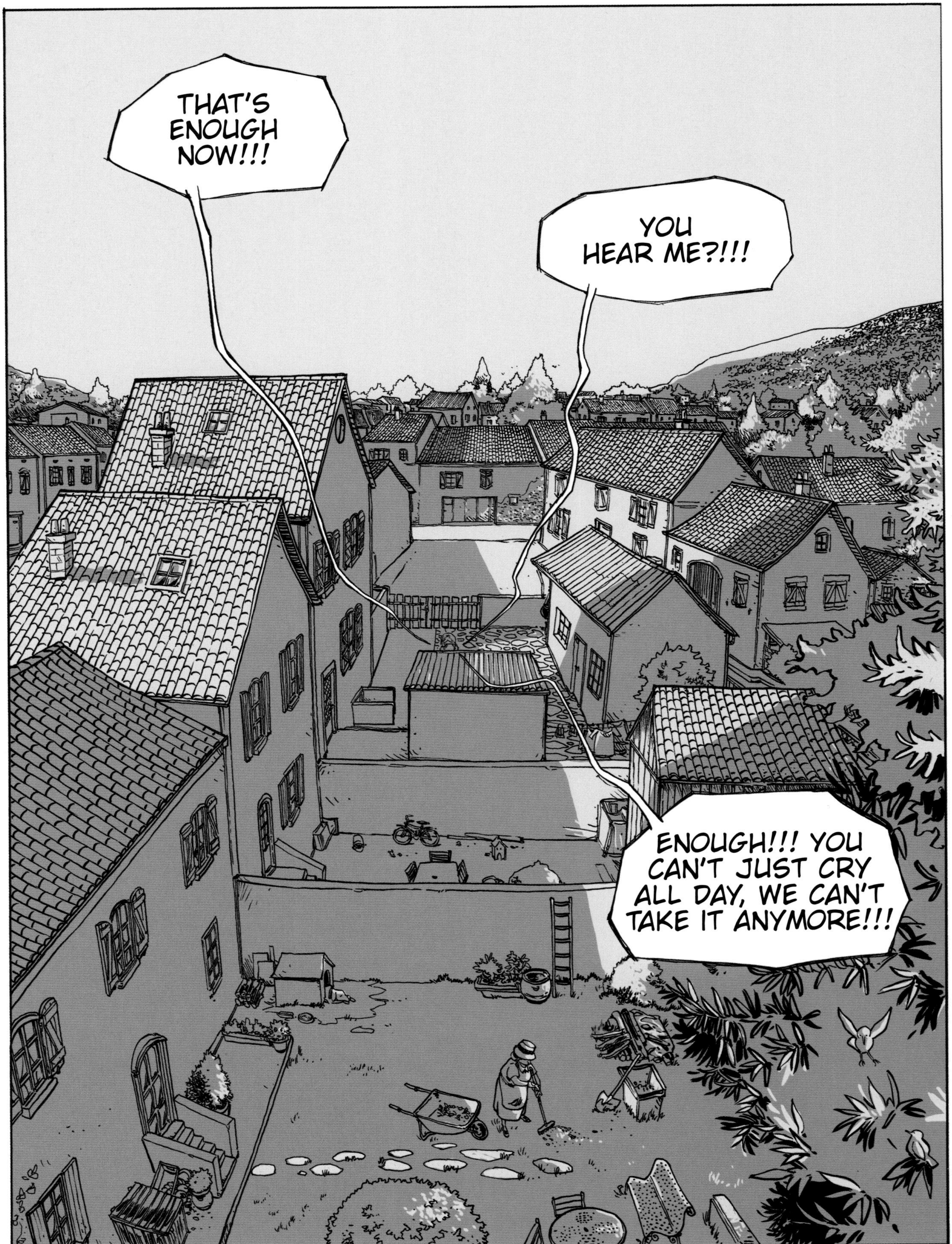
THAT'S ENOUGH NOW!!!
YOU HEAR ME?!!!
ENOUGH!!! YOU CAN'T JUST CRY ALL DAY, WE CAN'T TAKE IT ANYMORE!!!

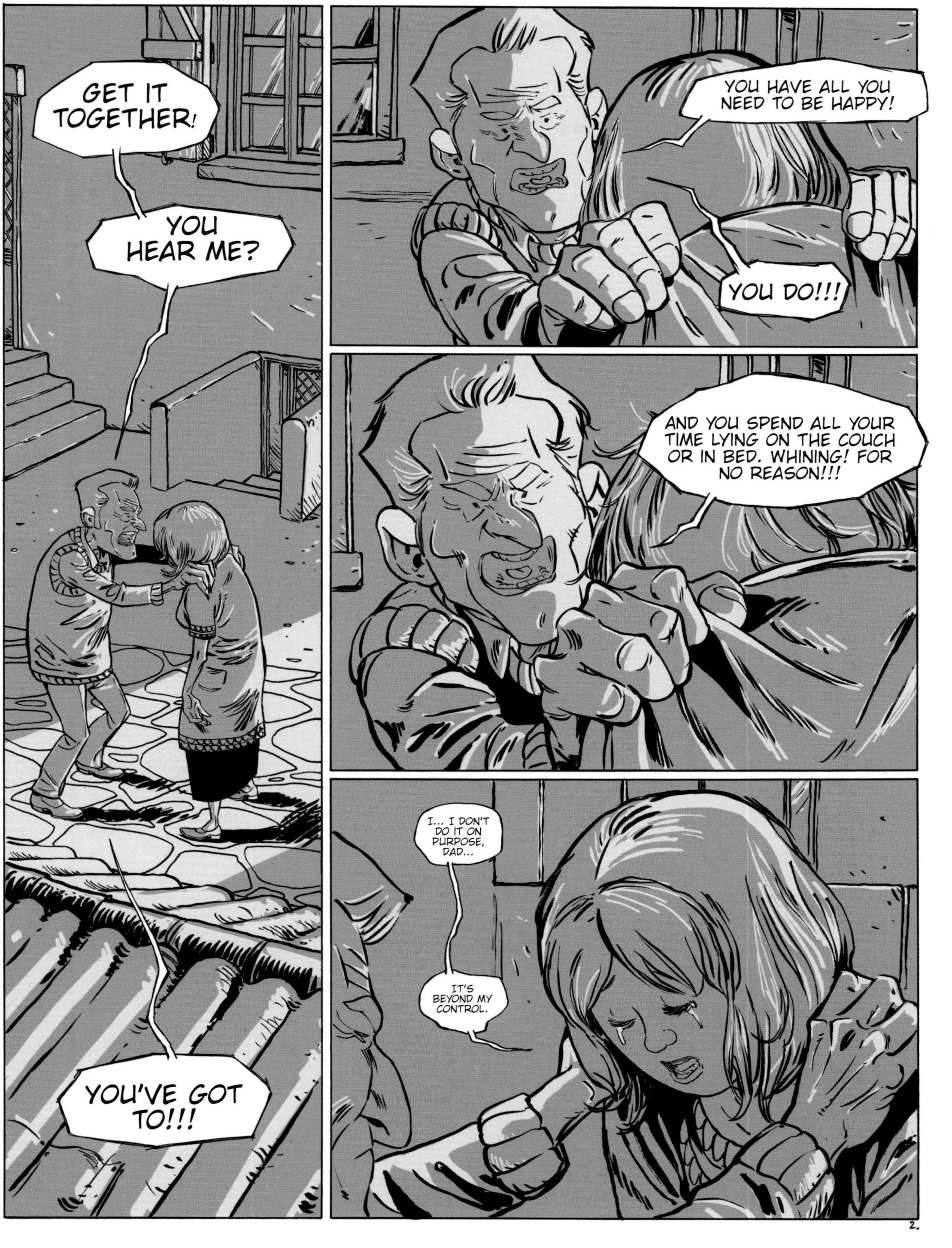
GET IT TOGETHER!
YOU HEAR ME?
YOU'VE GOT TO!!!
YOU HAVE ALL YOU NEED TO BE HAPPY!
YOU DO!!!
AND YOU SPEND ALL YOUR TIME LYING ON THE COUCH OR IN BED. WHINING! FOR NO REASON!!!
I... I DON'T DO IT ON PURPOSE, DAD...
IT'S BEYOND MY CONTROL.
2.

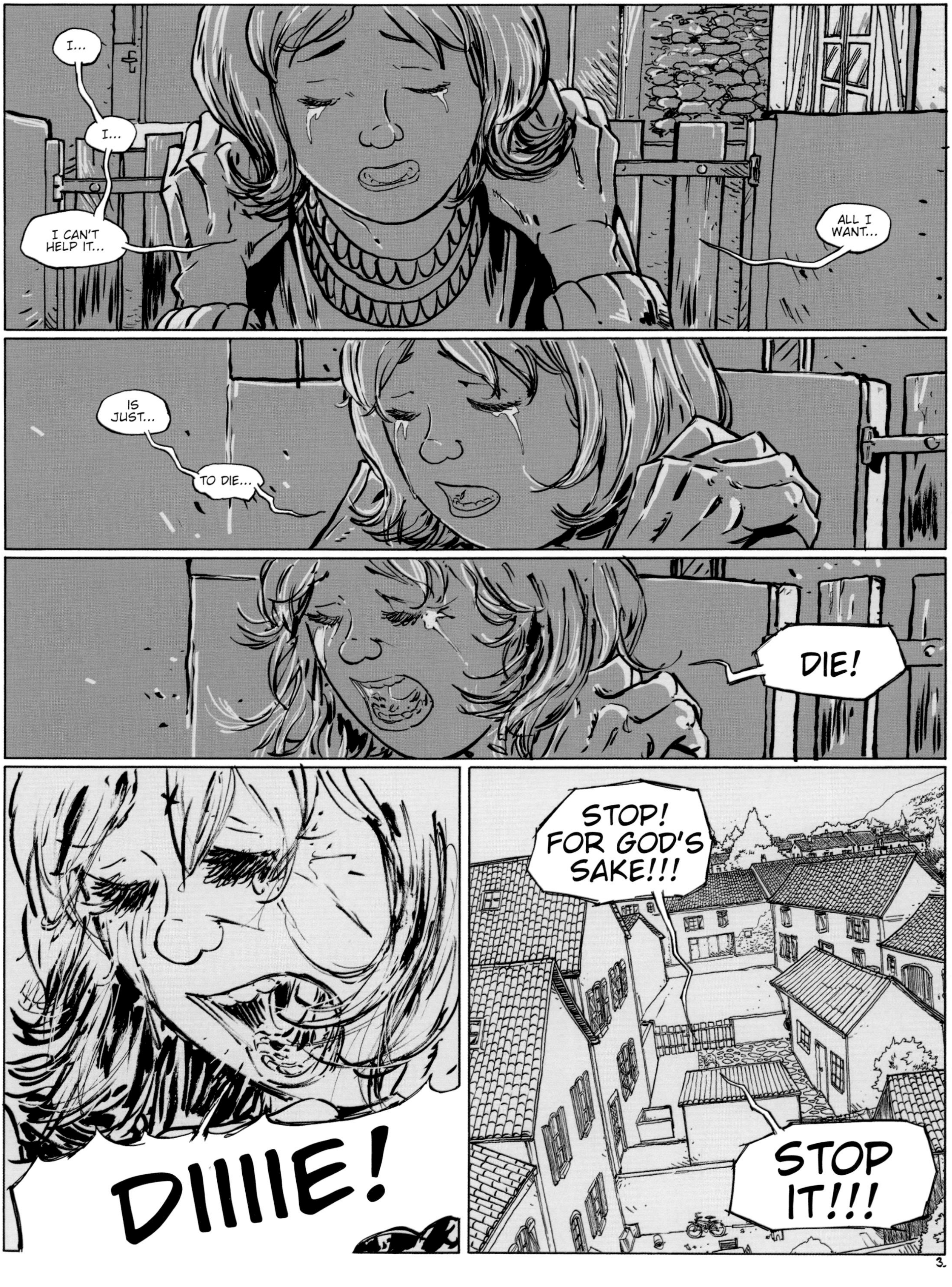
I...
I...
I CAN'T HELP IT...
ALL I WANT...
IS JUST...
TO DIE...
DIE!
DIIIIE!
STOP! FOR GOD'S SAKE!!!
STOP IT!!!

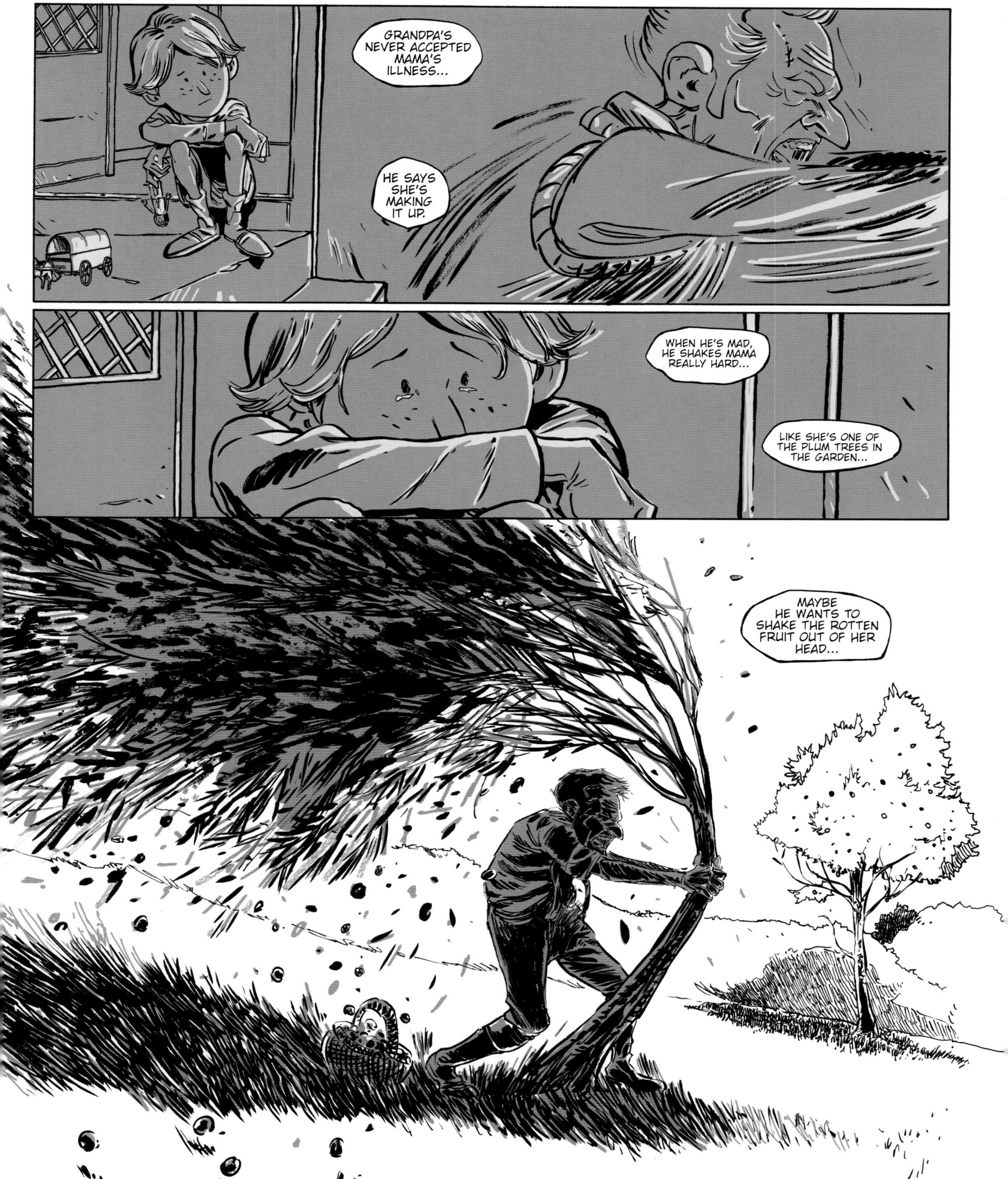
GRANDPA'S NEVER ACCEPTED MAMA'S ILLNESS...
HE SAYS SHE'S MAKING IT UP.
WHEN HE'S MAD, HE SHAKES MAMA REALLY HARD...
LIKE SHE'S ONE OF THE PLUM TREES IN THE GARDEN...
MAYBE HE WANTS TO SHAKE THE ROTTEN FRUIT OUT OF HER HEAD...

BABY BLUES

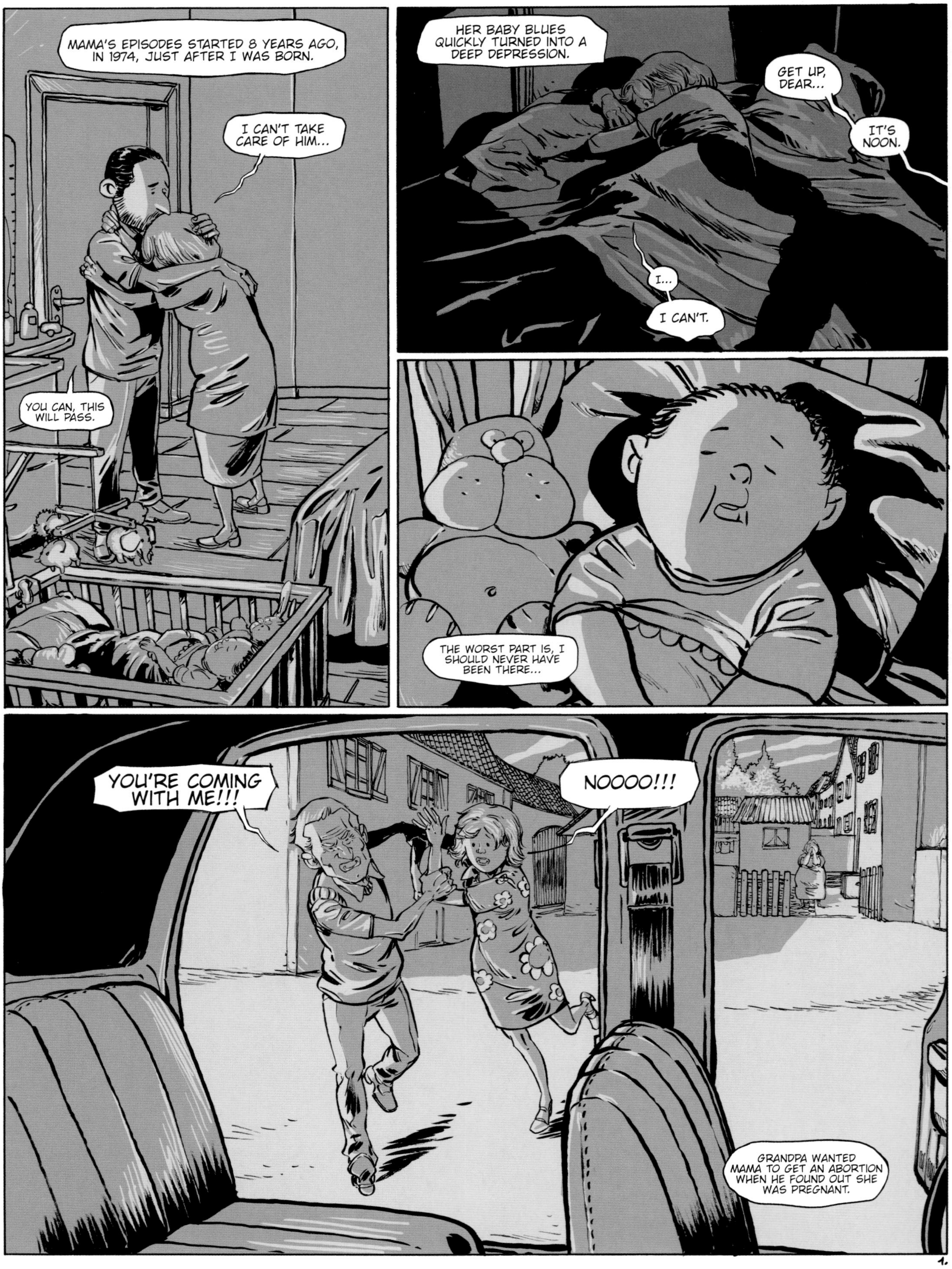
MAMA'S EPISODES STARTED 8 YEARS AGO, IN 1974, JUST AFTER I WAS BORN.
I CAN'T TAKE CARE OF HIM...
YOU CAN, THIS WILL PASS.
HER BABY BLUES QUICKLY TURNED INTO A DEEP DEPRESSION.
GET UP, DEAR...
IT'S NOON.
I...
I CAN'T.
THE WORST PART IS, I SHOULD NEVER HAVE BEEN THERE...
YOU'RE COMING WITH ME!!!
NOOOO!!!
GRANDPA WANTED MAMA TO GET AN ABORTION WHEN HE FOUND OUT SHE WAS PREGNANT.
1.

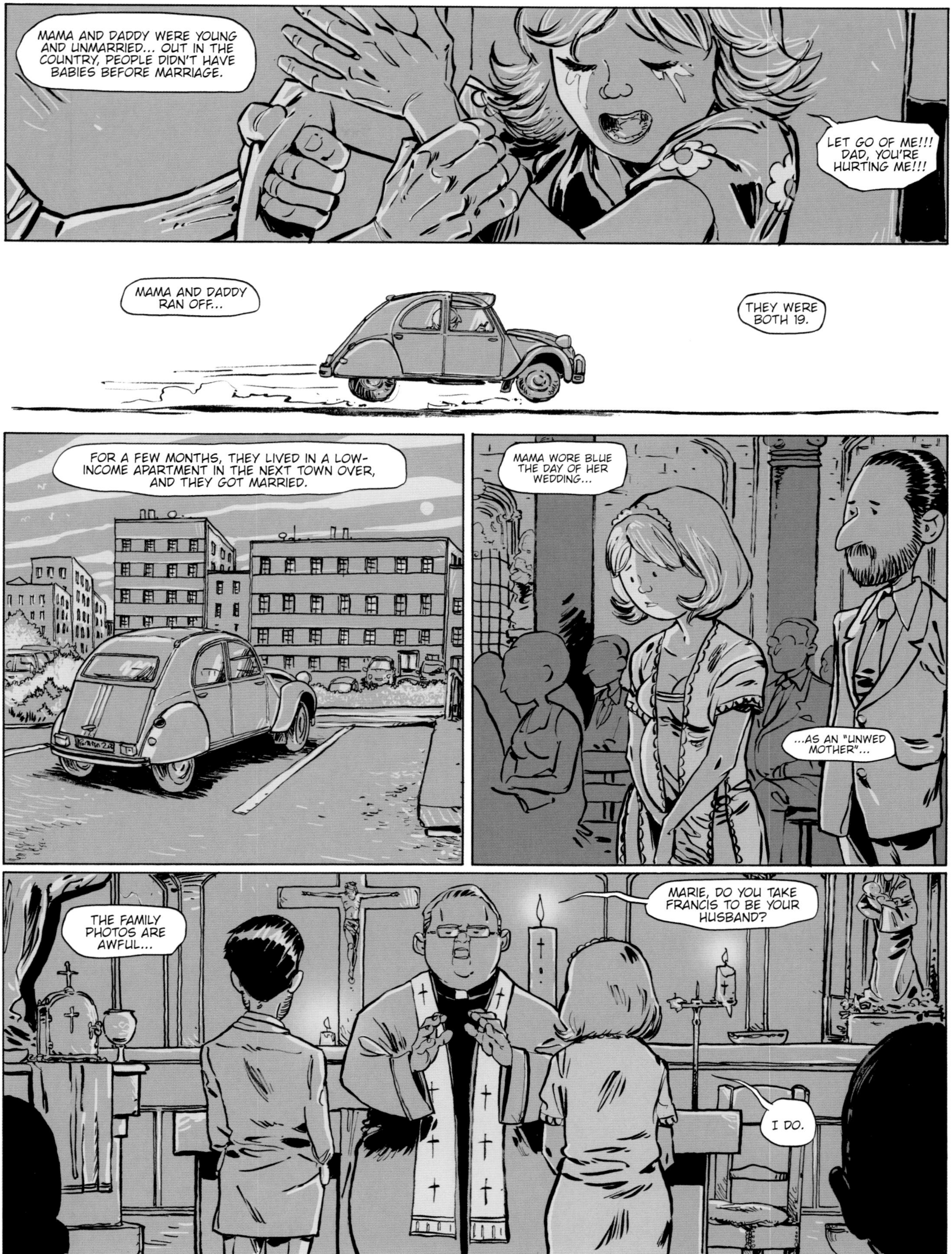
MAMA AND DADDY WERE YOUNG AND UNMARRIED... OUT IN THE COUNTRY, PEOPLE DIDN'T HAVE BABIES BEFORE MARRIAGE.
LET GO OF ME!!! DAD, YOU'RE HURTING ME!!!
MAMA AND DADDY RAN OFF...
THEY WERE BOTH 19.
FOR A FEW MONTHS, THEY LIVED IN A LOW-INCOME APARTMENT IN THE NEXT TOWN OVER, AND THEY GOT MARRIED.
MAMA WORE BLUE THE DAY OF HER WEDDING...
...AS AN "UNWED MOTHER"...
THE FAMILY PHOTOS ARE AWFUL...
MARIE, DO YOU TAKE FRANCIS TO BE YOUR HUSBAND?
I DO.

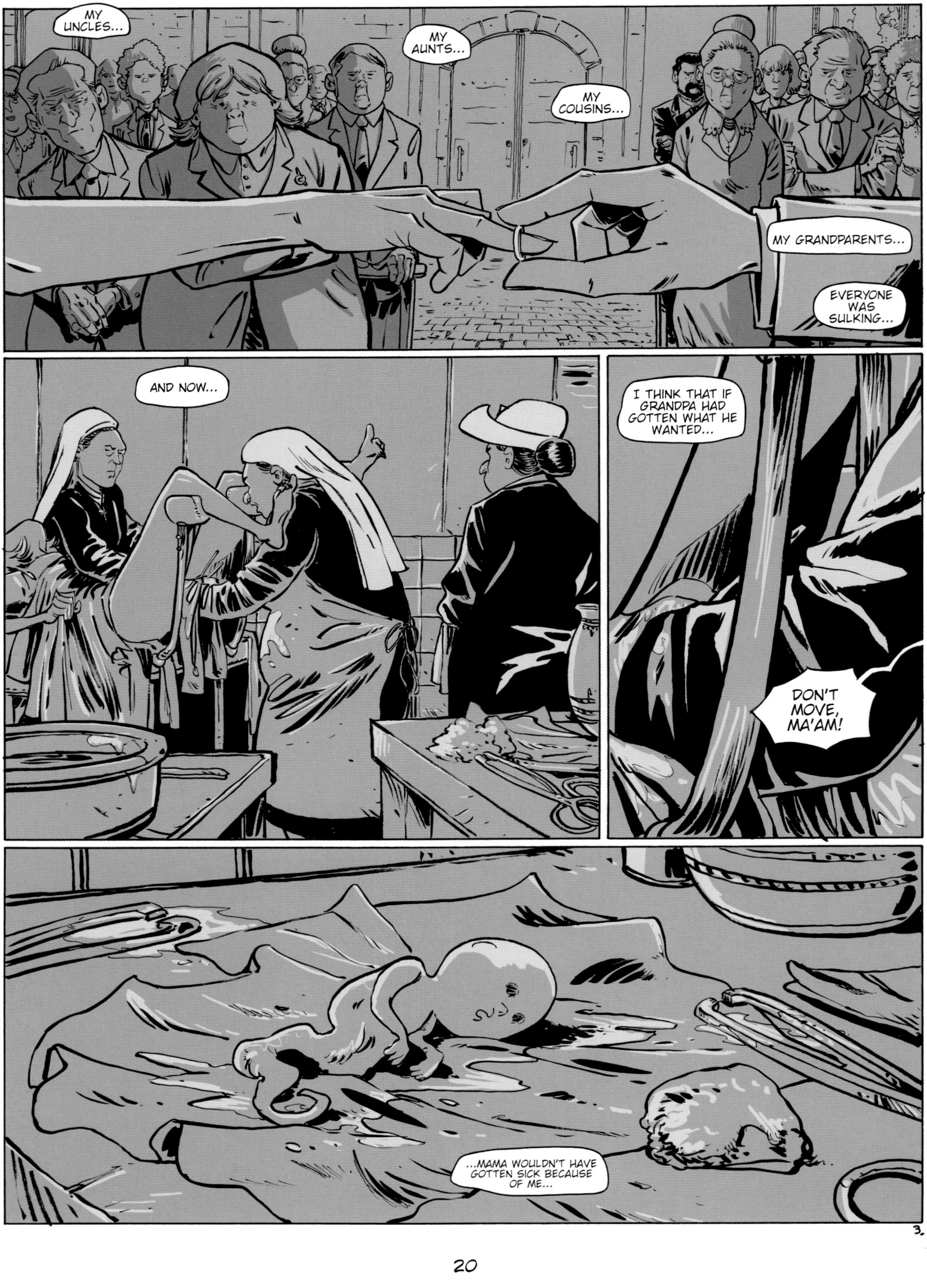
MY UNCLES...
MY AUNTS...
MY COUSINS...
MY GRANDPARENTS...
EVERYONE WAS SULKING...
AND NOW...
I THINK THAT IF GRANDPA HAD GOTTEN WHAT HE WANTED...
DON'T MOVE, MA'AM!
...MAMA WOULDN'T HAVE GOTTEN SICK BECAUSE OF ME...
3.

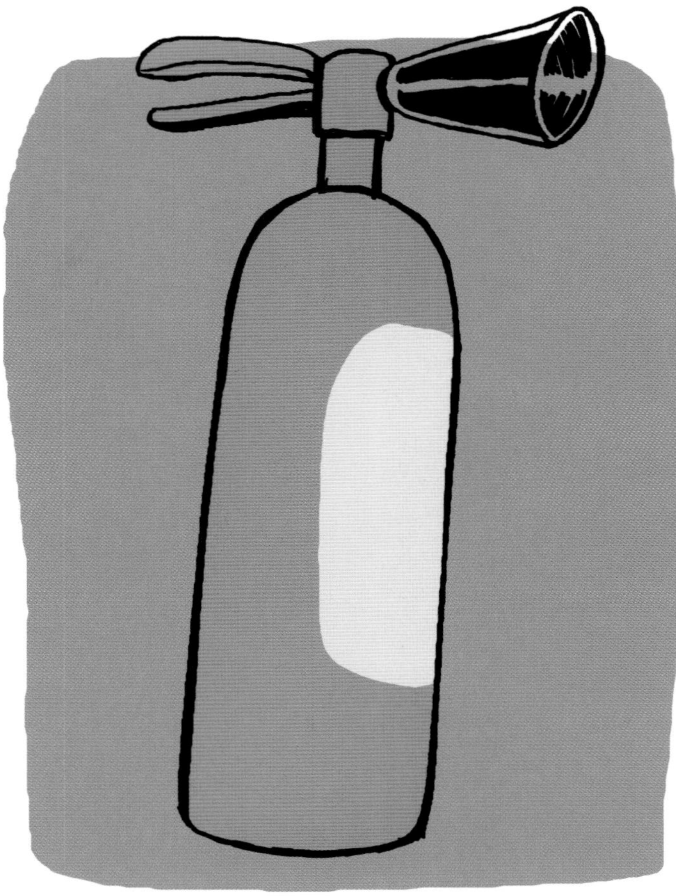

THE ES-TINGUISHER

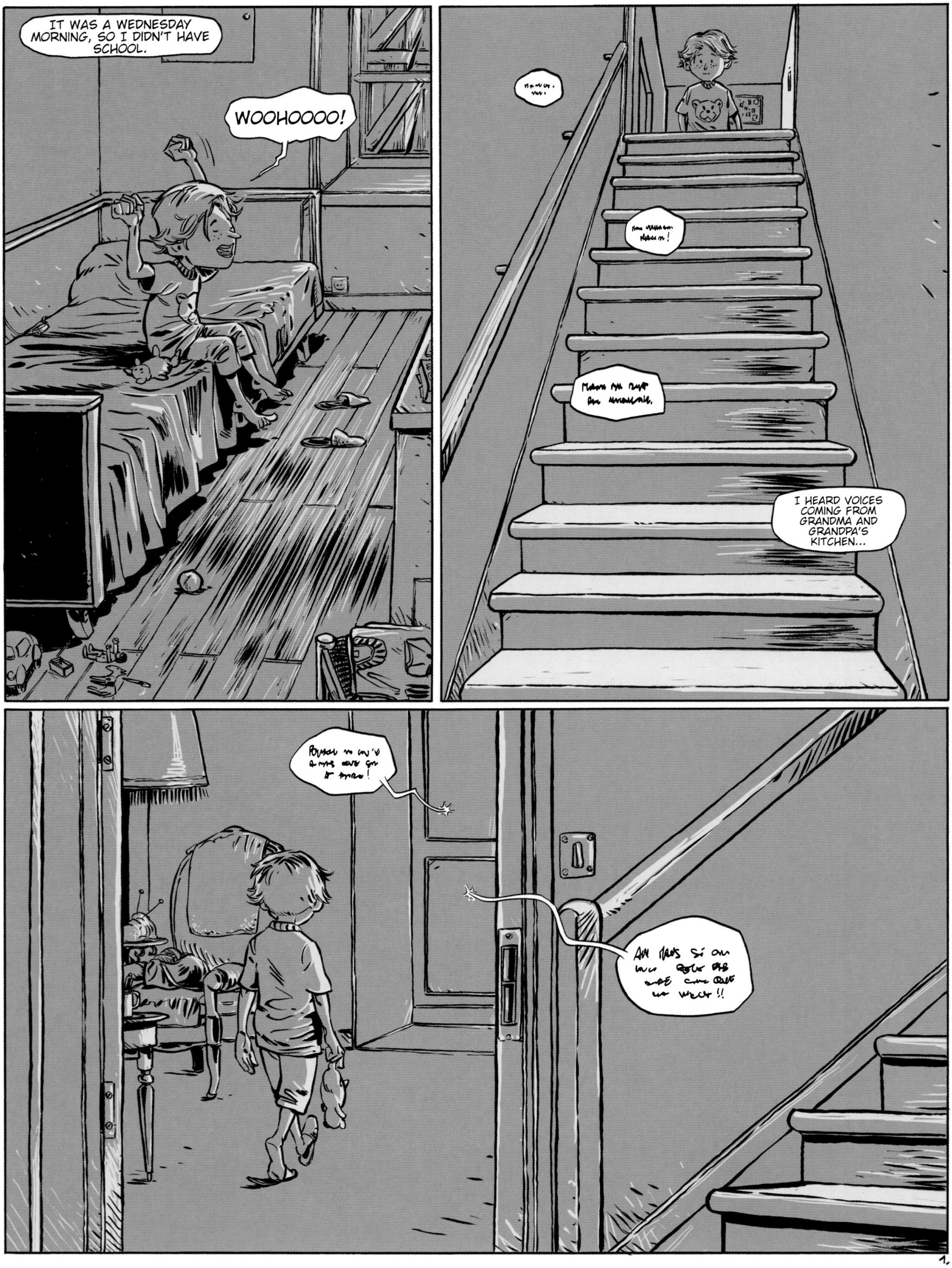

IT WAS A WEDNESDAY MORNING, SO I DIDN'T HAVE SCHOOL.
WOOHOOOO!
I HEARD VOICES COMING FROM GRANDMA AND GRANDPA'S KITCHEN...

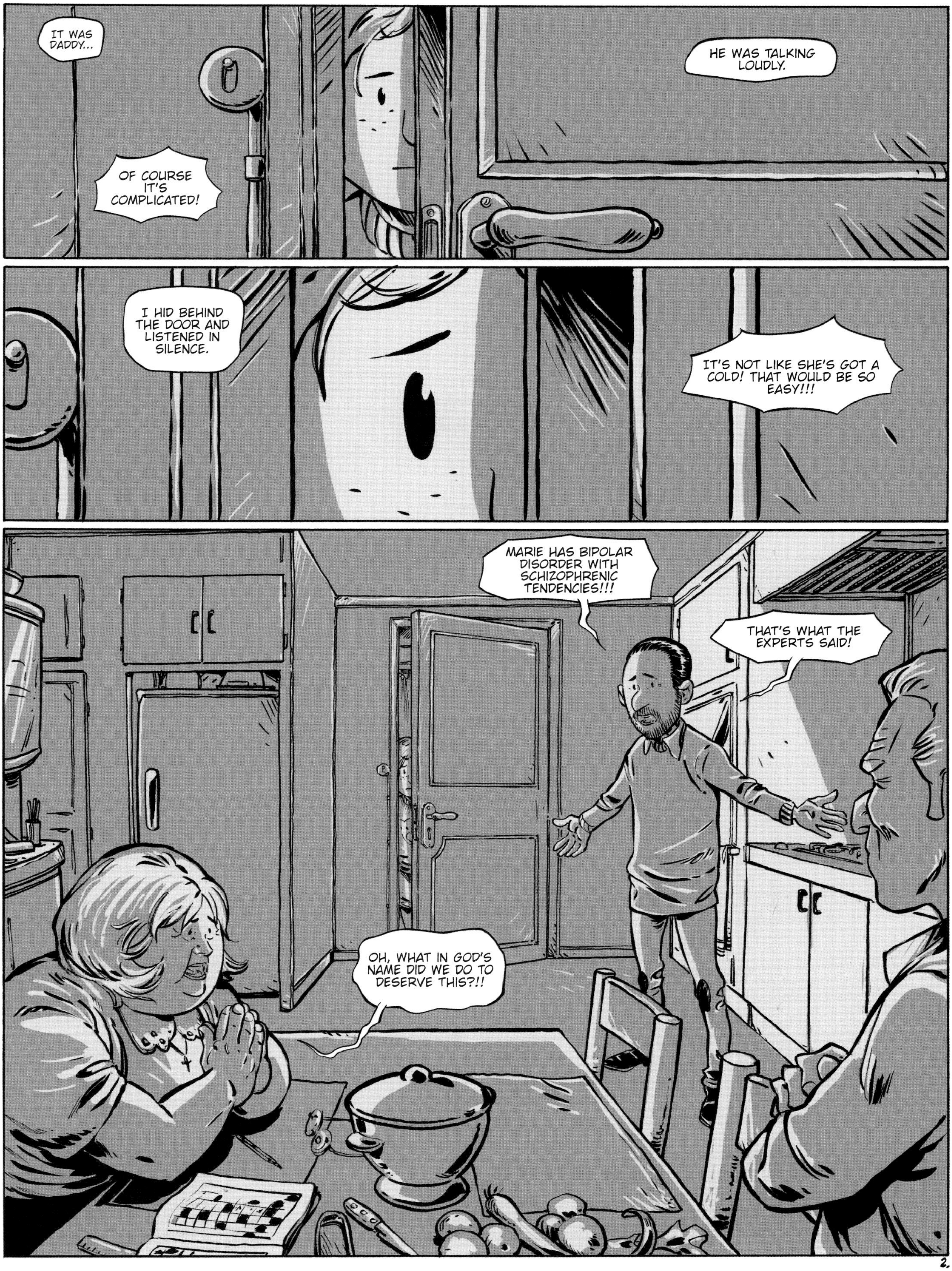
IT WAS DADDY...
HE WAS TALKING LOUDLY.
OF COURSE IT'S COMPLICATED!
I HID BEHIND THE DOOR AND LISTENED IN SILENCE.
IT'S NOT LIKE SHE'S GOT A COLD! THAT WOULD BE SO EASY!!!
MARIE HAS BIPOLAR DISORDER WITH SCHIZOPHRENIC TENDENCIES!!!
THAT'S WHAT THE EXPERTS SAID!
OH, WHAT IN GOD'S NAME DID WE DO TO DESERVE THIS?!!

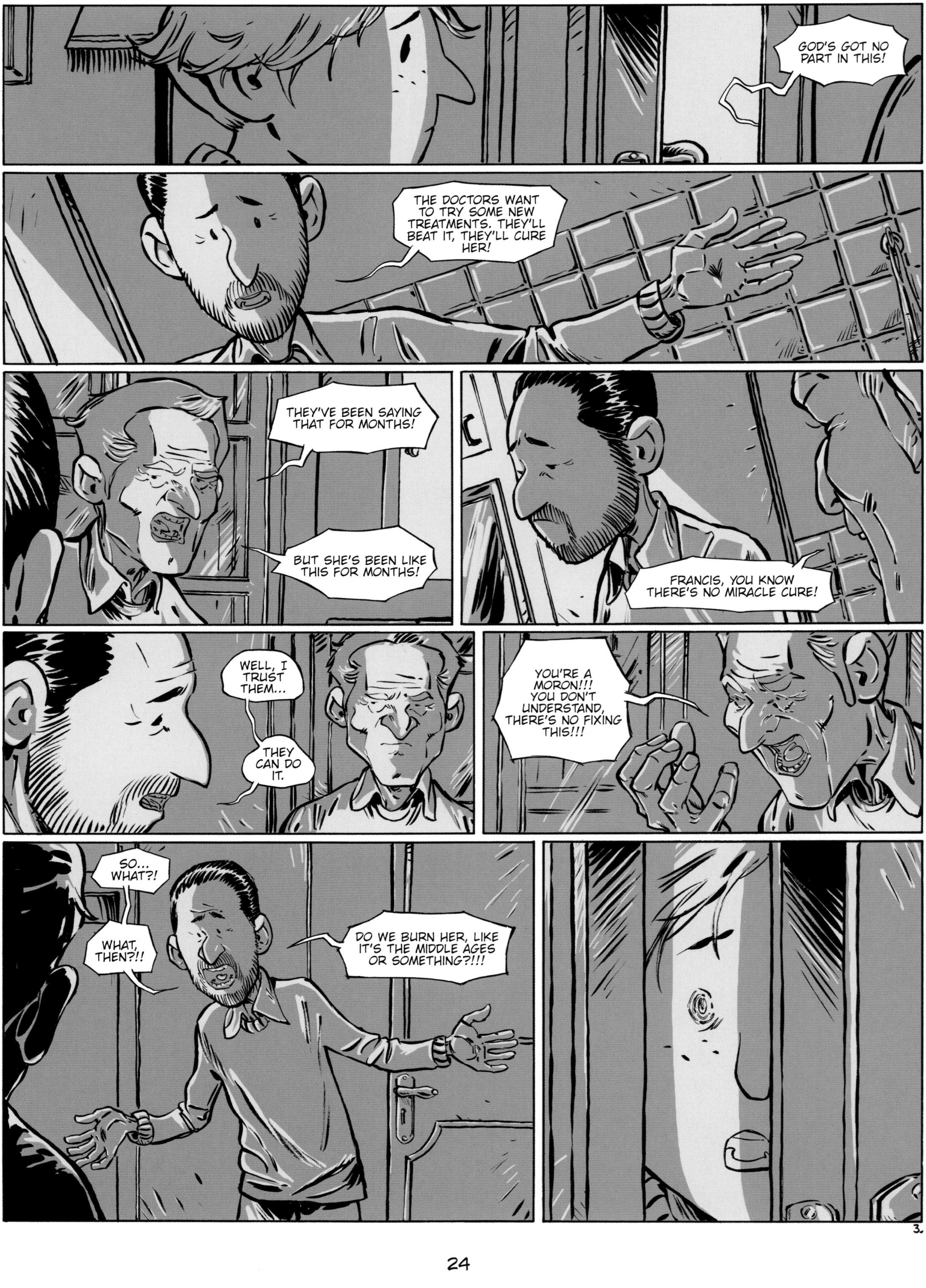
GOD'S GOT NO PART IN THIS!
THE DOCTORS WANT TO TRY SOME NEW TREATMENTS. THEY'LL BEAT IT, THEY'LL CURE HER!
THEY'VE BEEN SAYING THAT FOR MONTHS!
BUT SHE'S BEEN LIKE THIS FOR MONTHS!
FRANCIS, YOU KNOW THERE'S NO MIRACLE CURE!
WELL, I TRUST THEM...
THEY CAN DO IT.
YOU'RE A MORON!!! YOU DON'T UNDERSTAND, THERE'S NO FIXING THIS!!!
SO... WHAT?!
WHAT, THEN?!!
DO WE BURN HER, LIKE IT'S THE MIDDLE AGES OR SOMETHING?!!!
3.

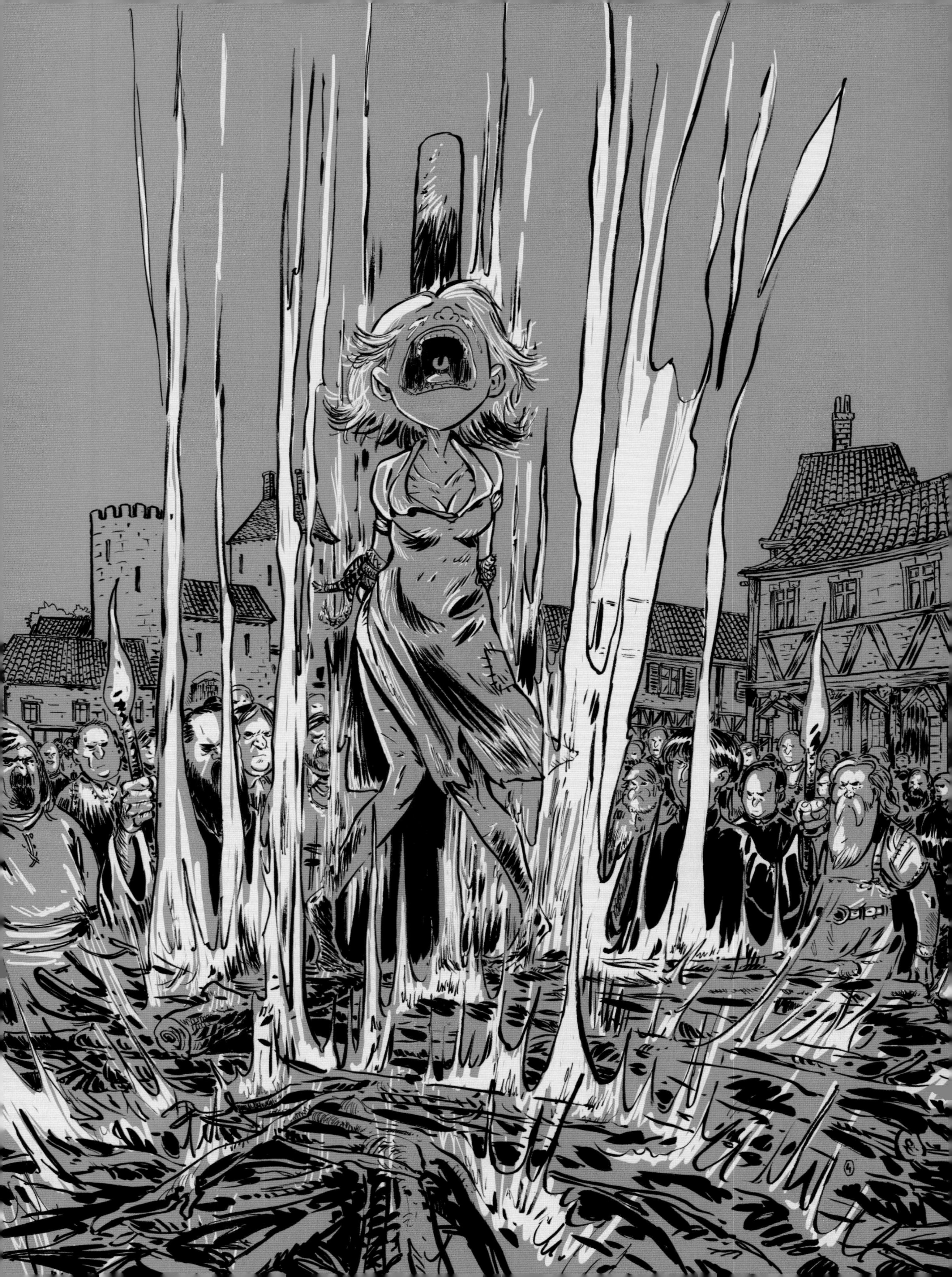

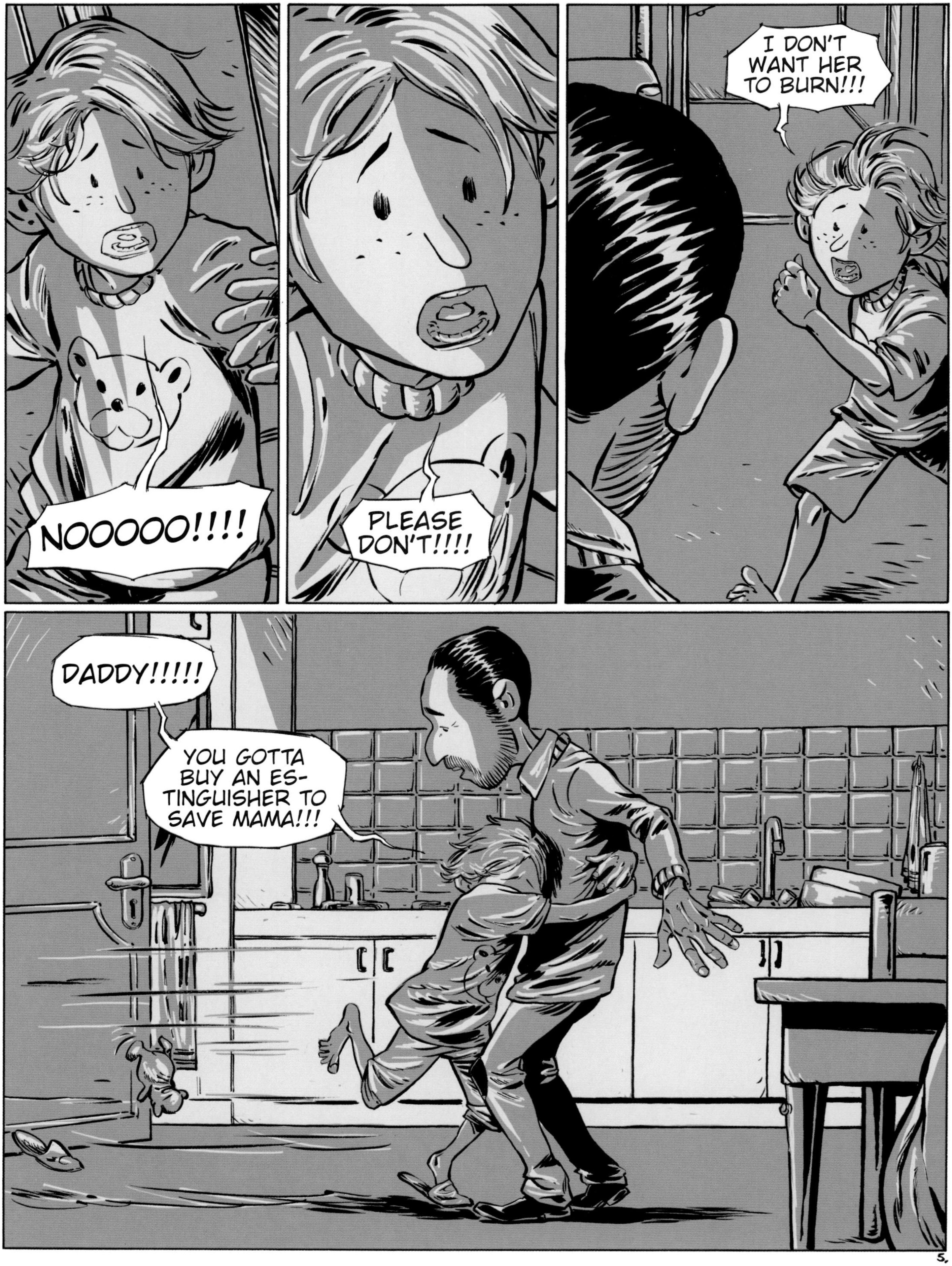
NOOOOO!!!!
PLEASE DON'T!!!!!
I DON'T WANT HER TO BURN!!!
DADDY!!!!!
YOU GOTTA BUY AN ES-TINGUISHER TO SAVE MAMA!!!
5.

MAMA'S TRIED
EVERYTHING

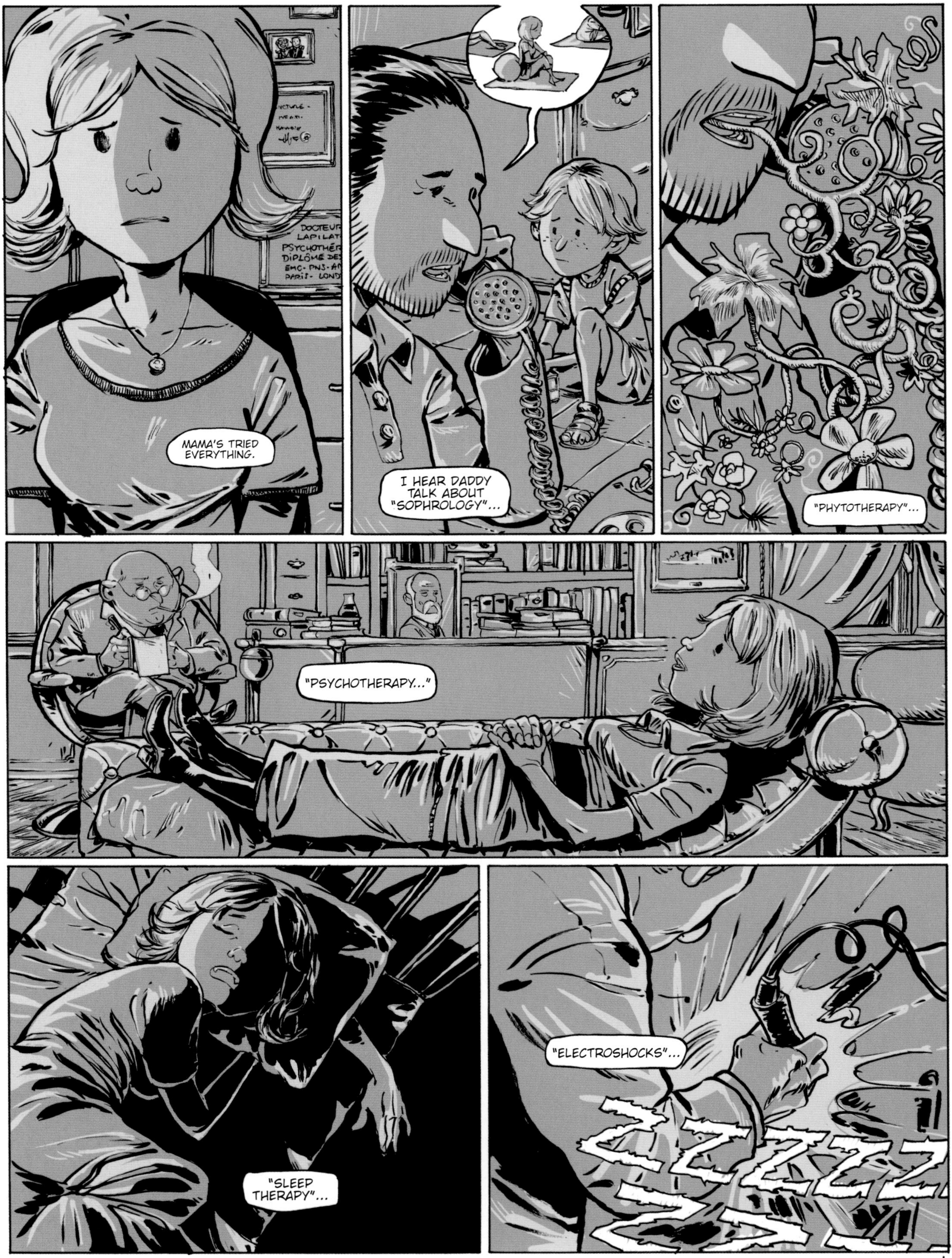
DOCTEUR
LAPILAT
PSYCHOTHÉR
DIPLÔMÉ DES
EMC-PNS-AN
PARIS-LOND
MAMA'S TRIED EVERYTHING.
I HEAR DADDY TALK ABOUT "SOPHROLOGY"...
"PHYTOTHERAPY"...
"PSYCHOTHERAPY..."
"SLEEP THERAPY"...
"ELECTROSHOCKS"...
ZZZZZ
ZZ

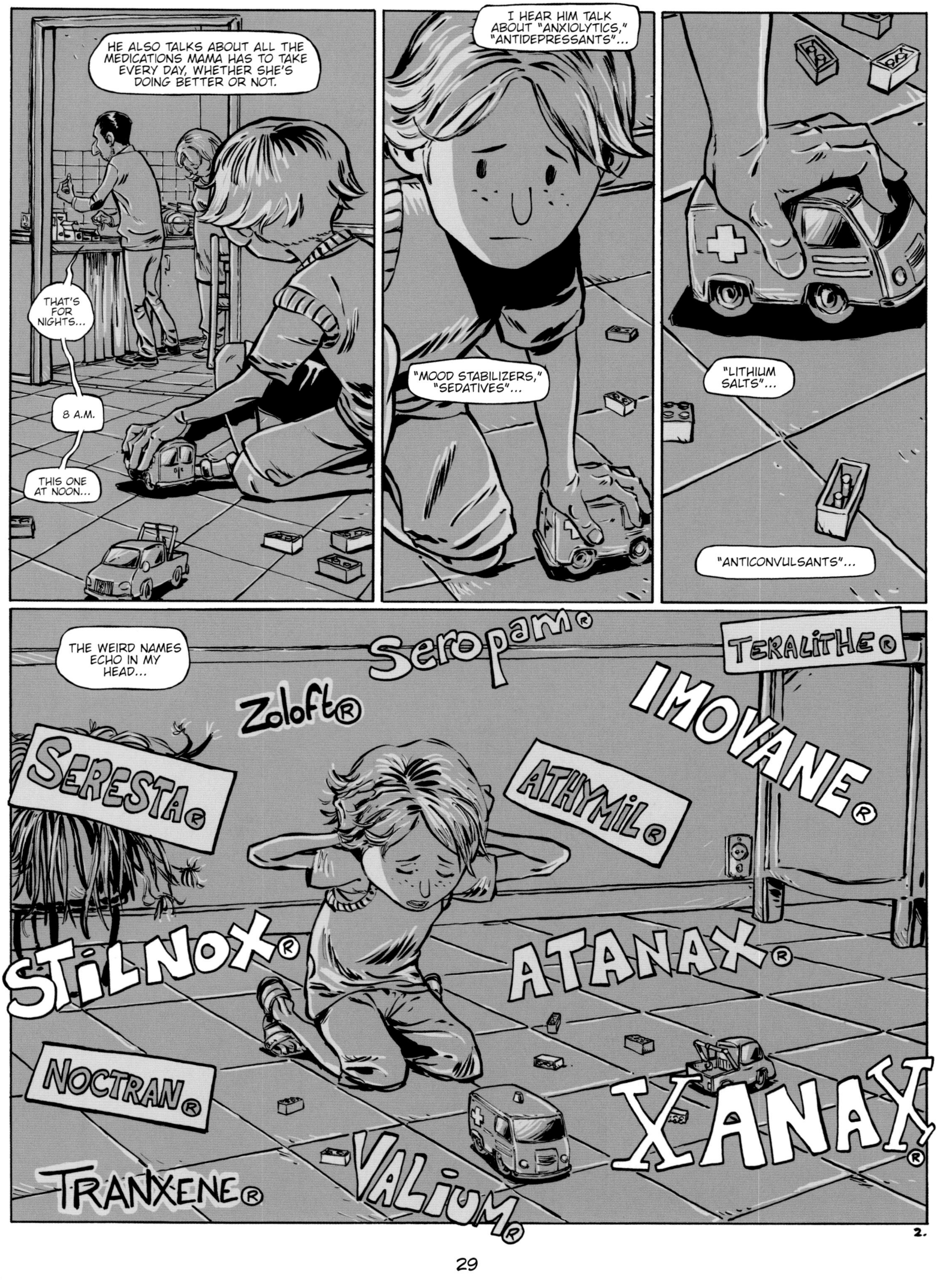

HE ALSO TALKS ABOUT ALL THE MEDICATIONS MAMA HAS TO TAKE EVERY DAY, WHETHER SHE'S DOING BETTER OR NOT.
THAT'S FOR NIGHTS...
8 A.M.
THIS ONE AT NOON...
I HEAR HIM TALK ABOUT "ANXIOLYTICS," "ANTIDEPRESSANTS"...
"MOOD STABILIZERS," "SEDATIVES"...
"LITHIUM SALTS"...
"ANTICONVULSANTS"...
THE WEIRD NAMES ECHO IN MY HEAD...
Seropam®
TERALITHE®
Zoloft®
IMOVANE®
SERESTA®
ATHYMIL®
STILNOX®
ATANAX®
NOCTRAN®
XANAX®
TRANXENE®
VALIUM®
2.

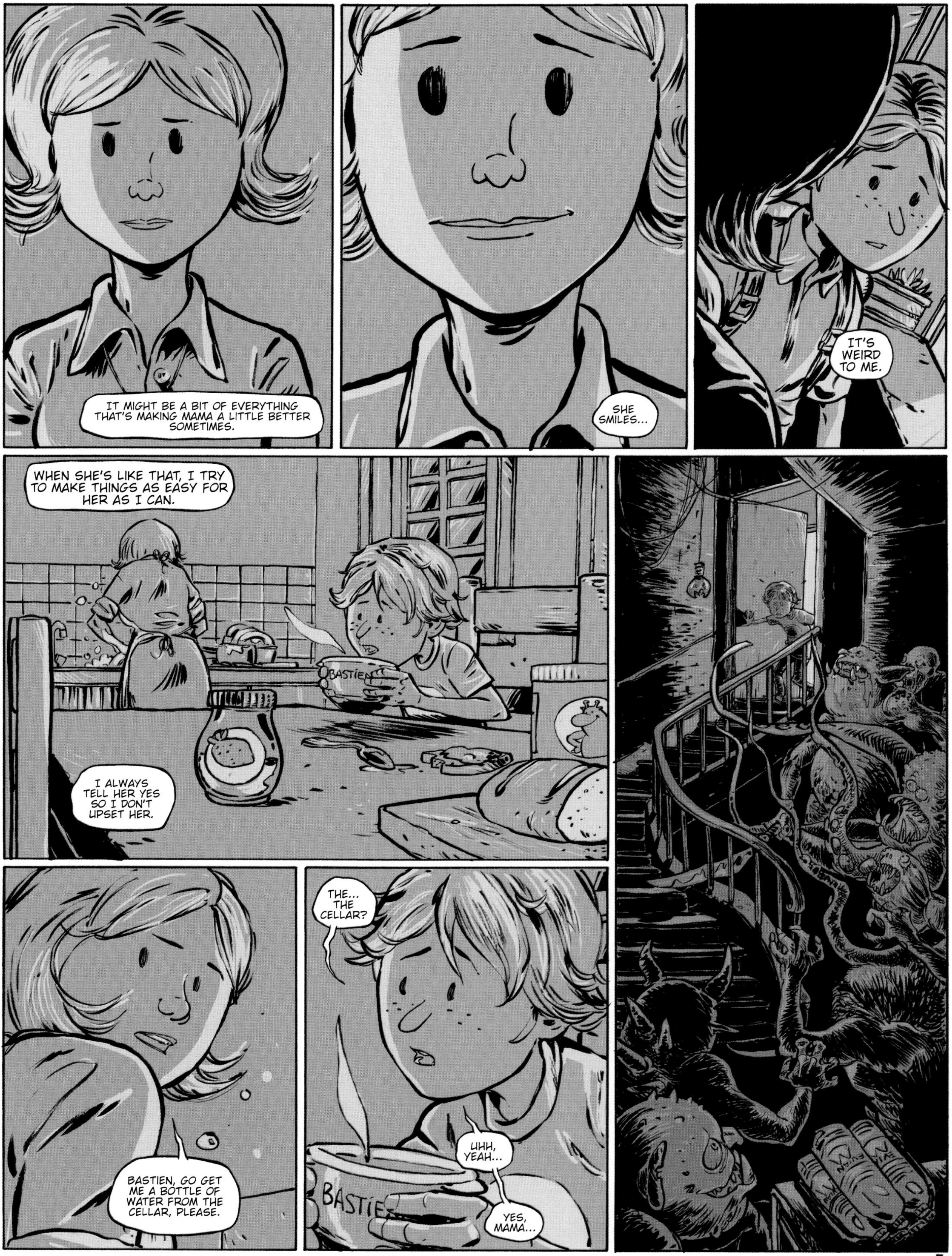
IT MIGHT BE A BIT OF EVERYTHING THAT'S MAKING MAMA A LITTLE BETTER SOMETIMES.
SHE SMILES...
IT'S WEIRD TO ME.
WHEN SHE'S LIKE THAT, I TRY TO MAKE THINGS AS EASY FOR HER AS I CAN.
BASTIEN
I ALWAYS TELL HER YES SO I DON'T UPSET HER.
BASTIEN, GO GET ME A BOTTLE OF WATER FROM THE CELLAR, PLEASE.
THE... THE CELLAR?
UHH, YEAH...
YES, MAMA...
BASTIE
3.

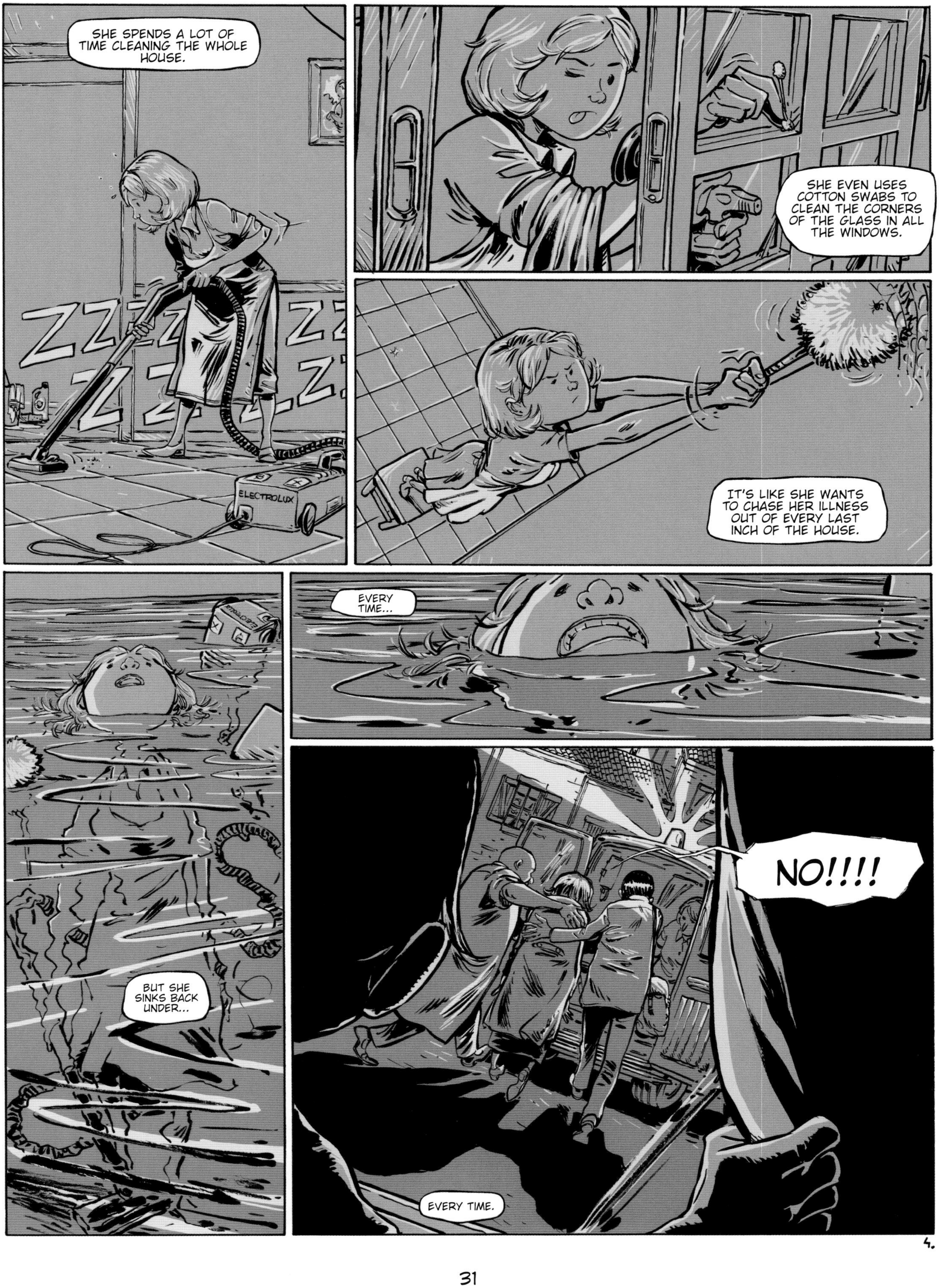
SHE SPENDS A LOT OF TIME CLEANING THE WHOLE HOUSE.
ZZZZZZZ
ELECTROLUX
SHE EVEN USES COTTON SWABS TO CLEAN THE CORNERS OF THE GLASS IN ALL THE WINDOWS.
IT'S LIKE SHE WANTS TO CHASE HER ILLNESS OUT OF EVERY LAST INCH OF THE HOUSE.
BUT SHE SINKS BACK UNDER...
EVERY TIME...
NO!!!!
EVERY TIME.
4.

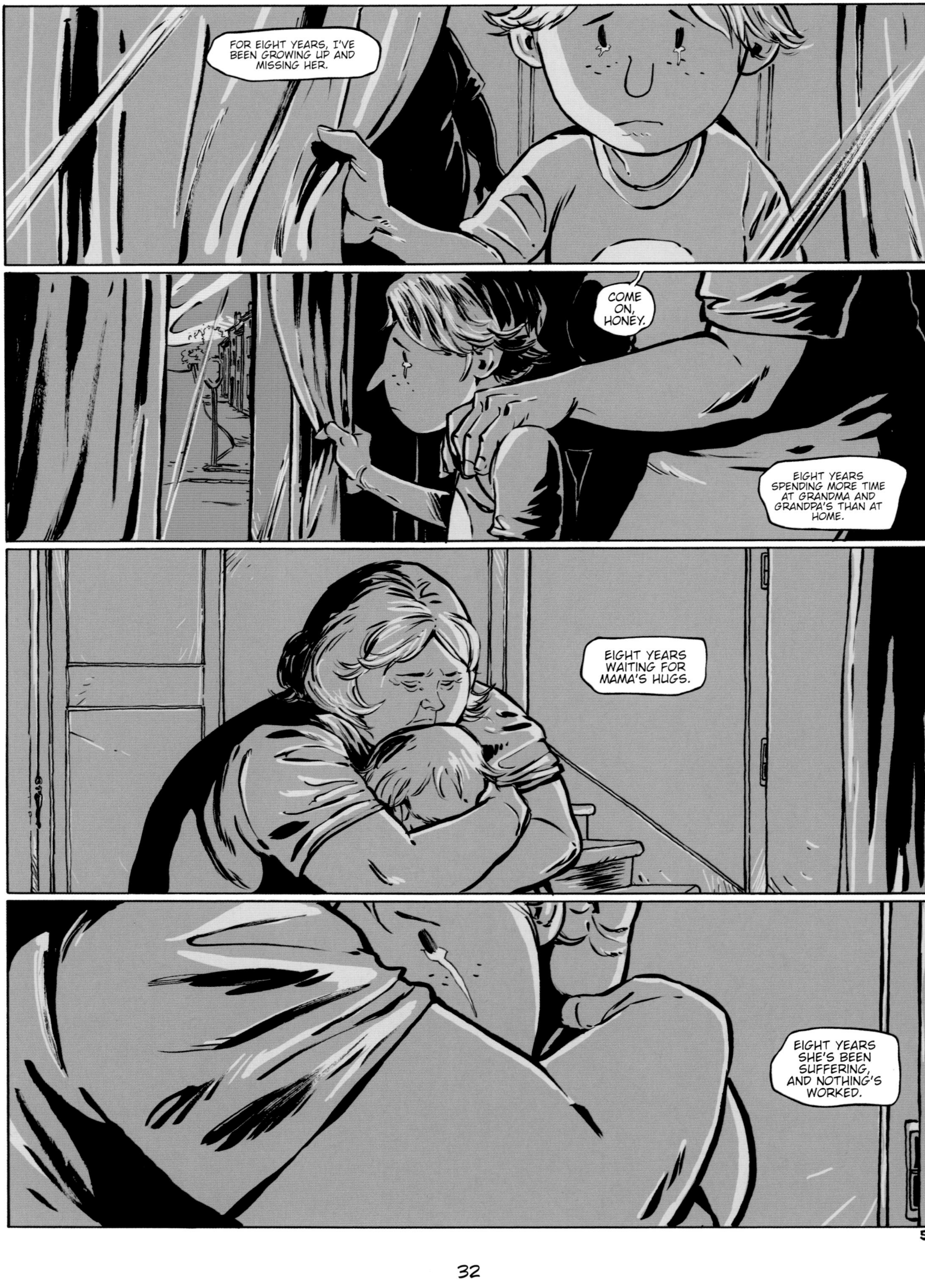
FOR EIGHT YEARS, I'VE BEEN GROWING UP AND MISSING HER.
COME ON, HONEY.
EIGHT YEARS SPENDING MORE TIME AT GRANDMA AND GRANDPA'S THAN AT HOME.
EIGHT YEARS WAITING FOR MAMA'S HUGS.
EIGHT YEARS SHE'S BEEN SUFFERING, AND NOTHING'S WORKED.
5-

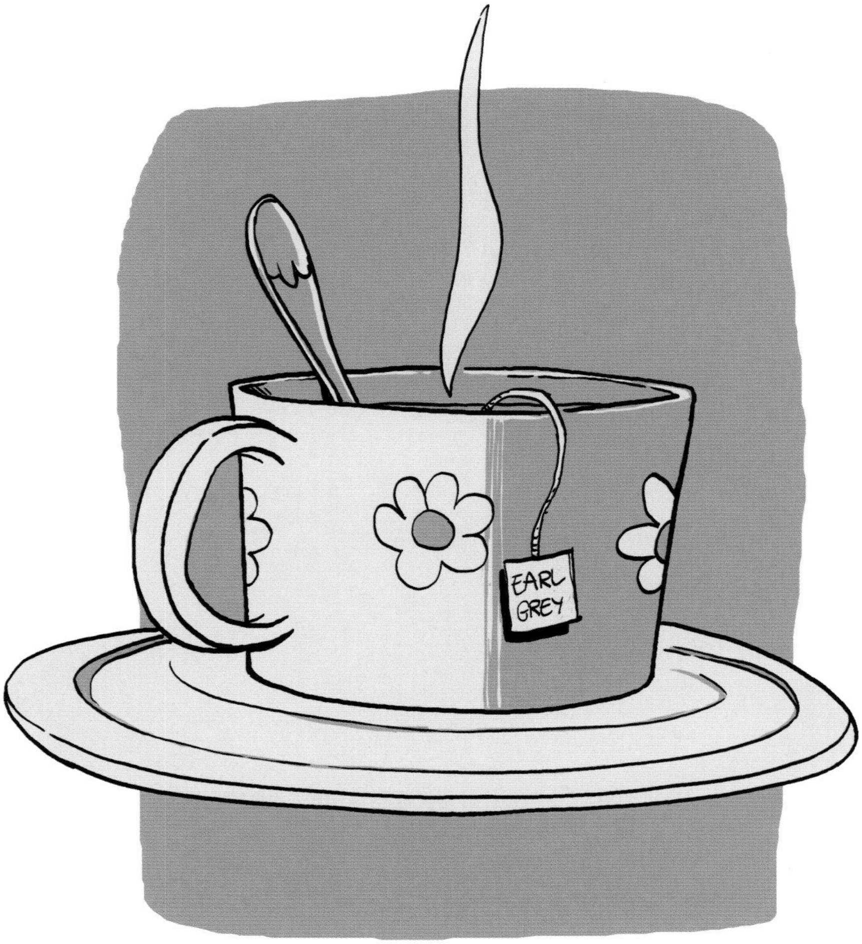
EARL GREY

GIRLFRIENDS

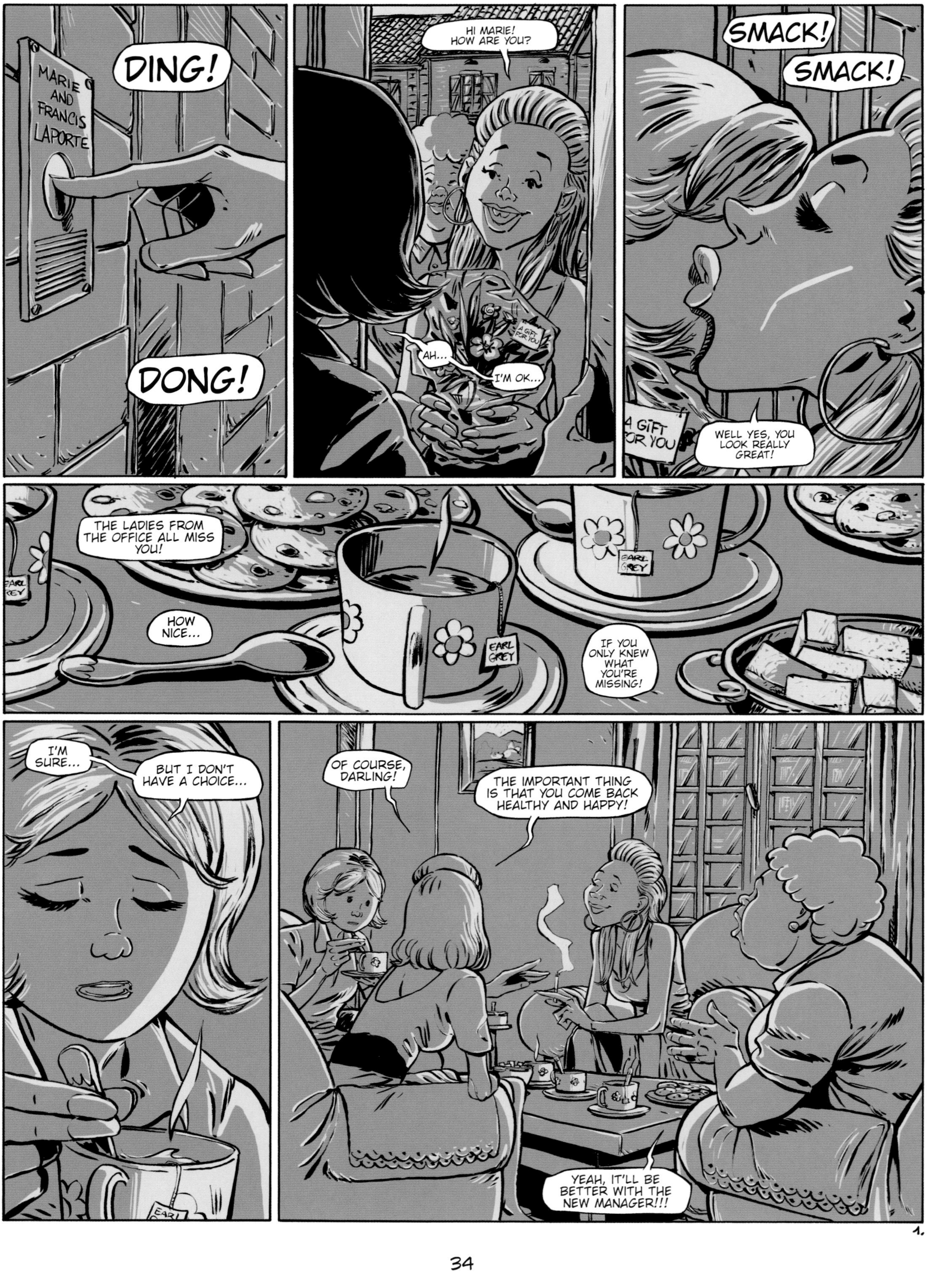
DING!
MARIE AND FRANCIS LAPORTE
DONG!
HI MARIE! HOW ARE YOU?
A GIFT FOR YOU
AH...
I'M OK...
SMACK!
SMACK!
A GIFT FOR YOU
WELL YES, YOU LOOK REALLY GREAT!
THE LADIES FROM THE OFFICE ALL MISS YOU!
HOW NICE...
EARL GREY
IF YOU ONLY KNEW WHAT YOU'RE MISSING!
I'M SURE...
BUT I DON'T HAVE A CHOICE...
OF COURSE, DARLING!
THE IMPORTANT THING IS THAT YOU COME BACK HEALTHY AND HAPPY!
YEAH, IT'LL BE BETTER WITH THE NEW MANAGER!!!
1.

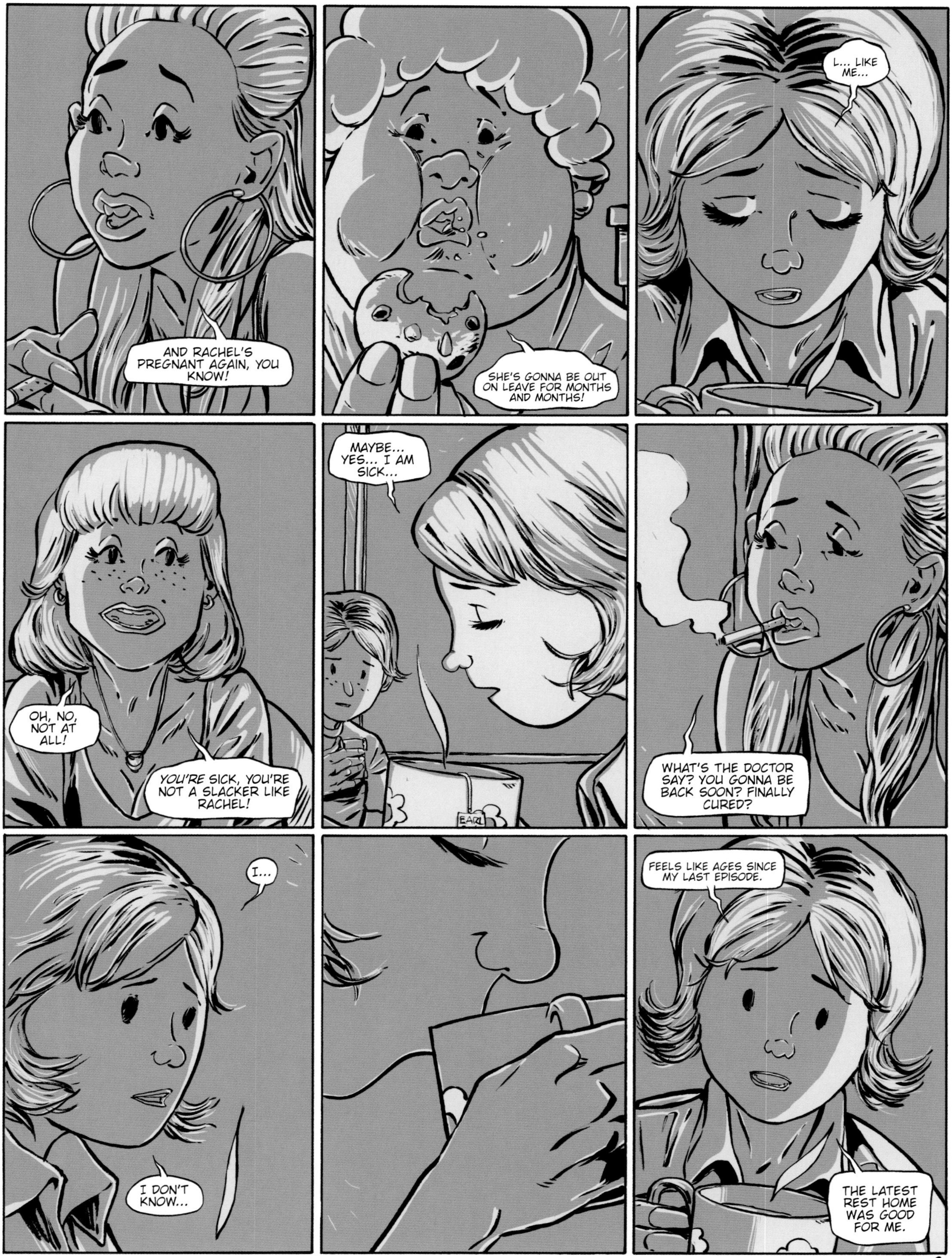
AND RACHEL'S PREGNANT AGAIN, YOU KNOW!
SHE'S GONNA BE OUT ON LEAVE FOR MONTHS AND MONTHS!
L... LIKE ME...
OH, NO, NOT AT ALL!
YOU'RE SICK, YOU'RE NOT A SLACKER LIKE RACHEL!
MAYBE... YES... I AM SICK...
EARL
WHAT'S THE DOCTOR SAY? YOU GONNA BE BACK SOON? FINALLY CURED?
I...
I DON'T KNOW...
FEELS LIKE AGES SINCE MY LAST EPISODE.
THE LATEST REST HOME WAS GOOD FOR ME.
2.

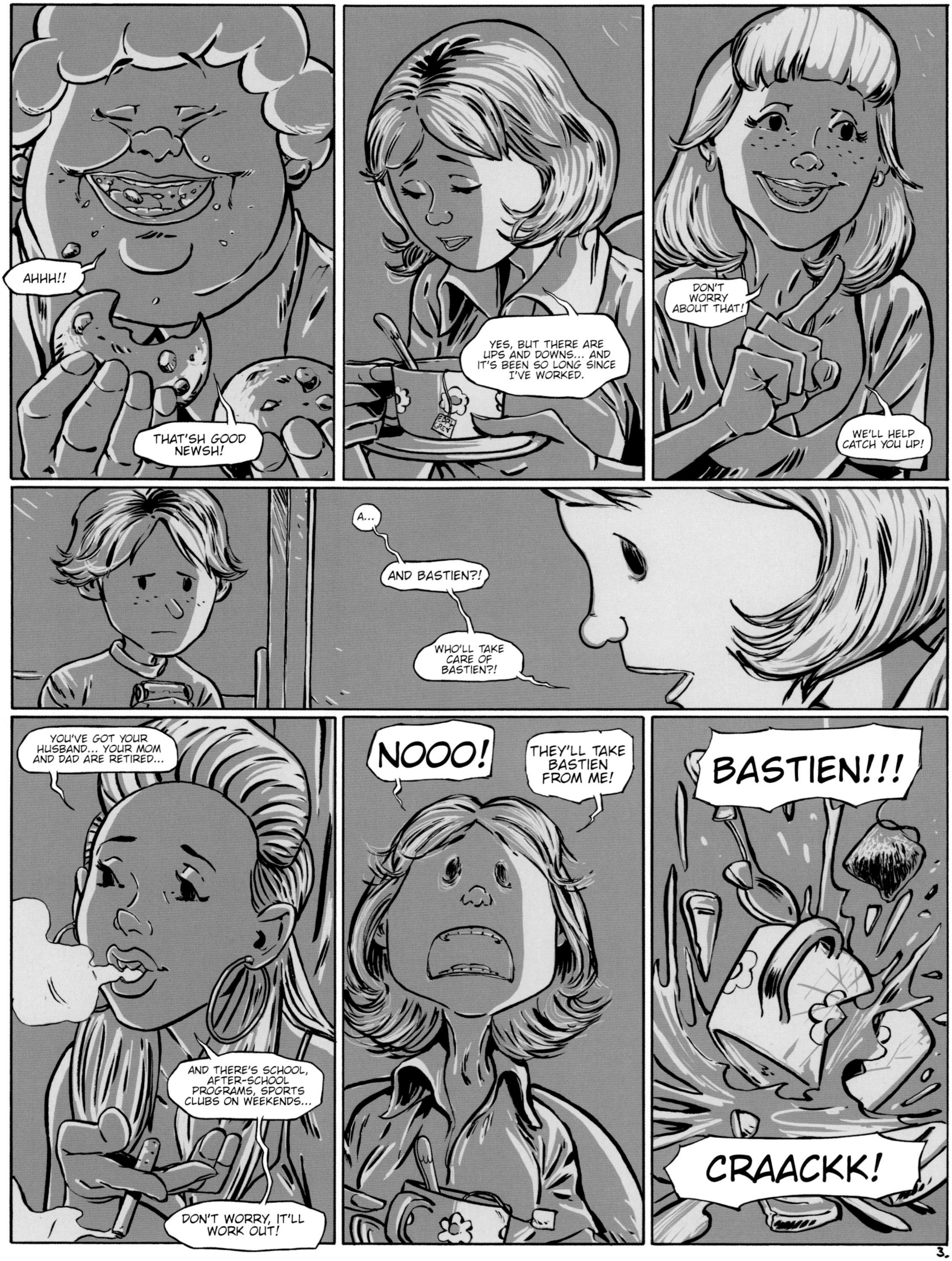
AHHH!!
THAT'SH GOOD NEWSH!
YES, BUT THERE ARE UPS AND DOWNS... AND IT'S BEEN SO LONG SINCE I'VE WORKED.
DON'T WORRY ABOUT THAT!
WE'LL HELP CATCH YOU UP!
A...
AND BASTIEN?!
WHO'LL TAKE CARE OF BASTIEN?!
YOU'VE GOT YOUR HUSBAND... YOUR MOM AND DAD ARE RETIRED...
AND THERE'S SCHOOL, AFTER-SCHOOL PROGRAMS, SPORTS CLUBS ON WEEKENDS...
DON'T WORRY, IT'LL WORK OUT!
NOOO!
THEY'LL TAKE BASTIEN FROM ME!
BASTIEN!!!
CRAACKK!

3.

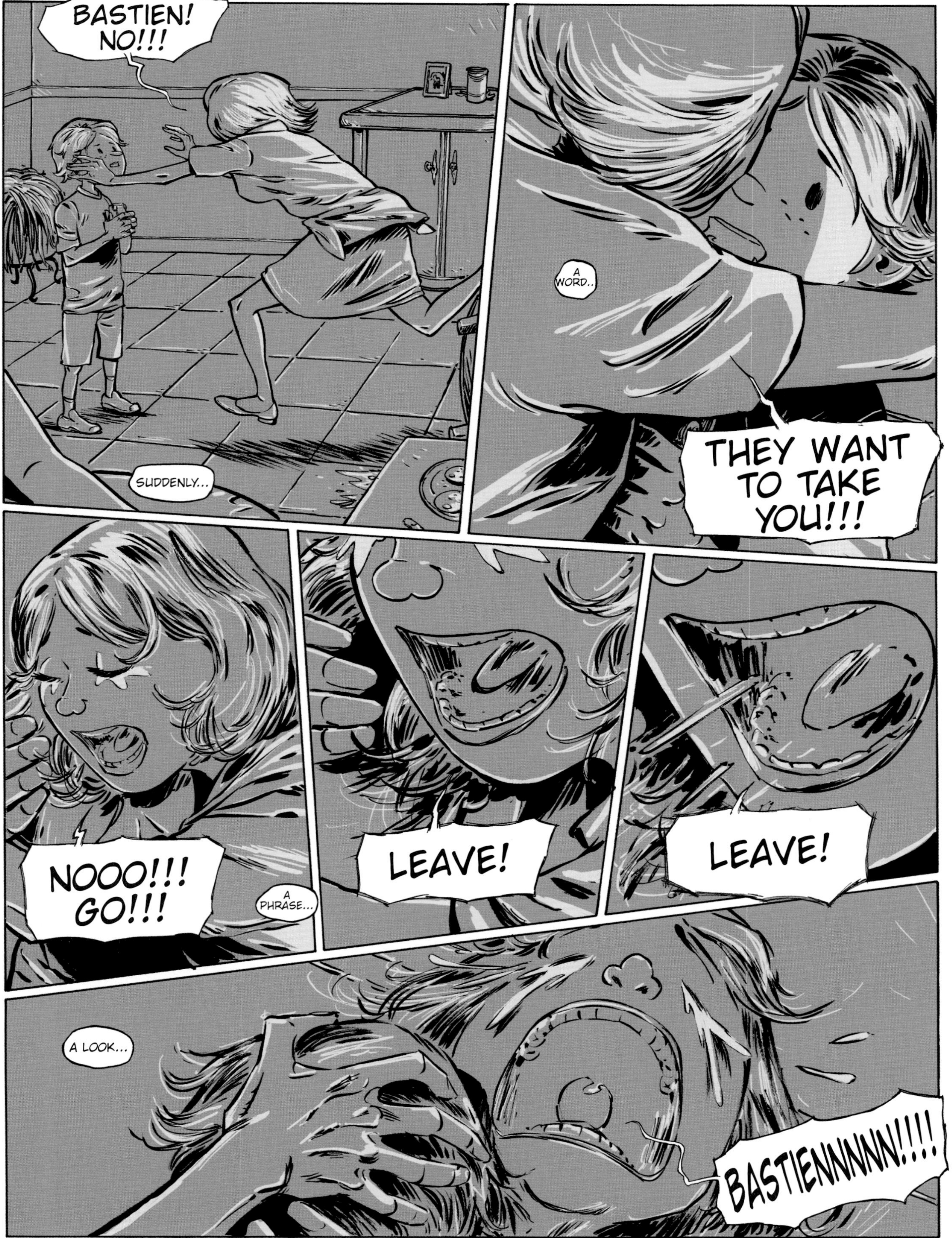

BASTIEN! NO!!!
SUDDENLY...
A WORD..
THEY WANT TO TAKE YOU!!!
NOOO!!! GO!!!
A PHRASE...
LEAVE!
LEAVE!
A LOOK...
BASTIENNNNN!!!!

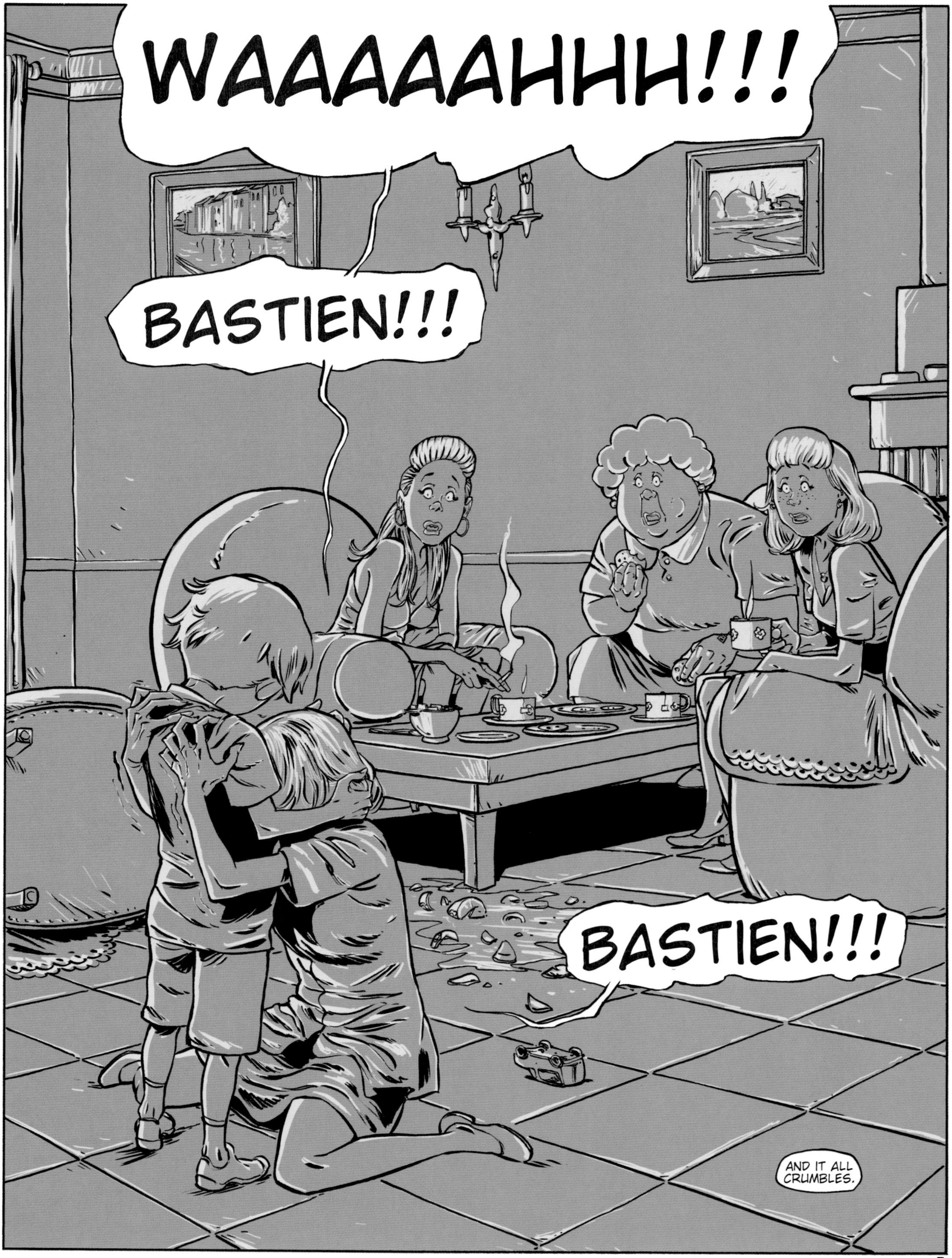
WAAAAAHHH!!!
BASTIEN!!!
BASTIEN!!!
AND IT ALL CRUMBLES.

5.

ELECTROSHOCKS

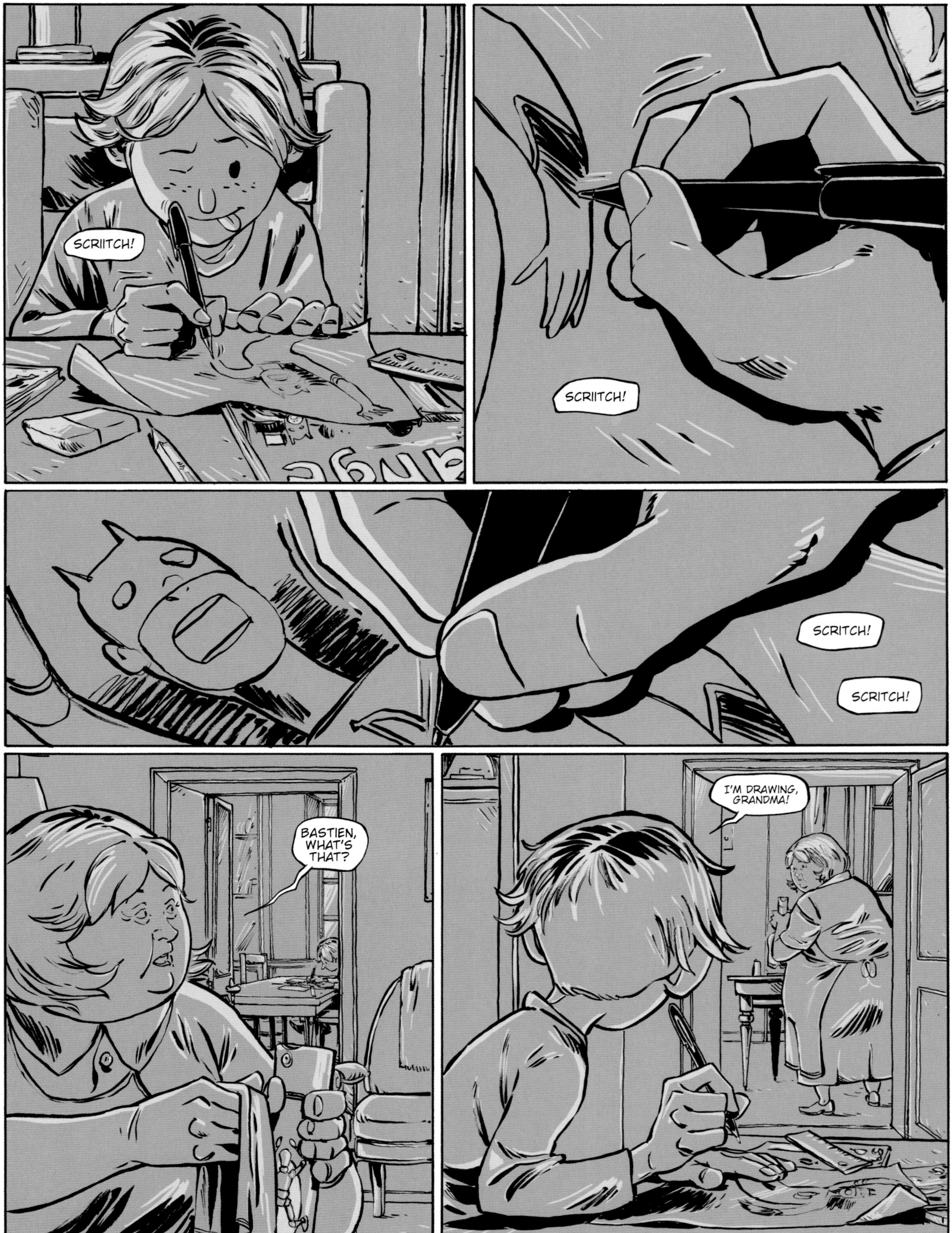
SCRIITCH!
SCRIITCH!
SCRITCH!
SCRITCH!
BASTIEN, WHAT'S THAT?
I'M DRAWING, GRANDMA!

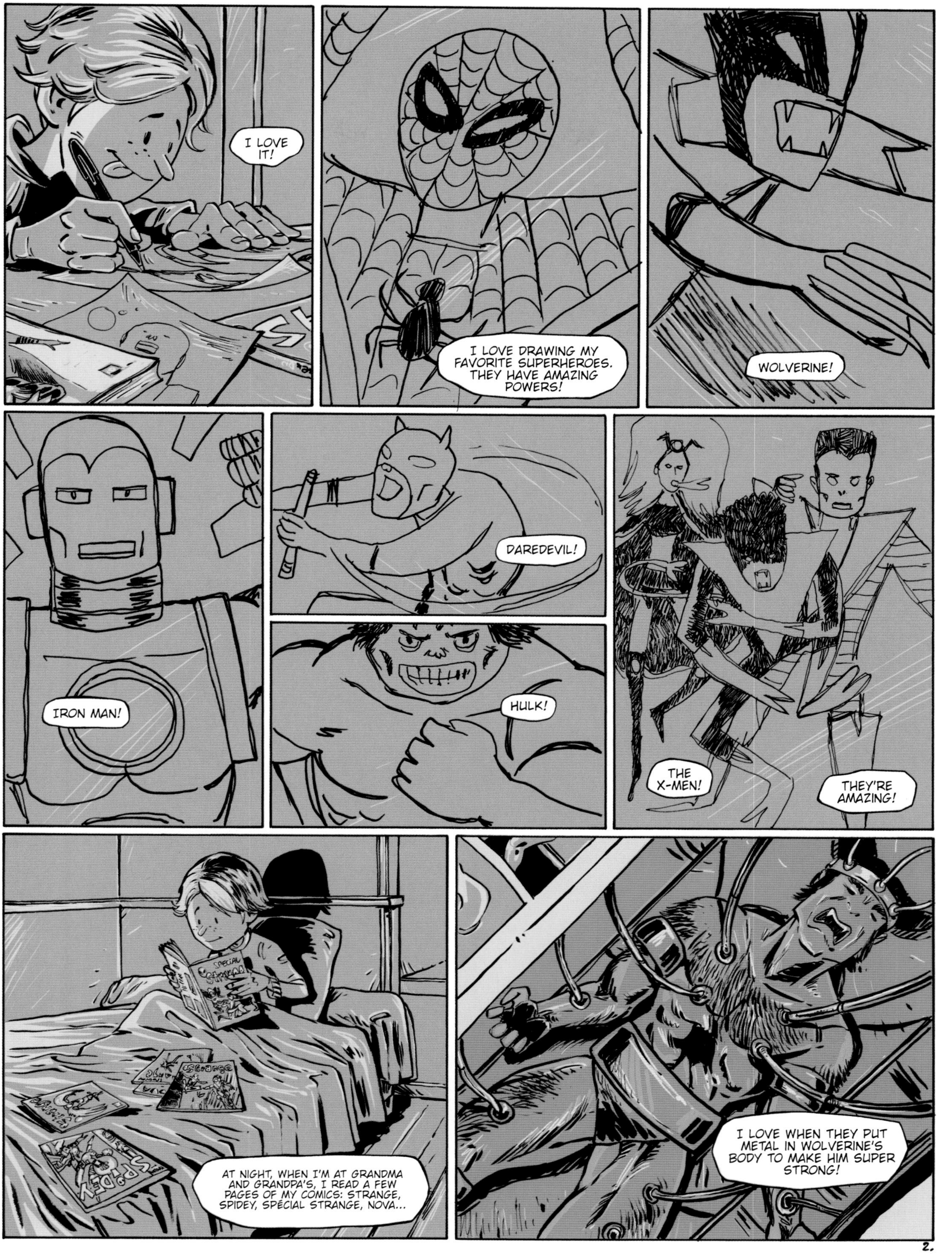
I LOVE IT!
I LOVE DRAWING MY FAVORITE SUPERHEROES. THEY HAVE AMAZING POWERS!
WOLVERINE!
IRON MAN!
DAREDEVIL!
HULK!
THE X-MEN!
THEY'RE AMAZING!
AT NIGHT, WHEN I'M AT GRANDMA AND GRANDPA'S, I READ A FEW PAGES OF MY COMICS: STRANGE, SPIDEY, SPÉCIAL STRANGE, NOVA...
I LOVE WHEN THEY PUT METAL IN WOLVERINE'S BODY TO MAKE HIM SUPER STRONG!
2.

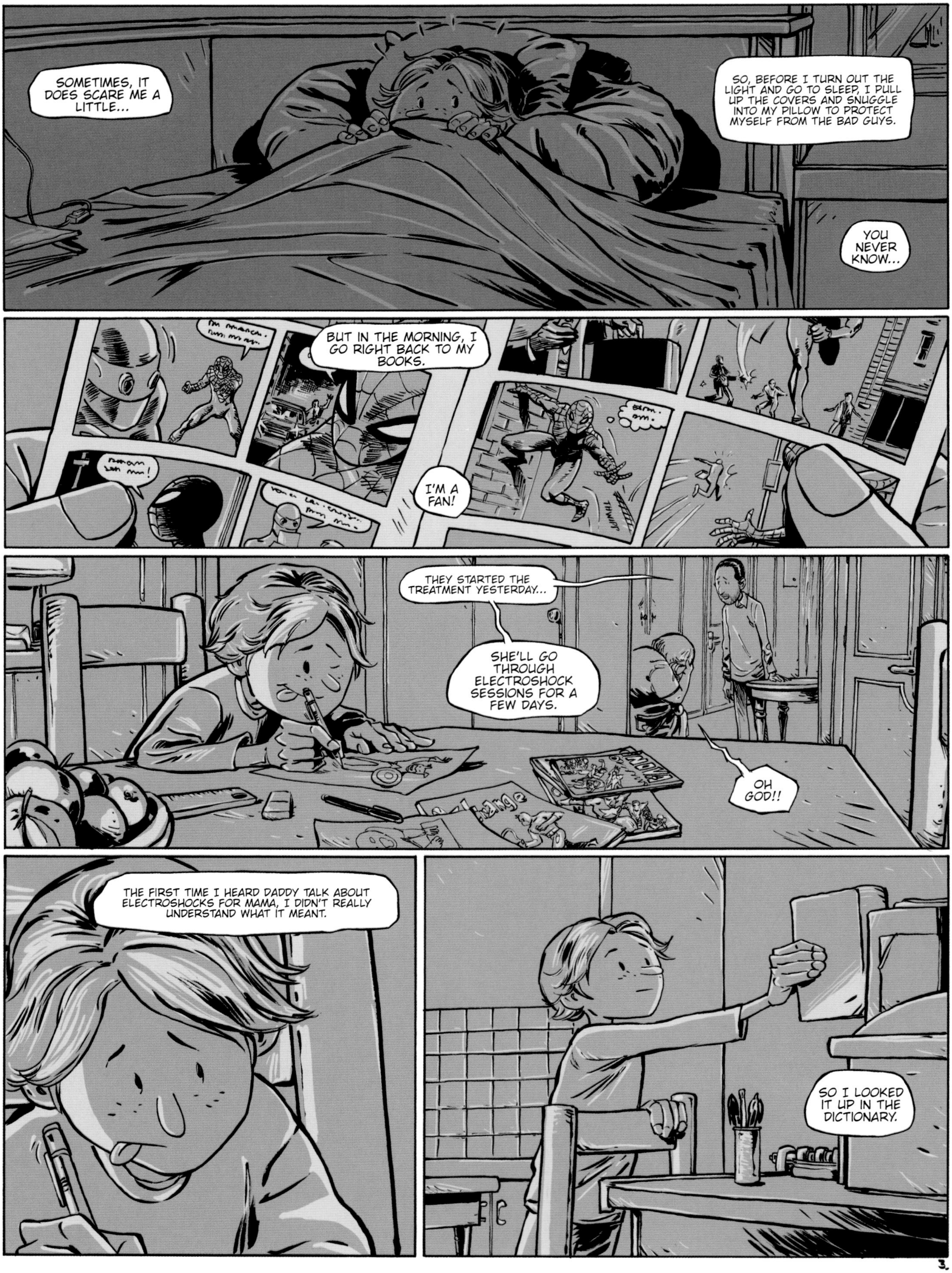
SOMETIMES, IT DOES SCARE ME A LITTLE...
SO, BEFORE I TURN OUT THE LIGHT AND GO TO SLEEP, I PULL UP THE COVERS AND SNUGGLE INTO MY PILLOW TO PROTECT MYSELF FROM THE BAD GUYS.
YOU NEVER KNOW...
BUT IN THE MORNING, I GO RIGHT BACK TO MY BOOKS.
I'M A FAN!
THEY STARTED THE TREATMENT YESTERDAY...
SHE'LL GO THROUGH ELECTROSHOCK SESSIONS FOR A FEW DAYS.
OH GOD!!
THE FIRST TIME I HEARD DADDY TALK ABOUT ELECTROSHOCKS FOR MAMA, I DIDN'T REALLY UNDERSTAND WHAT IT MEANT.
SO I LOOKED IT UP IN THE DICTIONARY.

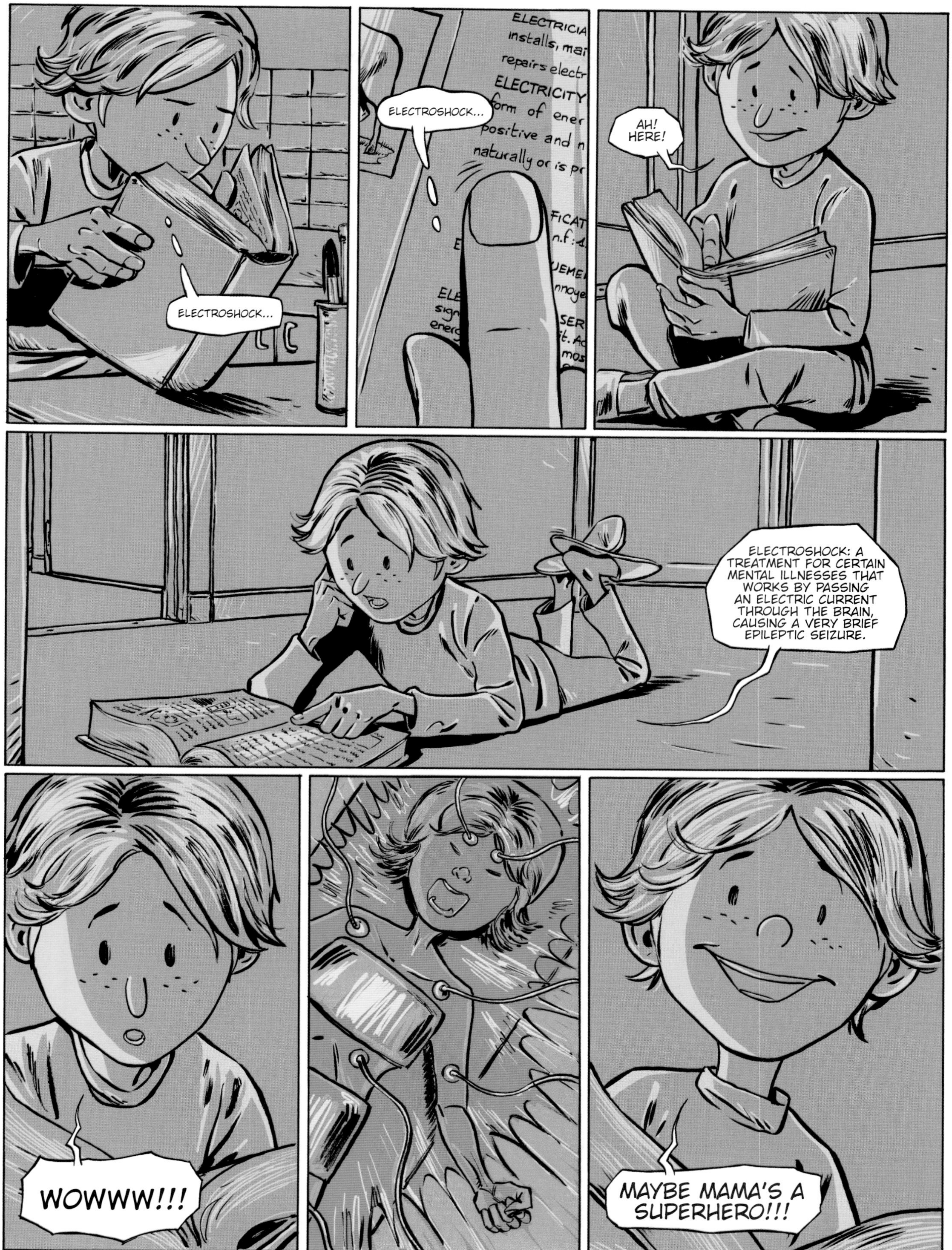

ELECTROSHOCK...
ELECTROSHOCK...
AH! HERE!
ELECTROSHOCK: A TREATMENT FOR CERTAIN MENTAL ILLNESSES THAT WORKS BY PASSING AN ELECTRIC CURRENT THROUGH THE BRAIN, CAUSING A VERY BRIEF EPILEPTIC SEIZURE.
WOWWW!!!
MAYBE MAMA'S A SUPERHERO!!!

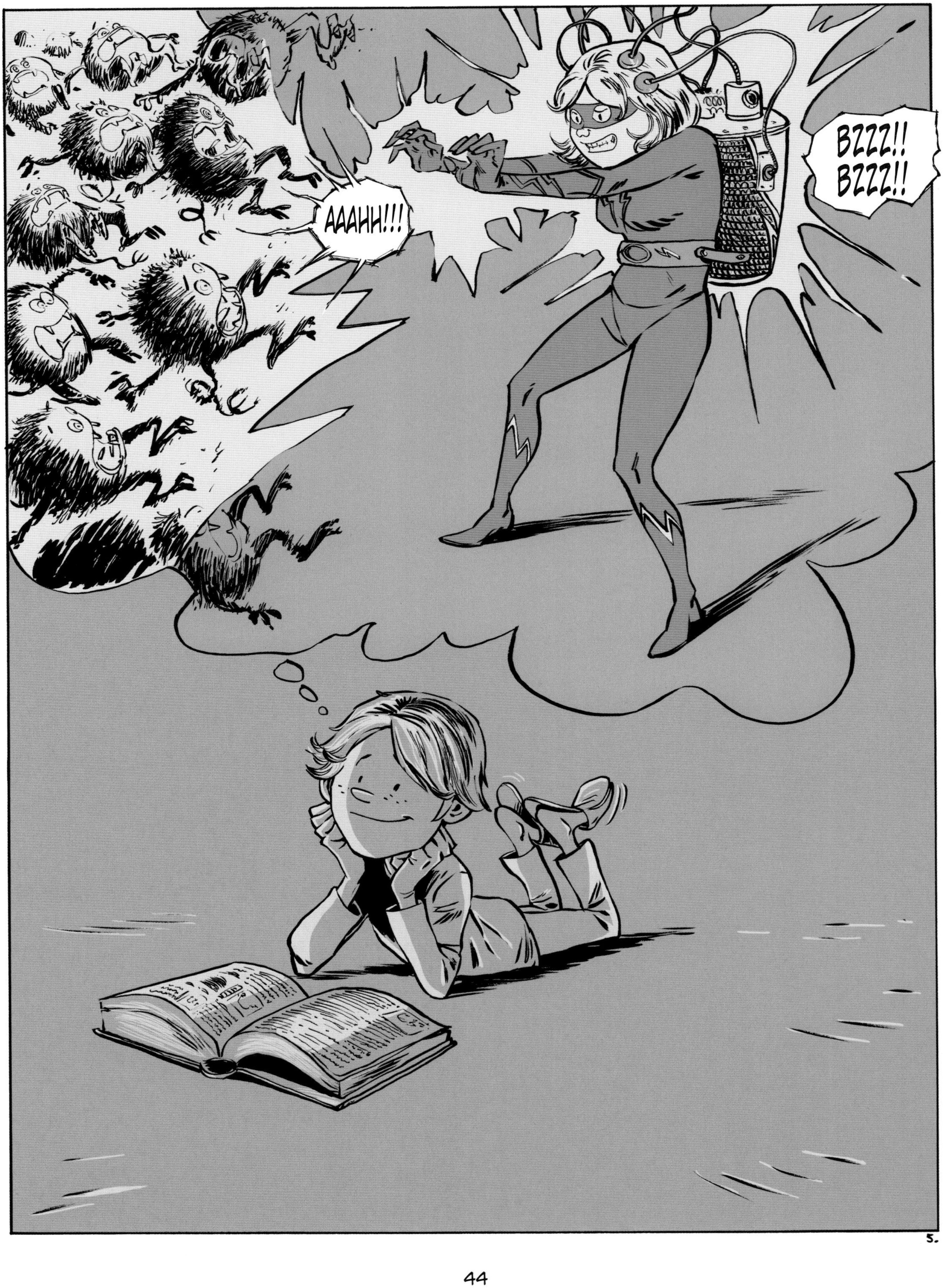
AAAHH!!!
BZZZ!!
BZZZ!!

5.

SCHOOL FRIENDS

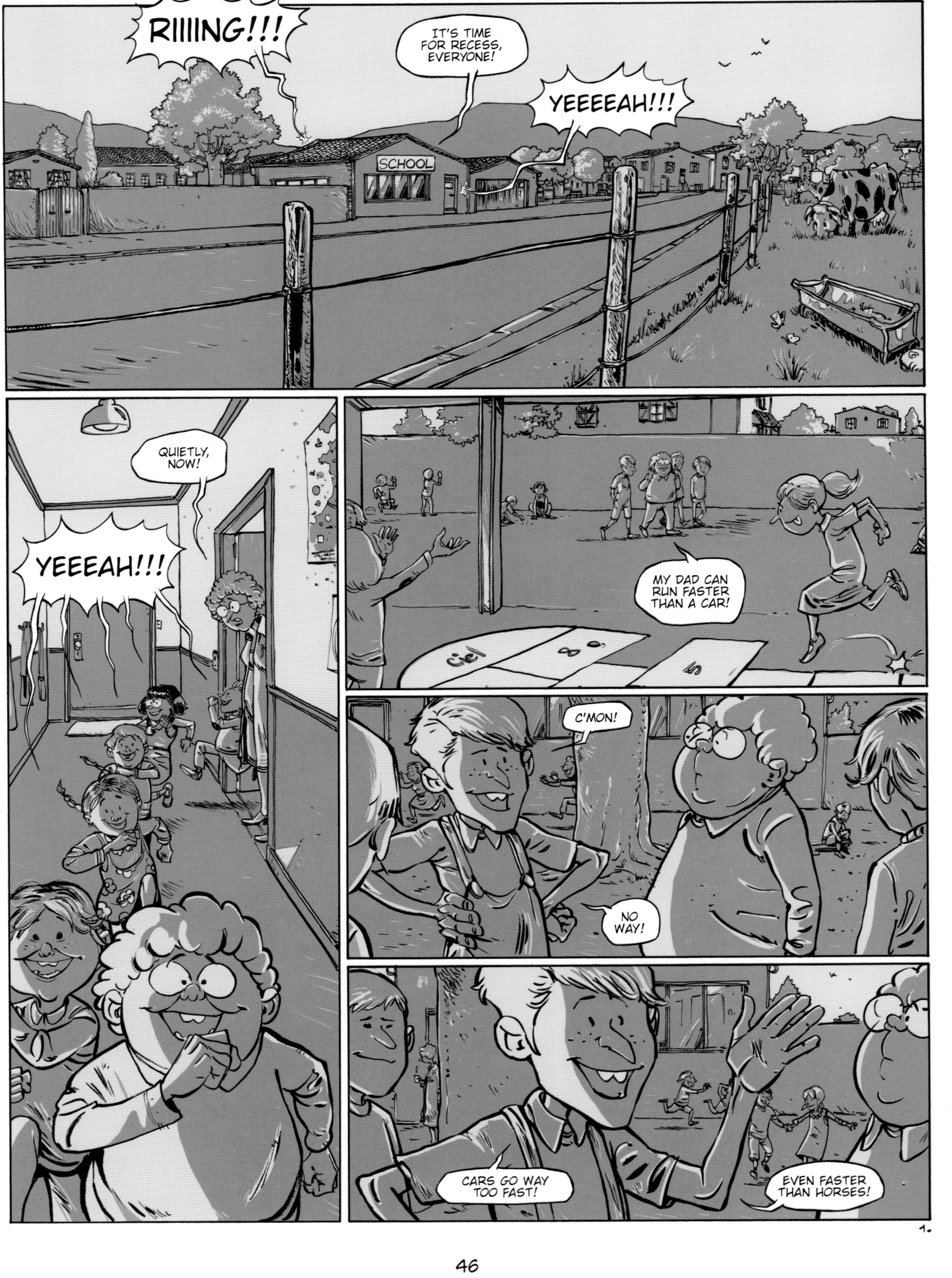
RIIIING!!!
IT'S TIME FOR RECESS, EVERYONE!
YEEEEAH!!!
SCHOOL
QUIETLY, NOW!
YEEEAH!!!
MY DAD CAN RUN FASTER THAN A CAR!
Ciel
8
5
C'MON!
NO WAY!
CARS GO WAY TOO FAST!
EVEN FASTER THAN HORSES!

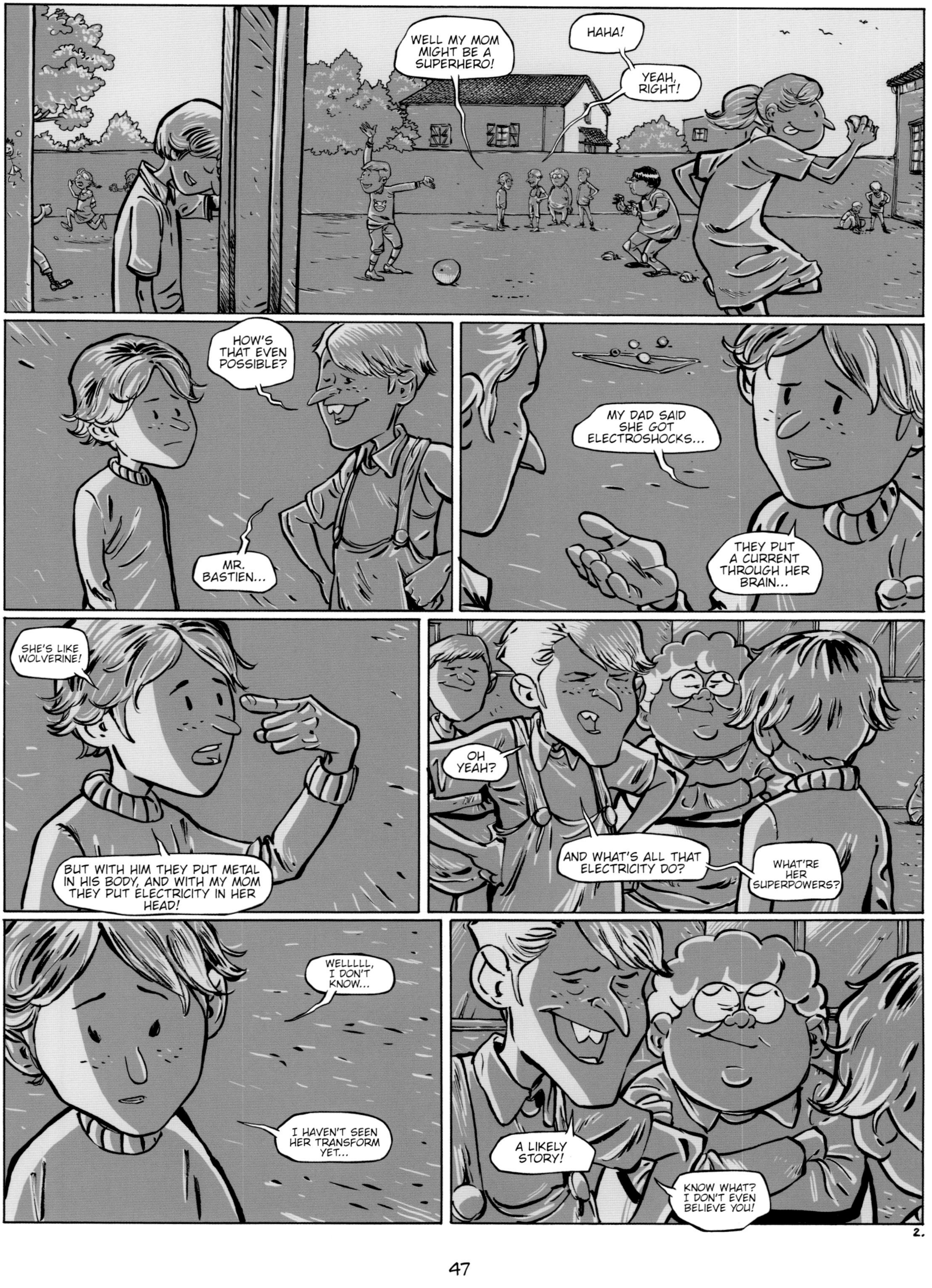
WELL MY MOM MIGHT BE A SUPERHERO!
HAHA!
YEAH, RIGHT!
HOW'S THAT EVEN POSSIBLE?
MR. BASTIEN...
MY DAD SAID SHE GOT ELECTROSHOCKS...
THEY PUT A CURRENT THROUGH HER BRAIN...
SHE'S LIKE WOLVERINE!
BUT WITH HIM THEY PUT METAL IN HIS BODY, AND WITH MY MOM THEY PUT ELECTRICITY IN HER HEAD!
OH YEAH?
AND WHAT'S ALL THAT ELECTRICITY DO?
WHAT'RE HER SUPERPOWERS?
WELLLLL, I DON'T KNOW...
I HAVEN'T SEEN HER TRANSFORM YET...
A LIKELY STORY!
KNOW WHAT? I DON'T EVEN BELIEVE YOU!
2.

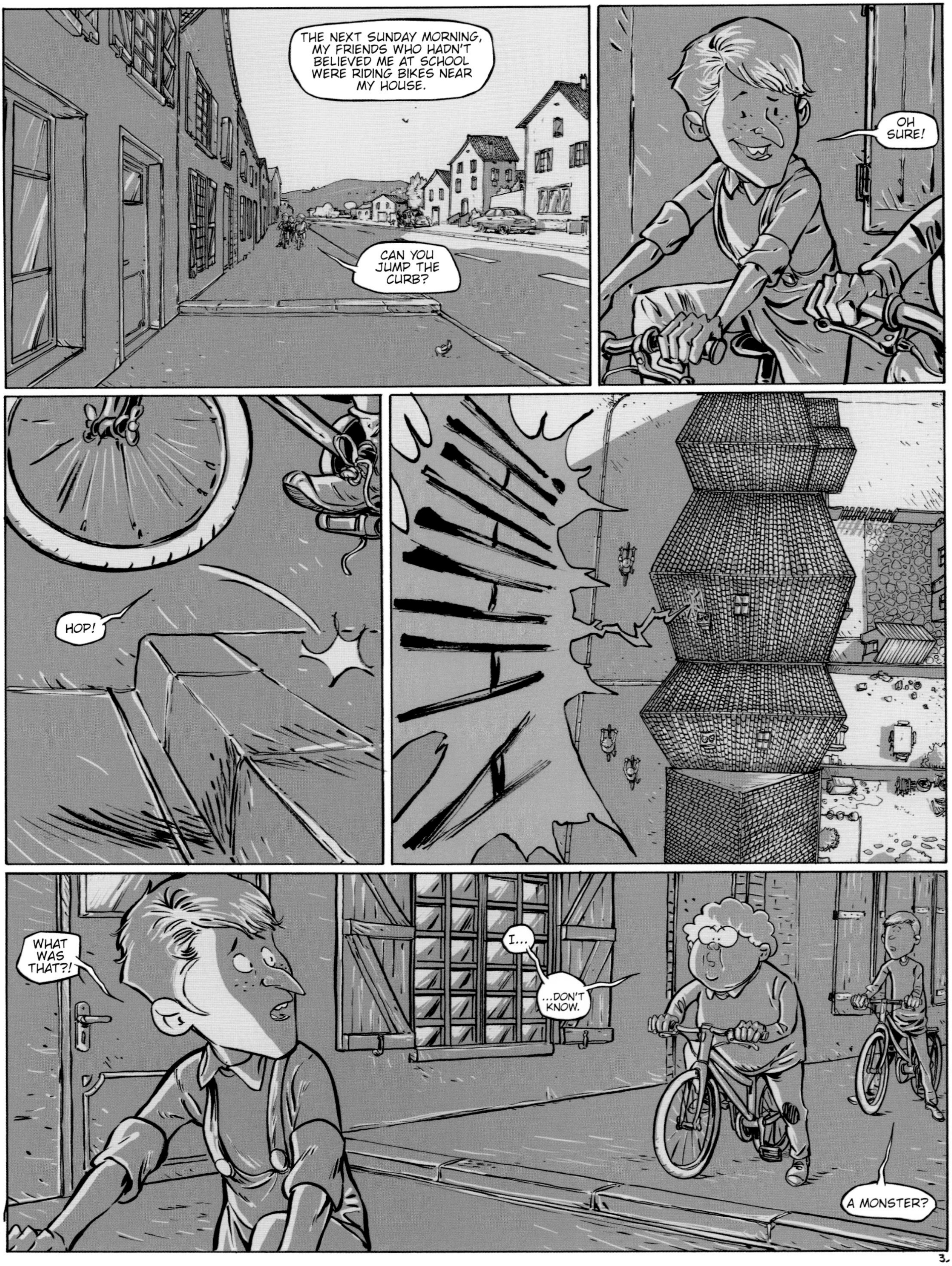
THE NEXT SUNDAY MORNING, MY FRIENDS WHO HADN'T BELIEVED ME AT SCHOOL WERE RIDING BIKES NEAR MY HOUSE.
CAN YOU JUMP THE CURB?
OH SURE!
HOP!
WHAT WAS THAT?!
I...
...DON'T KNOW.
A MONSTER?

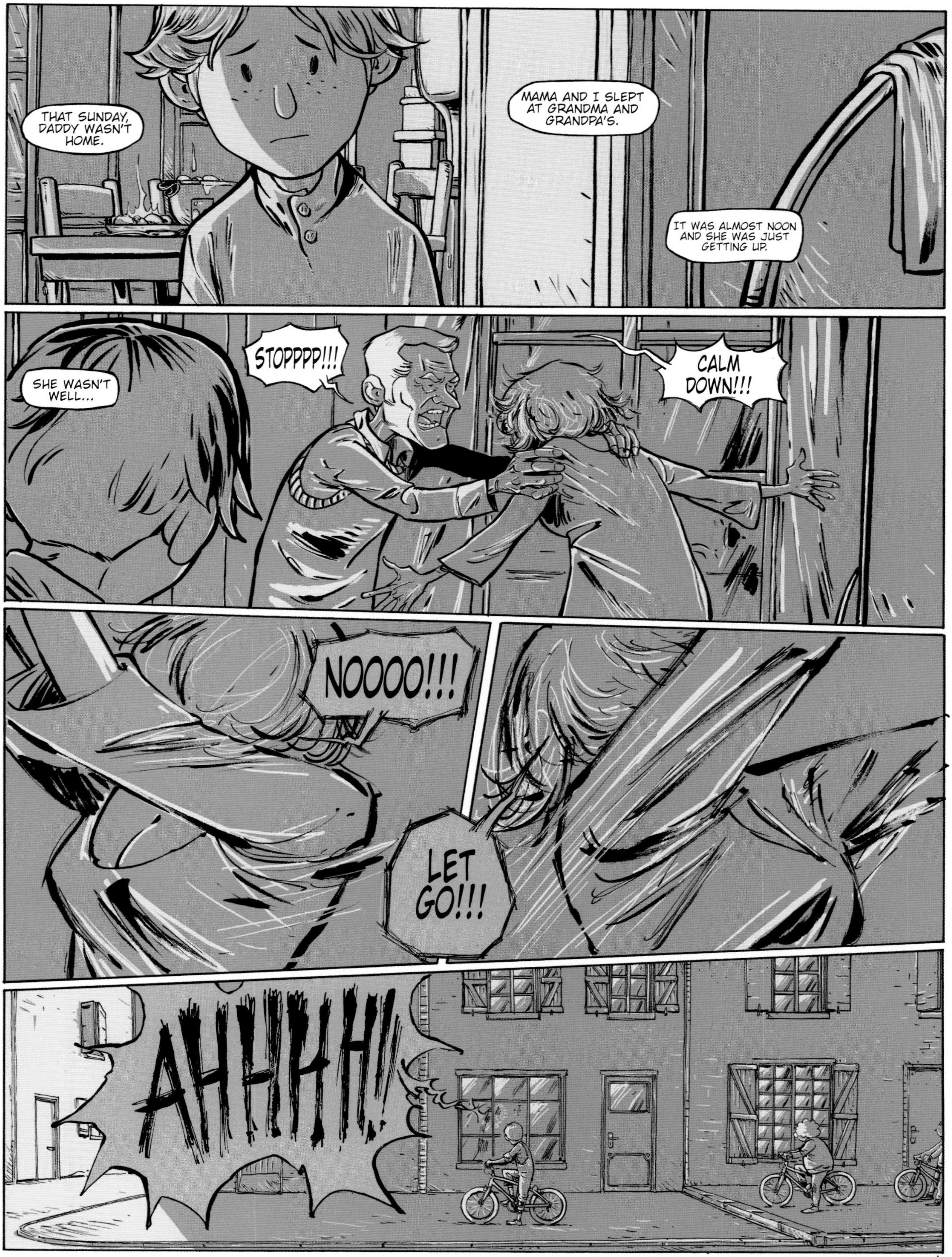
THAT SUNDAY, DADDY WASN'T HOME.
MAMA AND I SLEPT AT GRANDMA AND GRANDPA'S.
IT WAS ALMOST NOON AND SHE WAS JUST GETTING UP.
SHE WASN'T WELL...
STOPPPP!!!
CALM DOWN!!!
NOOOO!!!
LET GO!!!
AHHHH!!
4.

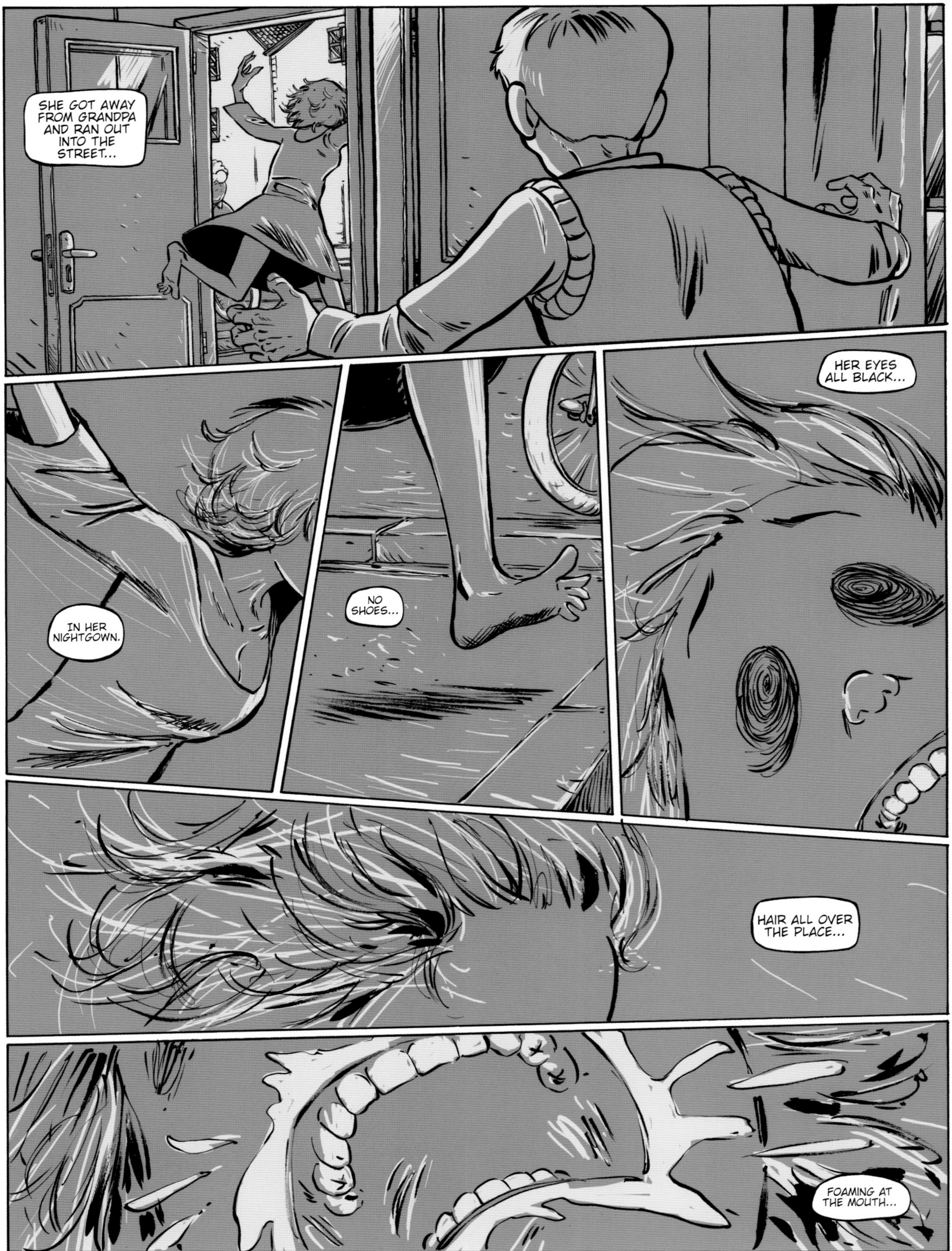
SHE GOT AWAY FROM GRANDPA AND RAN OUT INTO THE STREET...
IN HER NIGHTGOWN.
NO SHOES...
HER EYES ALL BLACK...
HAIR ALL OVER THE PLACE...
FOAMING AT THE MOUTH...

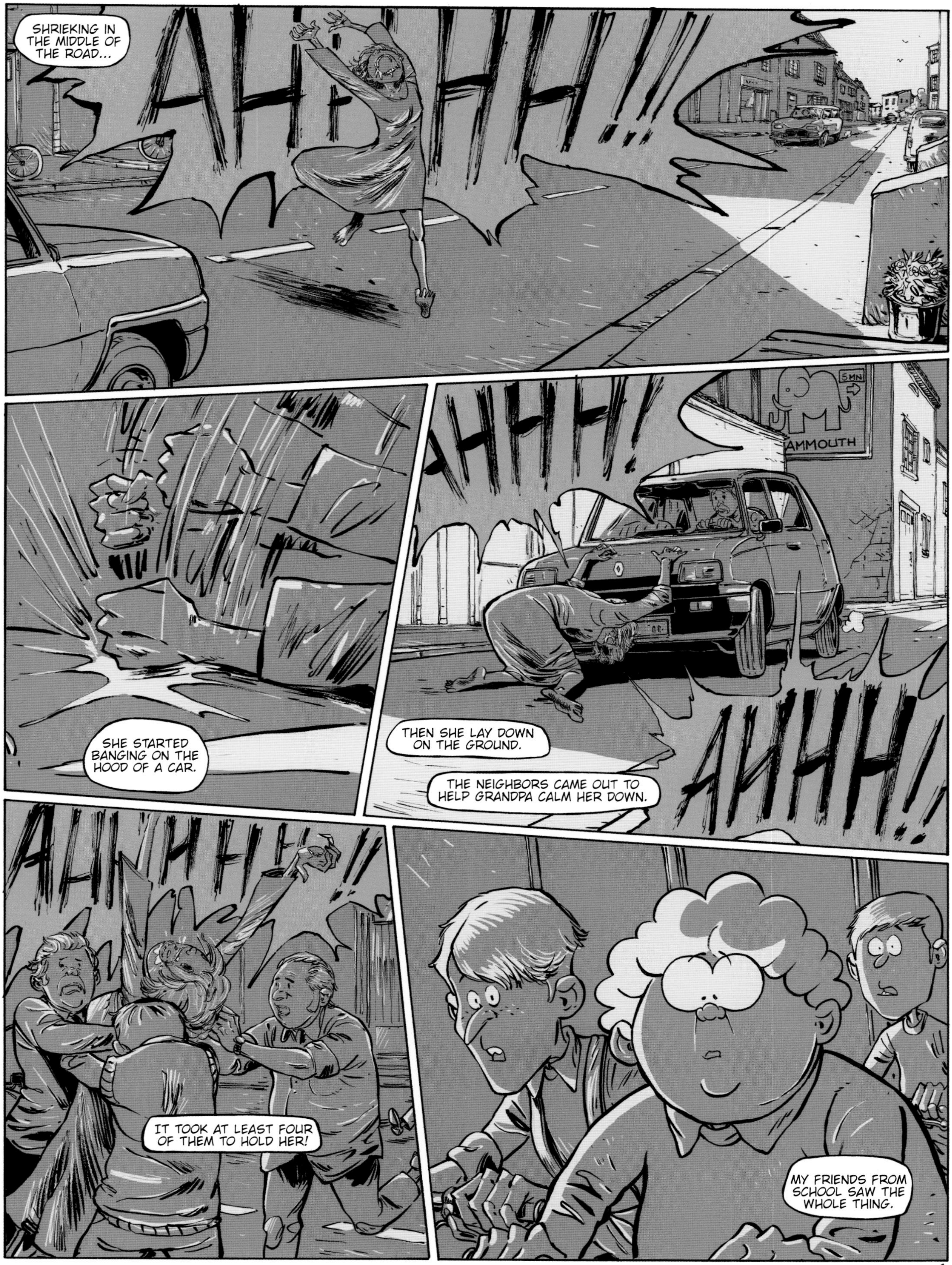
SHRIEKING IN THE MIDDLE OF THE ROAD...
SHE STARTED BANGING ON THE HOOD OF A CAR.
5 MN
AMMOUTH
THEN SHE LAY DOWN ON THE GROUND.
THE NEIGHBORS CAME OUT TO HELP GRANDPA CALM HER DOWN.
IT TOOK AT LEAST FOUR OF THEM TO HOLD HER!
MY FRIENDS FROM SCHOOL SAW THE WHOLE THING.

6.

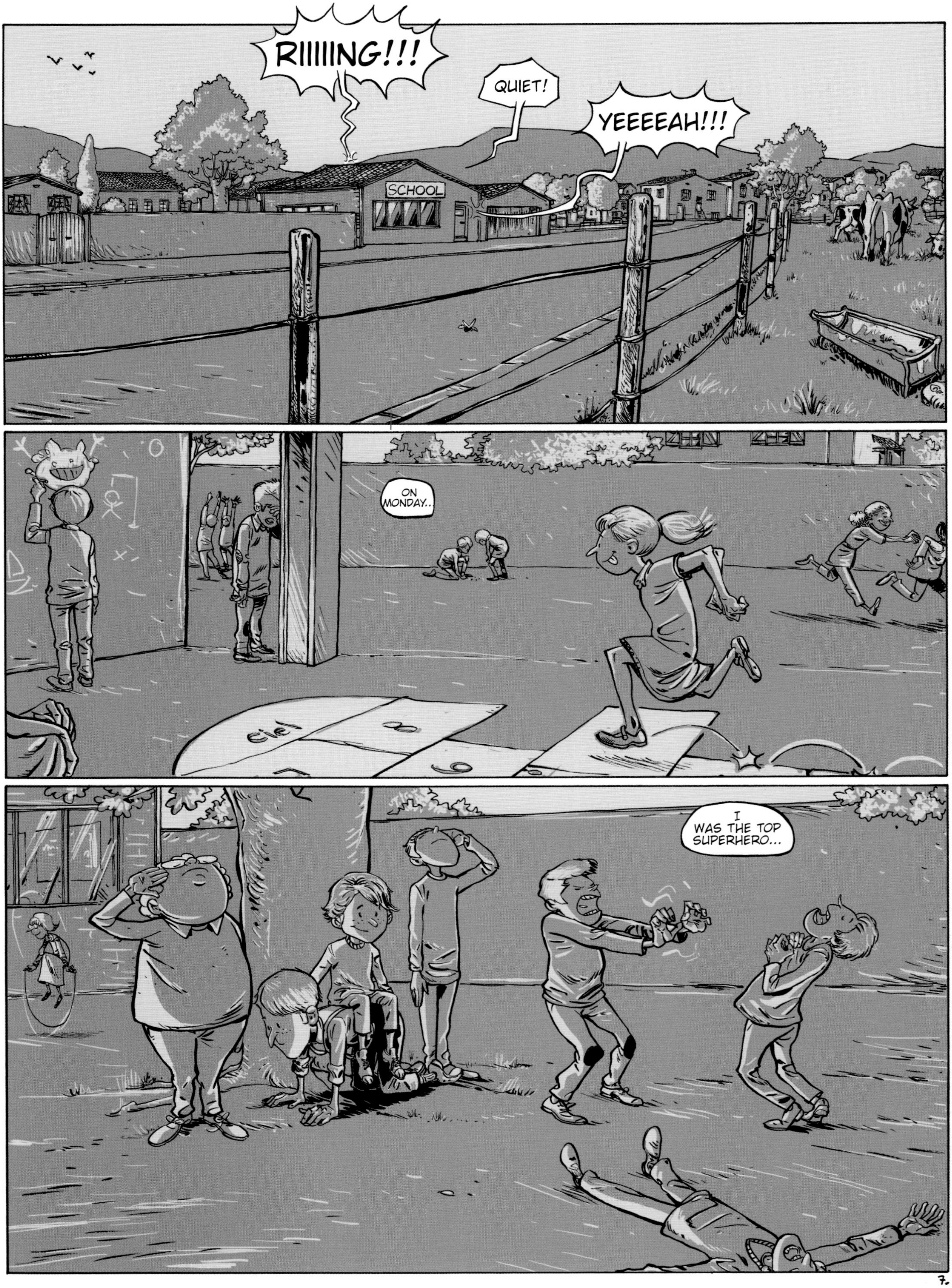
RIIIING!!!
SCHOOL
QUIET!
YEEEEAH!!!
ON MONDAY..
Ciel
I WAS THE TOP SUPERHERO...

7.

CHESTNUTS

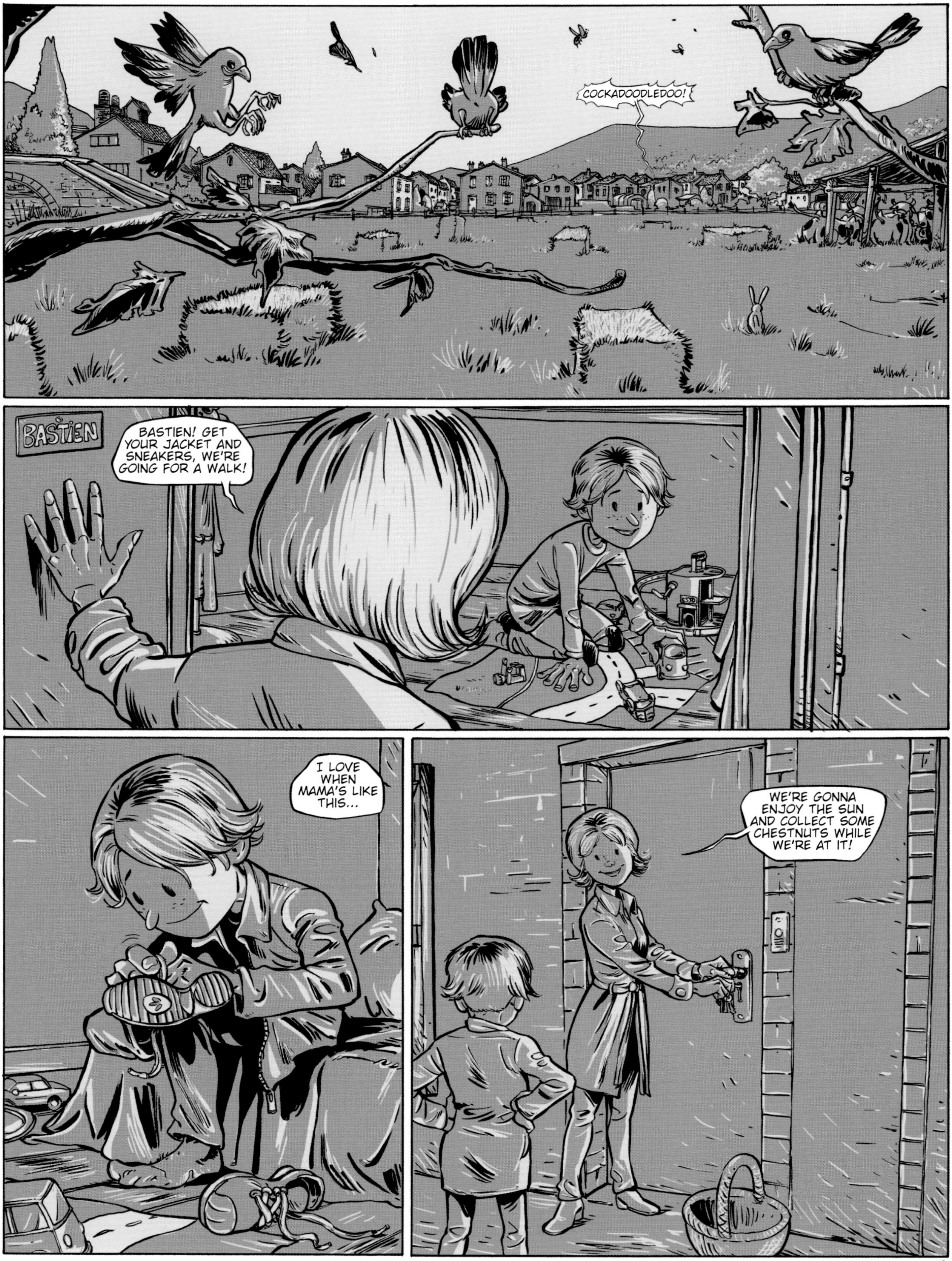
COCKADOODLEDOO!
BASTIEN
BASTIEN! GET YOUR JACKET AND SNEAKERS, WE'RE GOING FOR A WALK!
I LOVE WHEN MAMA'S LIKE THIS...
WE'RE GONNA ENJOY THE SUN AND COLLECT SOME CHESTNUTS WHILE WE'RE AT IT!

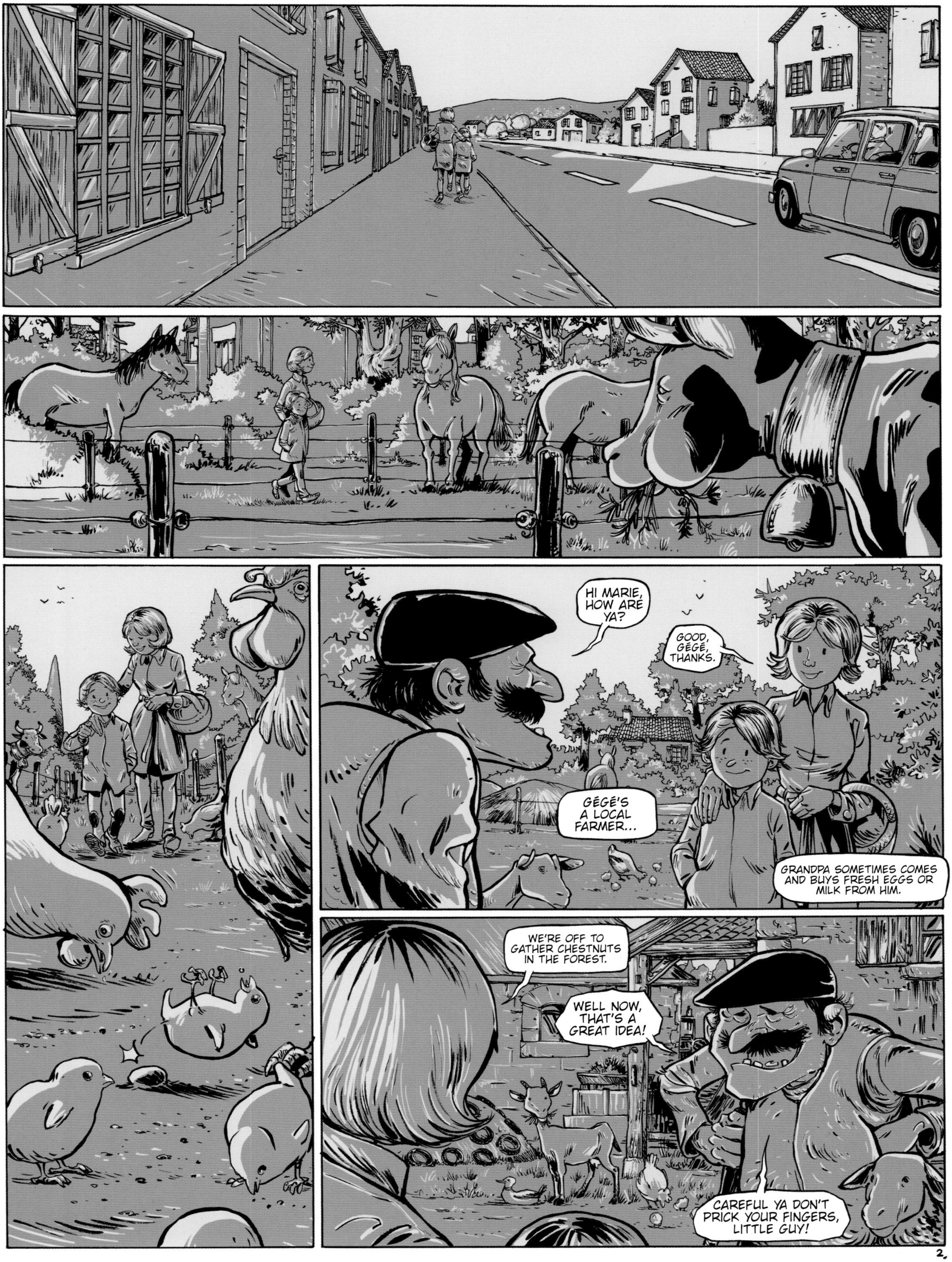
HI MARIE, HOW ARE YA?
GOOD, GÉGÉ, THANKS.
GÉGÉ'S A LOCAL FARMER...
GRANDPA SOMETIMES COMES AND BUYS FRESH EGGS OR MILK FROM HIM.
WE'RE OFF TO GATHER CHESTNUTS IN THE FOREST.
WELL NOW, THAT'S A GREAT IDEA!
CAREFUL YA DON'T PRICK YOUR FINGERS, LITTLE GUY!

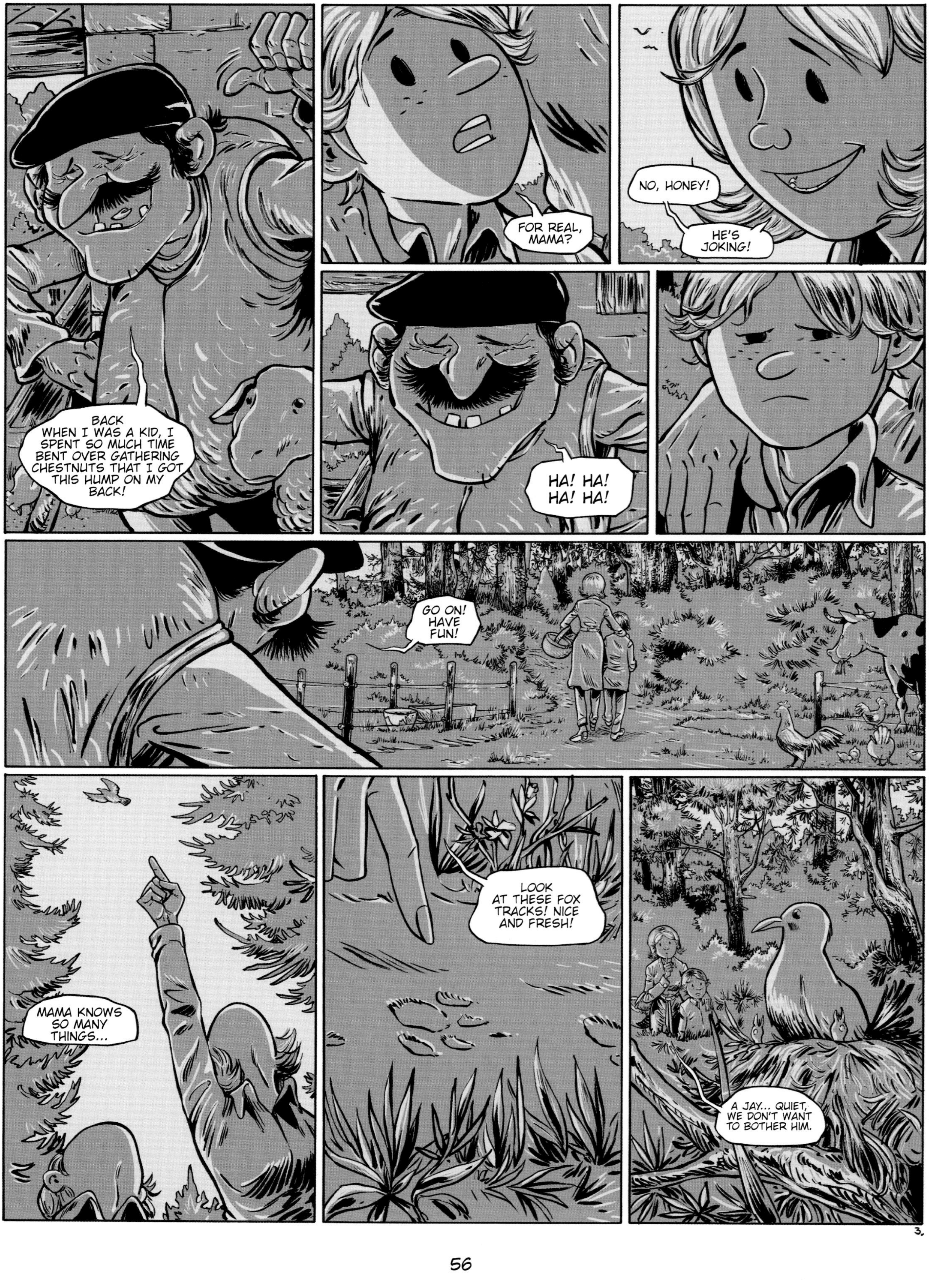
BACK WHEN I WAS A KID, I SPENT SO MUCH TIME BENT OVER GATHERING CHESTNUTS THAT I GOT THIS HUMP ON MY BACK!
FOR REAL, MAMA?
NO, HONEY!
HE'S JOKING!
HA! HA! HA! HA!
GO ON! HAVE FUN!
MAMA KNOWS SO MANY THINGS...
LOOK AT THESE FOX TRACKS! NICE AND FRESH!
A JAY... QUIET, WE DON'T WANT TO BOTHER HIM.
3.

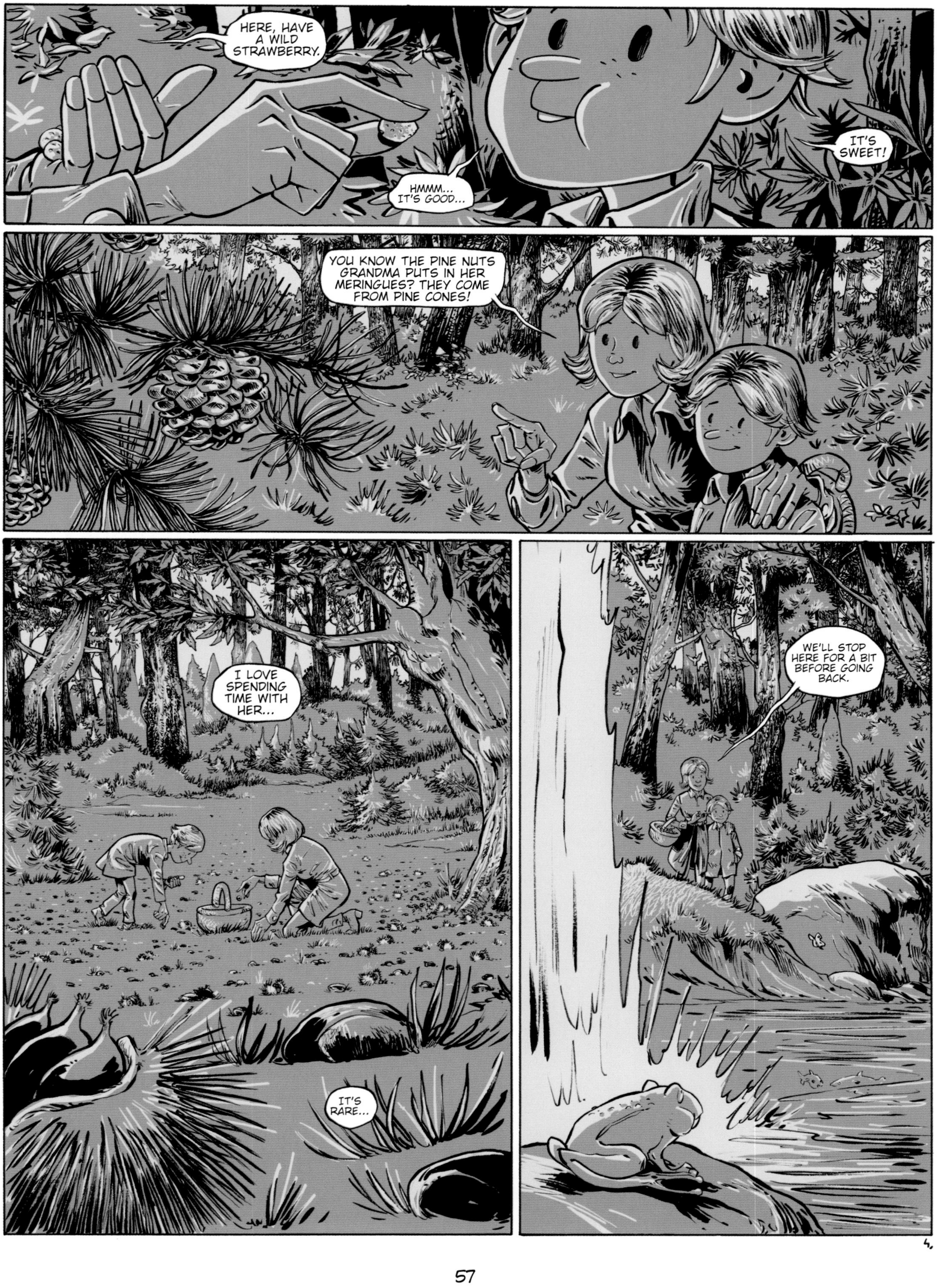
HERE, HAVE A WILD STRAWBERRY.
HMMM... IT'S GOOD...
IT'S SWEET!
YOU KNOW THE PINE NUTS GRANDMA PUTS IN HER MERINGUES? THEY COME FROM PINE CONES!
I LOVE SPENDING TIME WITH HER...
IT'S RARE...
WE'LL STOP HERE FOR A BIT BEFORE GOING BACK.

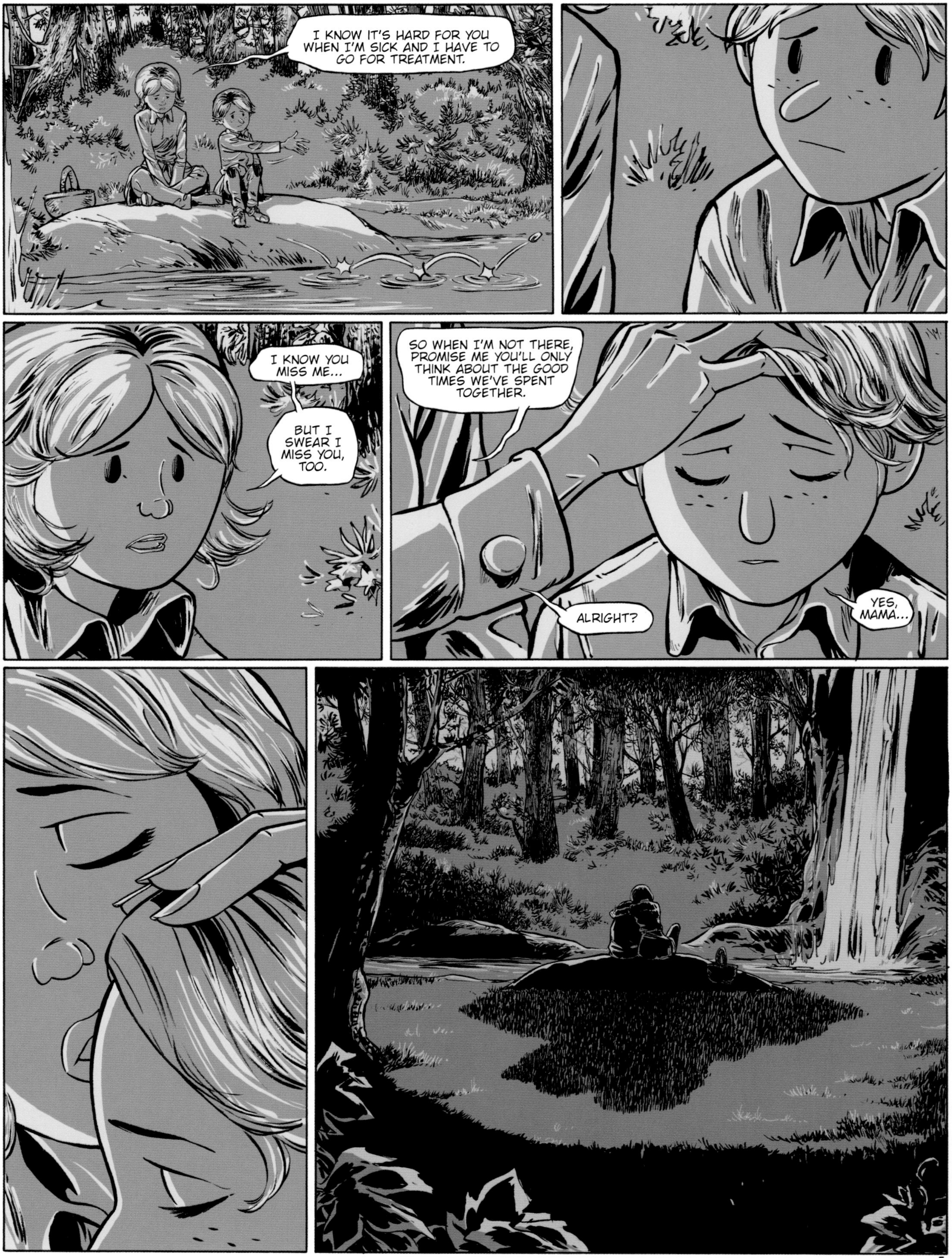
I KNOW IT'S HARD FOR YOU WHEN I'M SICK AND I HAVE TO GO FOR TREATMENT.
I KNOW YOU MISS ME...
BUT I SWEAR I MISS YOU, TOO.
SO WHEN I'M NOT THERE, PROMISE ME YOU'LL ONLY THINK ABOUT THE GOOD TIMES WE'VE SPENT TOGETHER.
ALRIGHT?
YES, MAMA...
5.

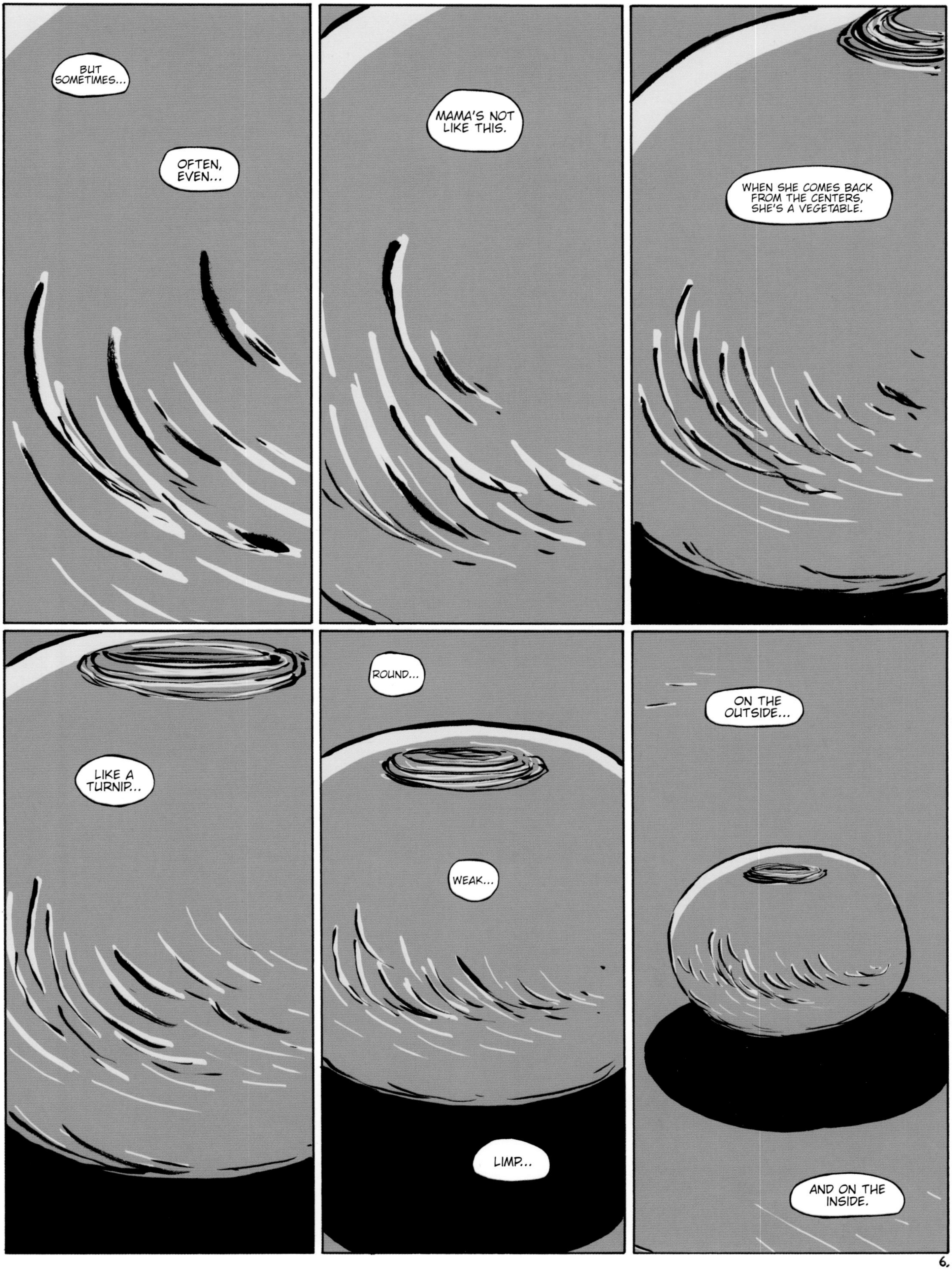
BUT SOMETIMES...
OFTEN, EVEN...
MAMA'S NOT LIKE THIS.
WHEN SHE COMES BACK FROM THE CENTERS, SHE'S A VEGETABLE.
LIKE A TURNIP...
ROUND...
WEAK...
LIMP...
ON THE OUTSIDE...
AND ON THE INSIDE.
6.

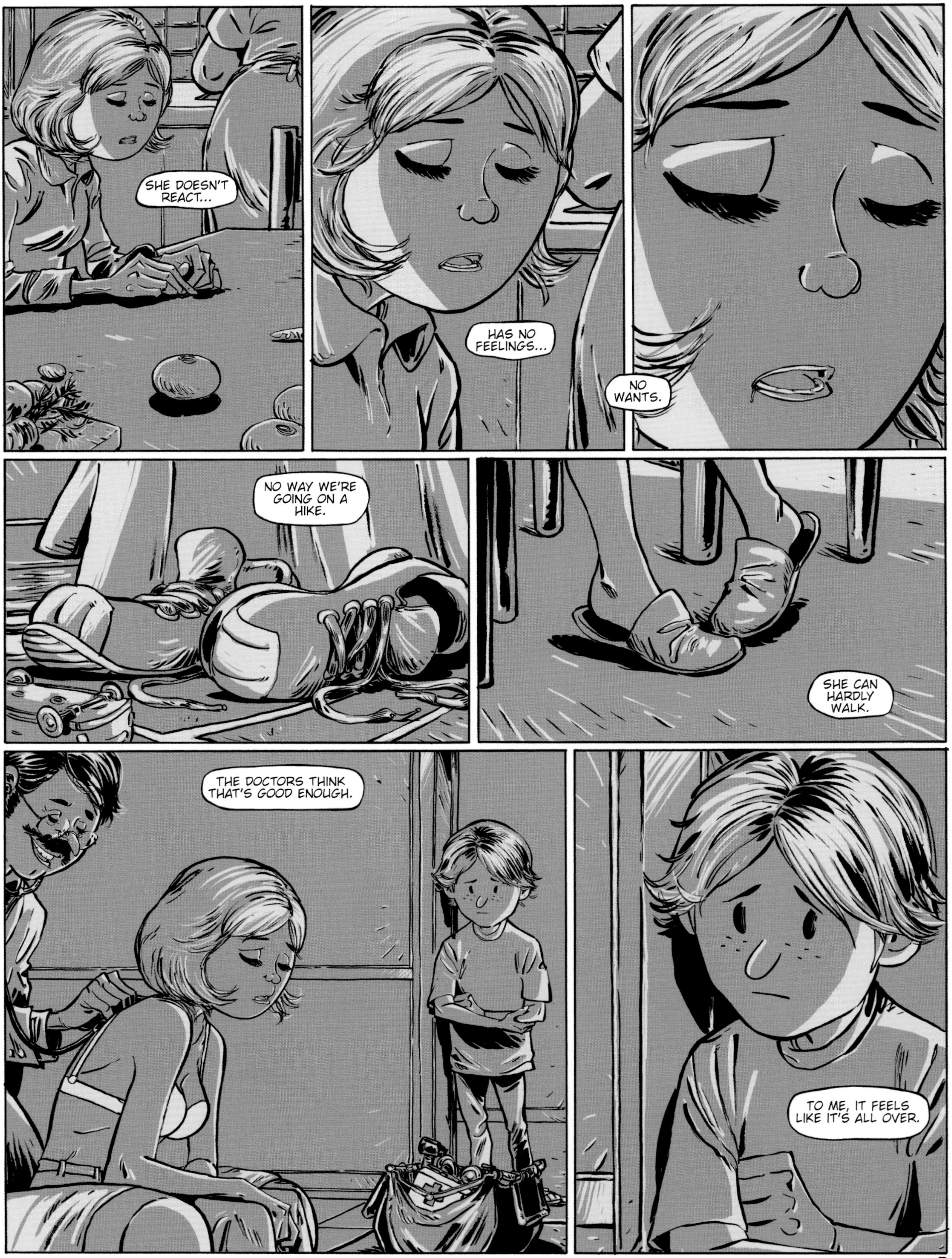
SHE DOESN'T REACT...
HAS NO FEELINGS...
NO WANTS.
NO WAY WE'RE GOING ON A HIKE.
SHE CAN HARDLY WALK.
THE DOCTORS THINK THAT'S GOOD ENOUGH.
TO ME, IT FEELS LIKE IT'S ALL OVER.
7.

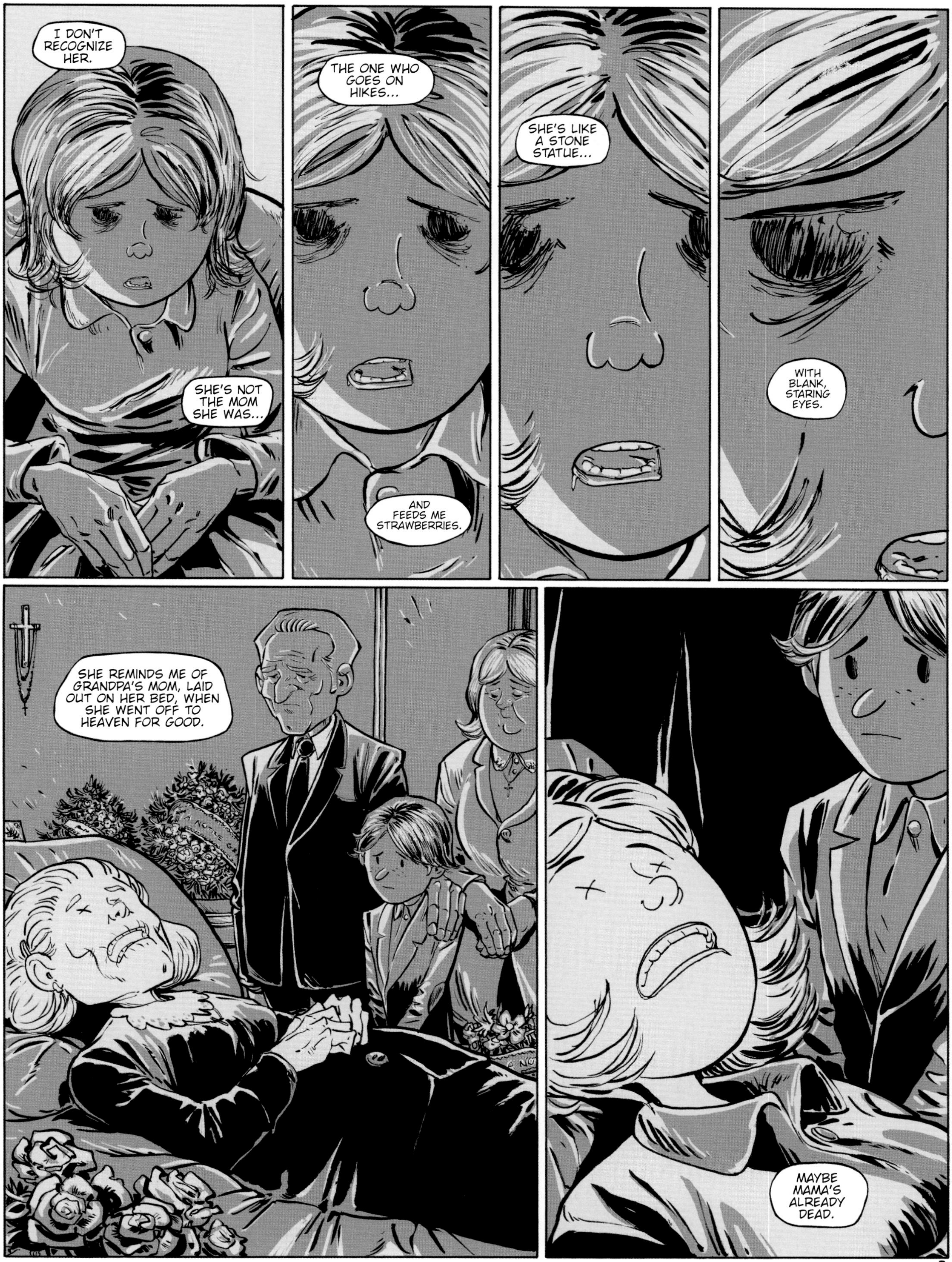
I DON'T RECOGNIZE HER.
SHE'S NOT THE MOM SHE WAS...
THE ONE WHO GOES ON HIKES...
AND FEEDS ME STRAWBERRIES.
SHE'S LIKE A STONE STATUE...
WITH BLANK, STARING EYES.
SHE REMINDS ME OF GRANDPA'S MOM, LAID OUT ON HER BED, WHEN SHE WENT OFF TO HEAVEN FOR GOOD.
MAYBE MAMA'S ALREADY DEAD.
8.

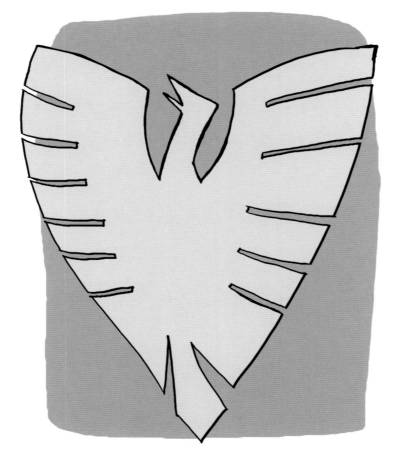

JEAN GREY

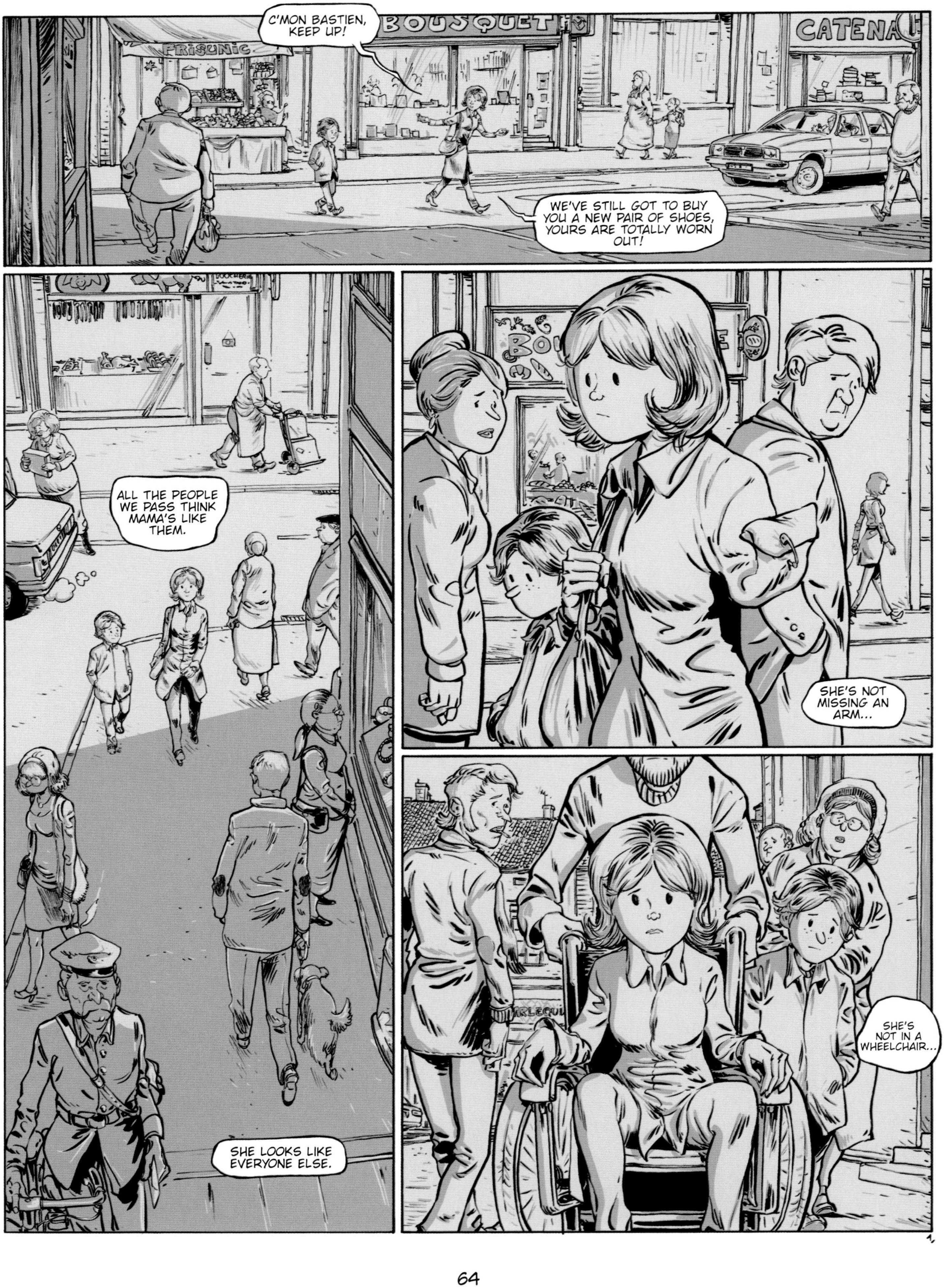
C'MON BASTIEN, KEEP UP!
PRISUNIC
BOUSQUET
CATENA
WE'VE STILL GOT TO BUY YOU A NEW PAIR OF SHOES, YOURS ARE TOTALLY WORN OUT!
ALL THE PEOPLE WE PASS THINK MAMA'S LIKE THEM.
SHE LOOKS LIKE EVERYONE ELSE.
SHE'S NOT MISSING AN ARM...
SHE'S NOT IN A WHEELCHAIR...

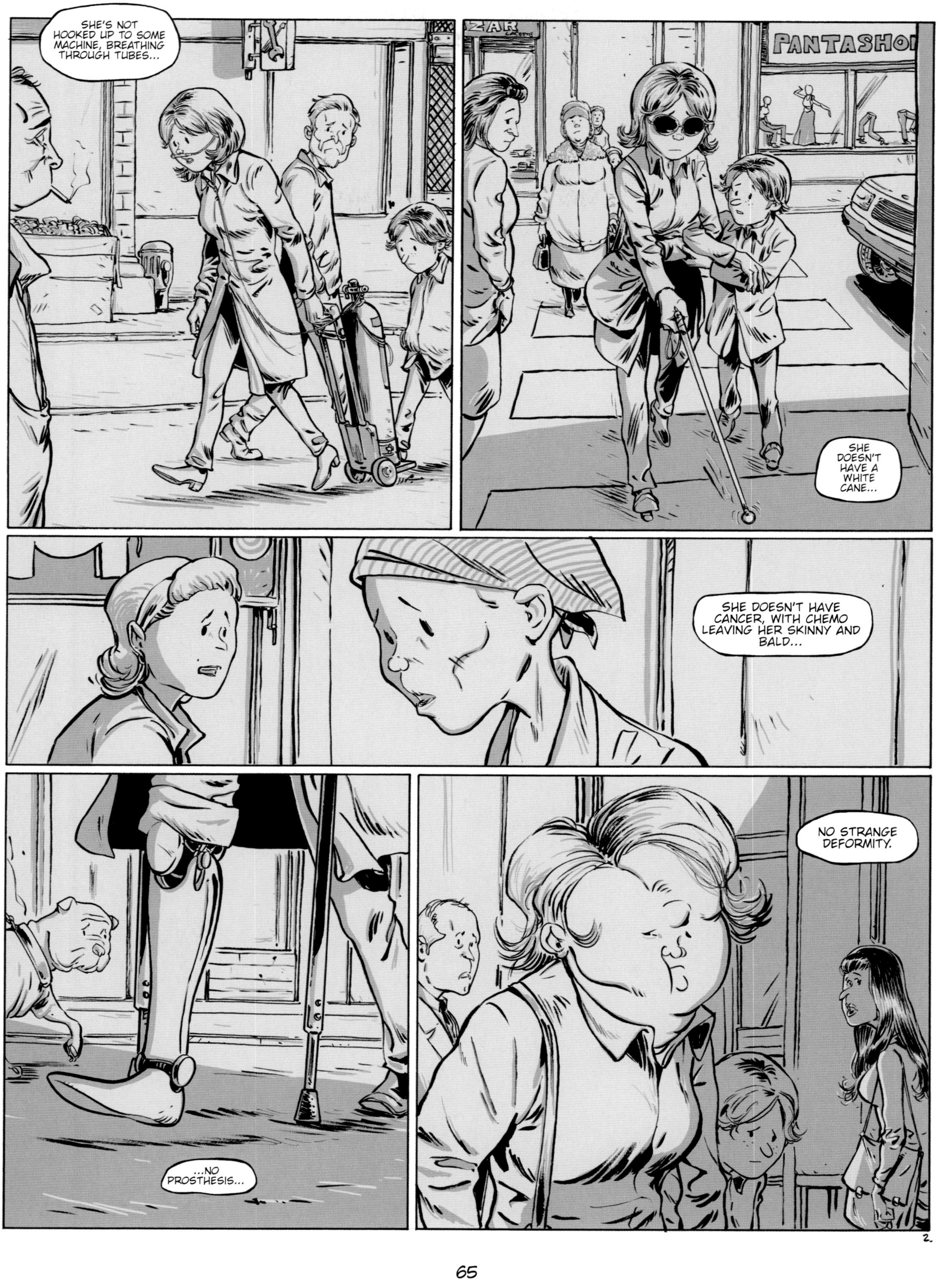
SHE'S NOT HOOKED UP TO SOME MACHINE, BREATHING THROUGH TUBES...
PANTASHO
SHE DOESN'T HAVE A WHITE CANE...
SHE DOESN'T HAVE CANCER, WITH CHEMO LEAVING HER SKINNY AND BALD...
...NO PROSTHESIS...
NO STRANGE DEFORMITY.
2.

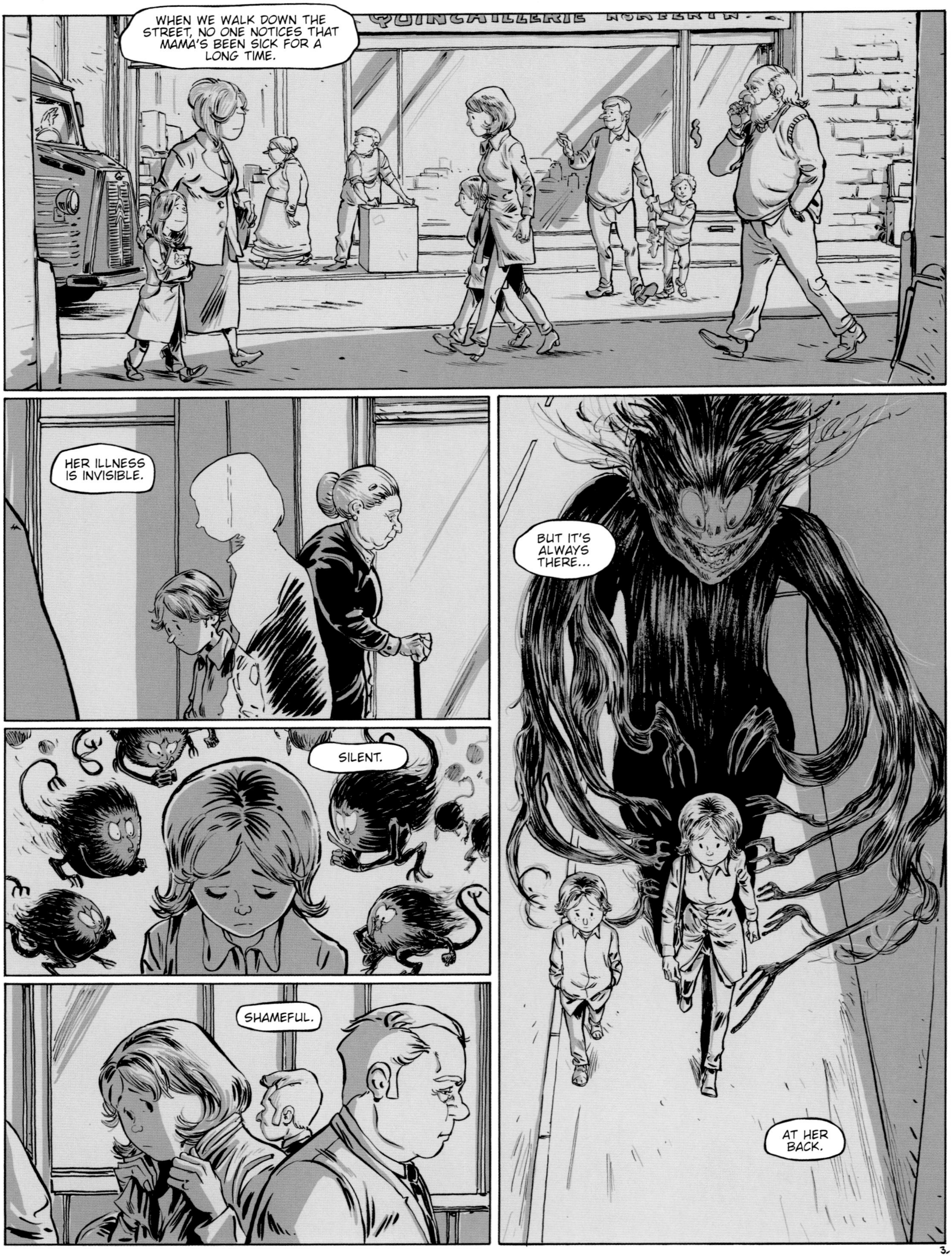
QUINCAILLERIE
WHEN WE WALK DOWN THE STREET, NO ONE NOTICES THAT MAMA'S BEEN SICK FOR A LONG TIME.
HER ILLNESS IS INVISIBLE.
SILENT.
SHAMEFUL.
BUT IT'S ALWAYS THERE...
AT HER BACK.

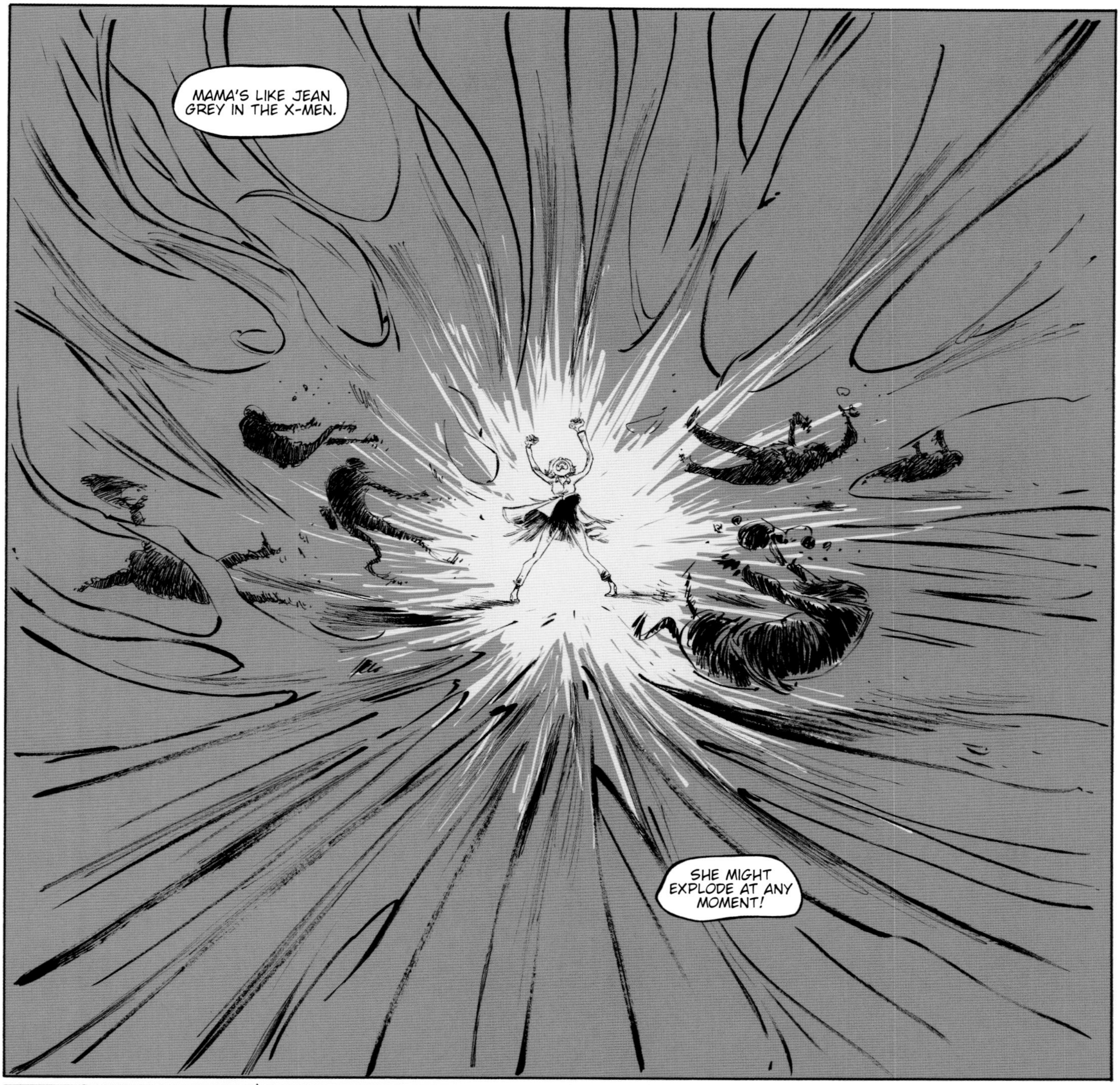
MAMA'S LIKE JEAN GREY IN THE X-MEN.
SHE MIGHT EXPLODE AT ANY MOMENT!

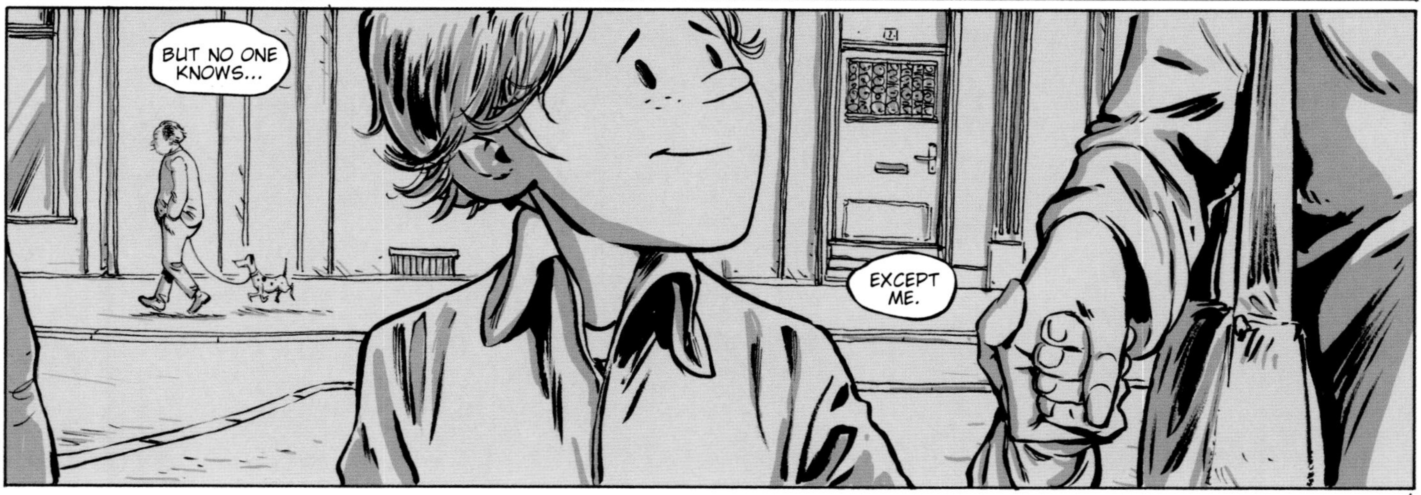
BUT NO ONE KNOWS...
EXCEPT ME.

THE SOCIAL SECURITY
INSPECTOR

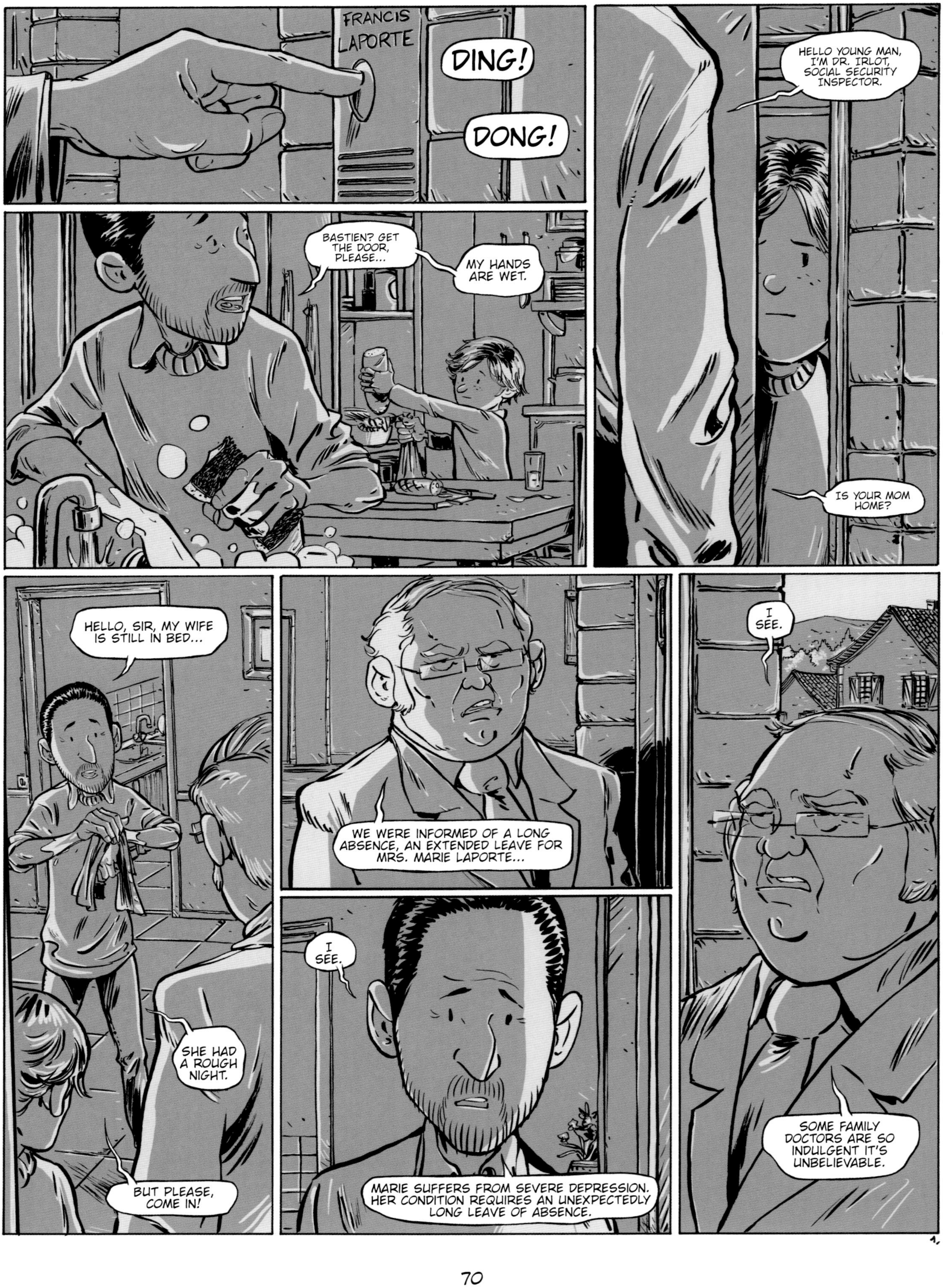
FRANCIS LAPORTE
DING!
DONG!
BASTIEN? GET THE DOOR, PLEASE...
MY HANDS ARE WET.
HELLO YOUNG MAN, I'M DR. IRLOT, SOCIAL SECURITY INSPECTOR.
IS YOUR MOM HOME?
HELLO, SIR, MY WIFE IS STILL IN BED...
SHE HAD A ROUGH NIGHT.
BUT PLEASE, COME IN!
WE WERE INFORMED OF A LONG ABSENCE, AN EXTENDED LEAVE FOR MRS. MARIE LAPORTE...
I SEE.
MARIE SUFFERS FROM SEVERE DEPRESSION. HER CONDITION REQUIRES AN UNEXPECTEDLY LONG LEAVE OF ABSENCE.
I SEE.
SOME FAMILY DOCTORS ARE SO INDULGENT IT'S UNBELIEVABLE.

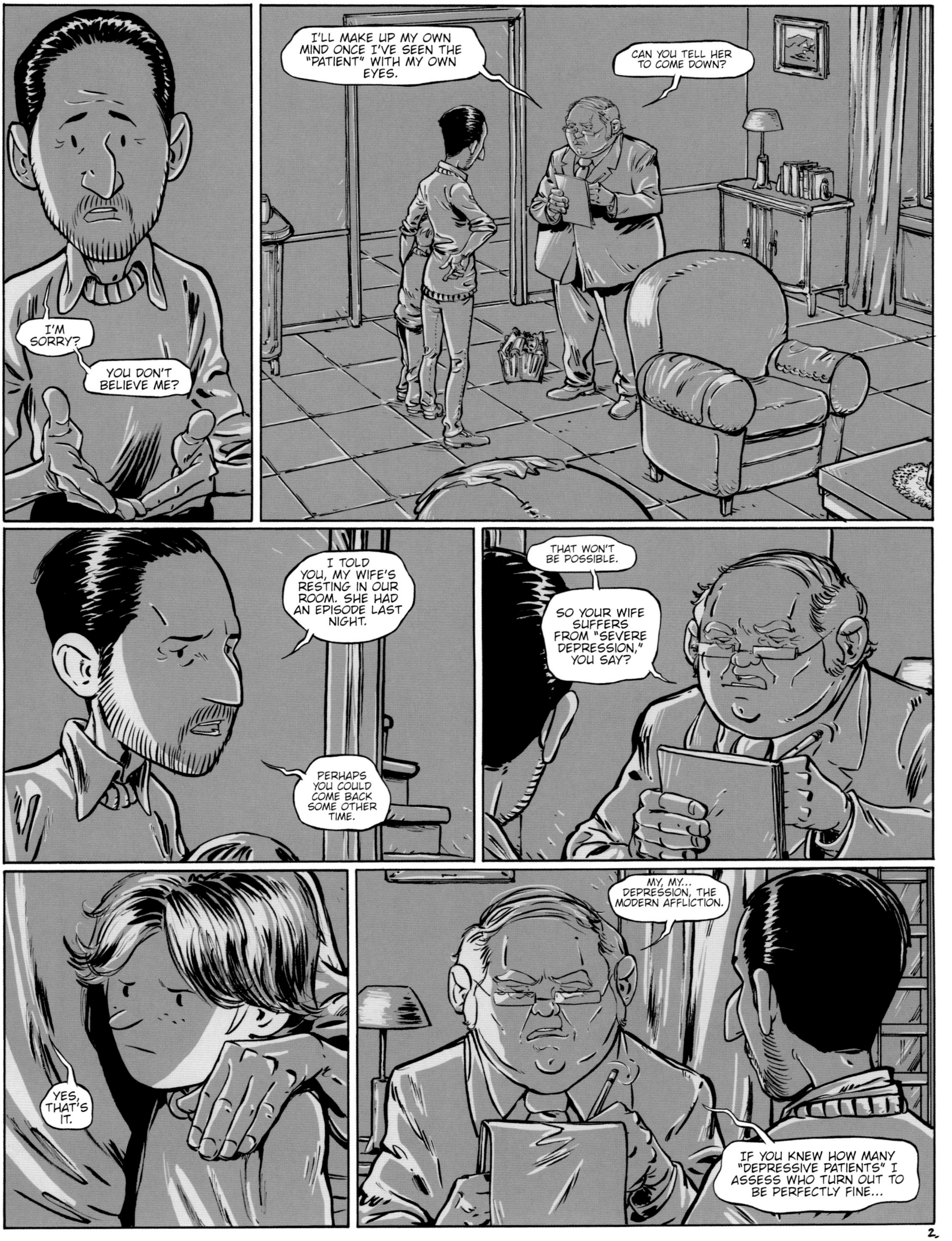
I'M SORRY?
YOU DON'T BELIEVE ME?
I'LL MAKE UP MY OWN MIND ONCE I'VE SEEN THE "PATIENT" WITH MY OWN EYES.
CAN YOU TELL HER TO COME DOWN?
I TOLD YOU, MY WIFE'S RESTING IN OUR ROOM. SHE HAD AN EPISODE LAST NIGHT.
PERHAPS YOU COULD COME BACK SOME OTHER TIME.
THAT WON'T BE POSSIBLE.
SO YOUR WIFE SUFFERS FROM "SEVERE DEPRESSION," YOU SAY?
YES, THAT'S IT.
MY, MY... DEPRESSION, THE MODERN AFFLICTION.
IF YOU KNEW HOW MANY "DEPRESSIVE PATIENTS" I ASSESS WHO TURN OUT TO BE PERFECTLY FINE...
2

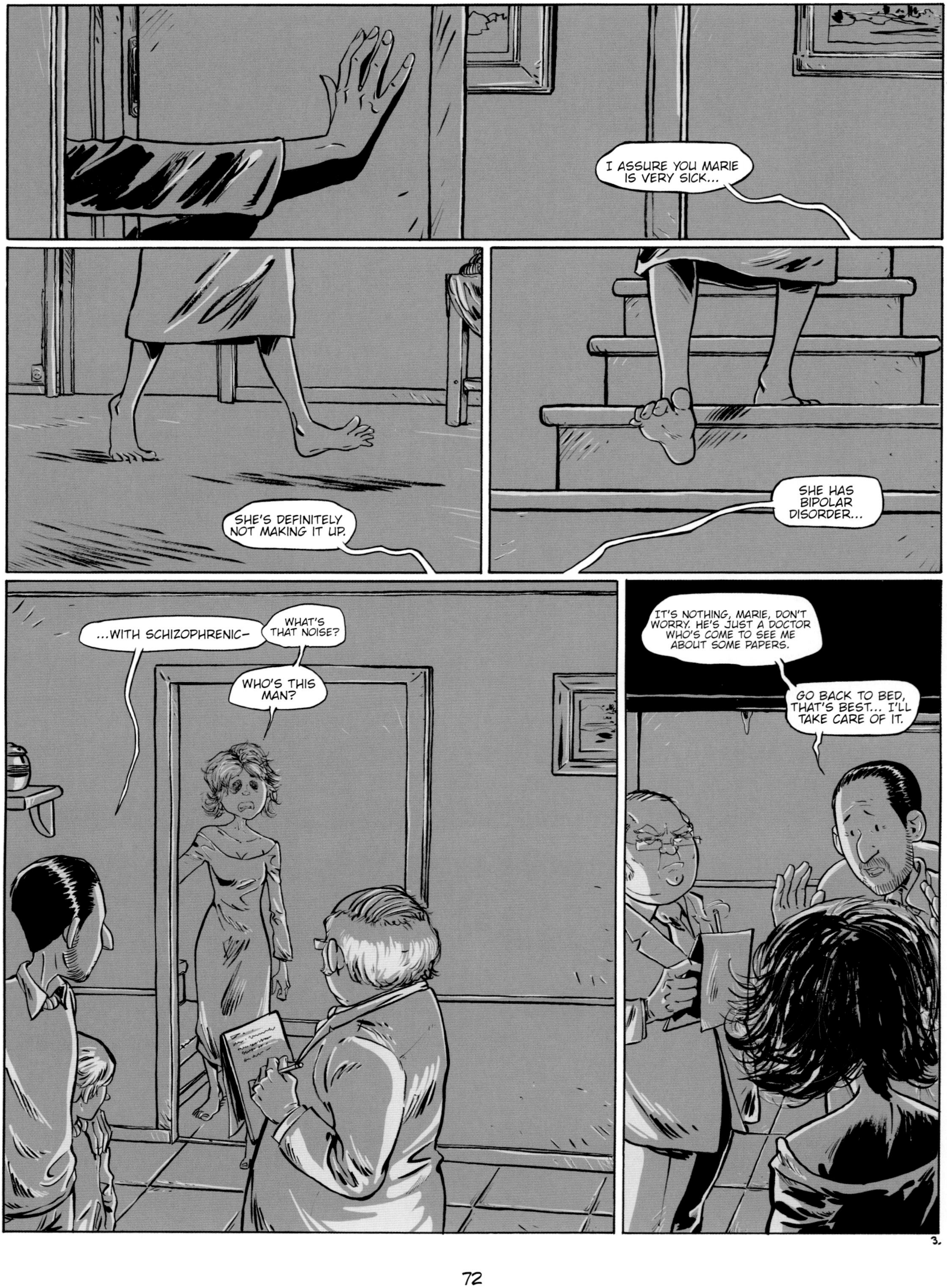
I ASSURE YOU MARIE IS VERY SICK...
SHE'S DEFINITELY NOT MAKING IT UP.
SHE HAS BIPOLAR DISORDER...
...WITH SCHIZOPHRENIC-
WHAT'S THAT NOISE?
WHO'S THIS MAN?
IT'S NOTHING, MARIE, DON'T WORRY. HE'S JUST A DOCTOR WHO'S COME TO SEE ME ABOUT SOME PAPERS.
GO BACK TO BED, THAT'S BEST... I'LL TAKE CARE OF IT.
3.

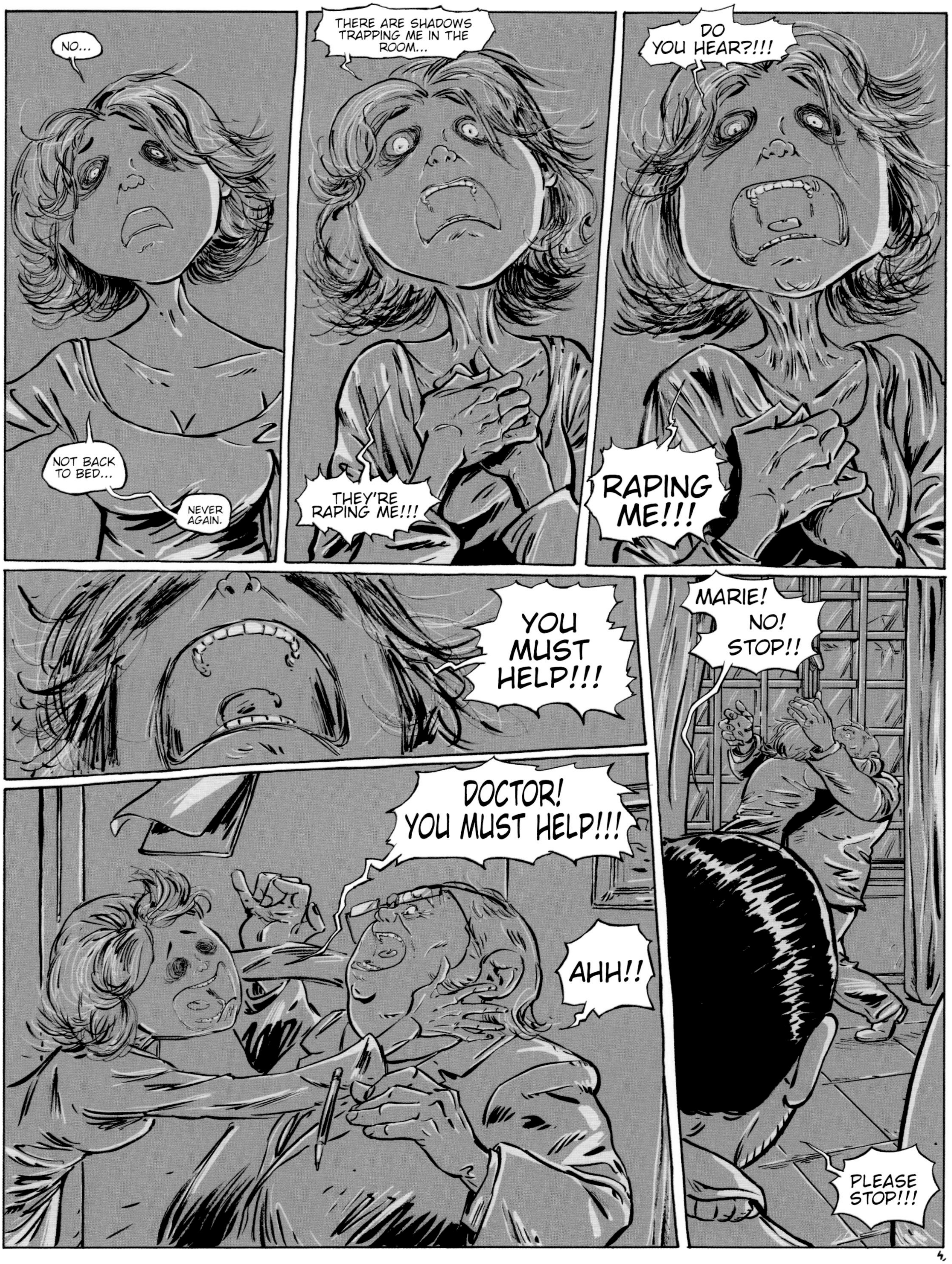
NO...
NOT BACK TO BED...
NEVER AGAIN.
THERE ARE SHADOWS TRAPPING ME IN THE ROOM...
THEY'RE RAPING ME!!!
DO YOU HEAR?!!!
RAPING ME!!!
YOU MUST HELP!!!
DOCTOR! YOU MUST HELP!!!
AHH!!
MARIE!
NO! STOP!!
PLEASE STOP!!!

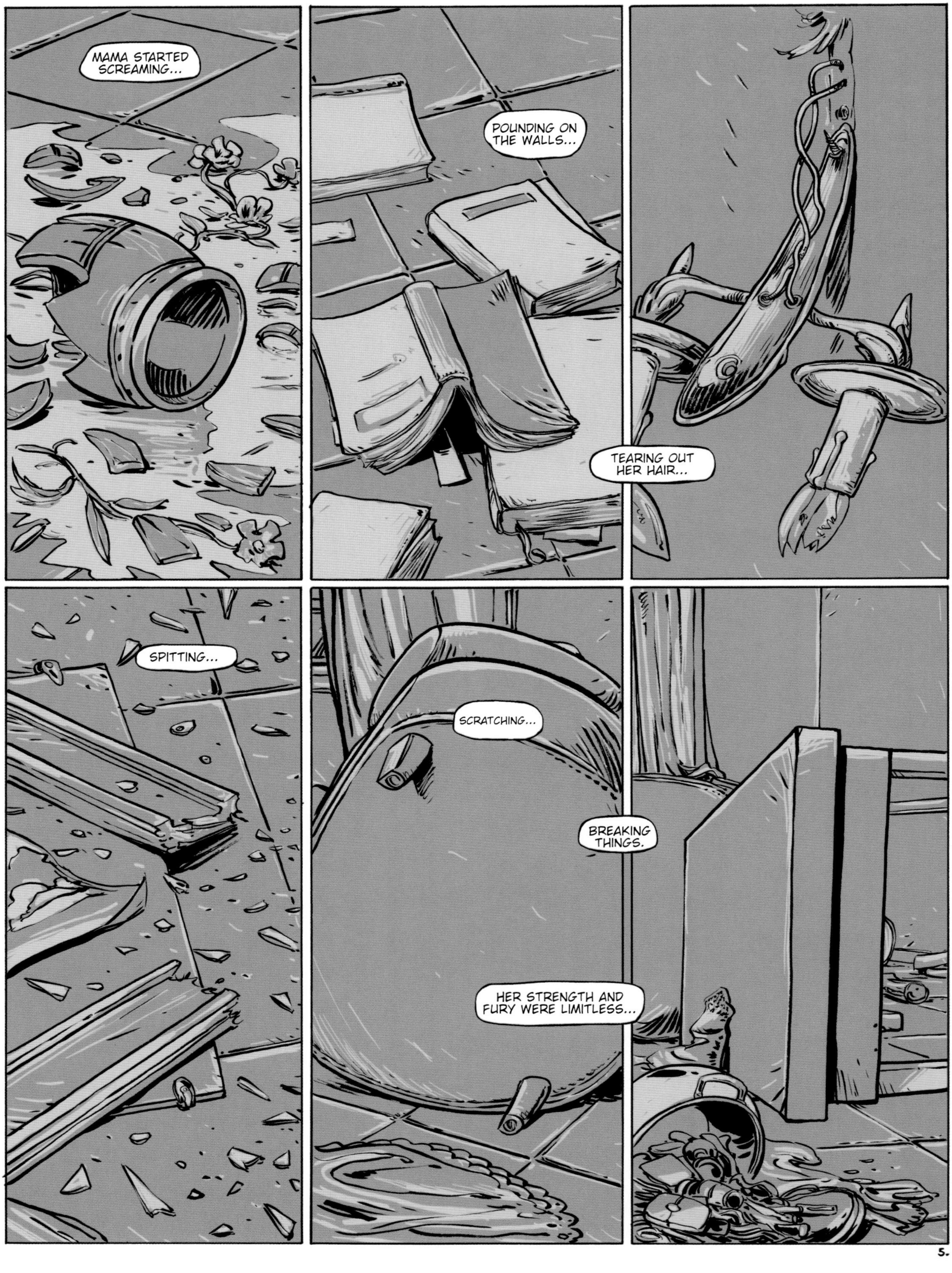
MAMA STARTED SCREAMING...
POUNDING ON THE WALLS...
TEARING OUT HER HAIR...
SPITTING...
SCRATCHING...
BREAKING THINGS.
HER STRENGTH AND FURY WERE LIMITLESS...
5.

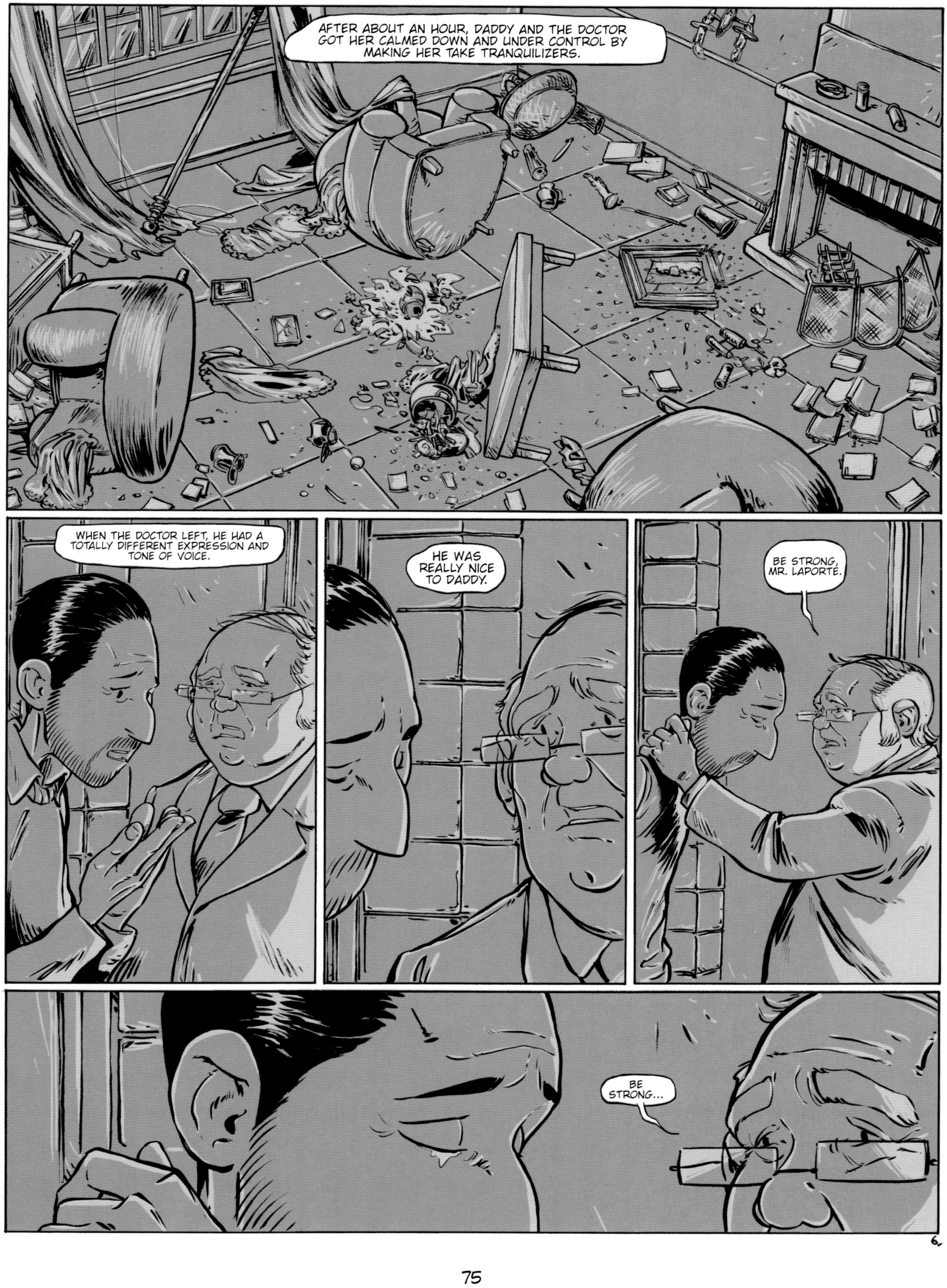
AFTER ABOUT AN HOUR, DADDY AND THE DOCTOR GOT HER CALMED DOWN AND UNDER CONTROL BY MAKING HER TAKE TRANQUILIZERS.
WHEN THE DOCTOR LEFT, HE HAD A TOTALLY DIFFERENT EXPRESSION AND TONE OF VOICE.
HE WAS REALLY NICE TO DADDY.
BE STRONG, MR. LAPORTE.
BE STRONG...
6.

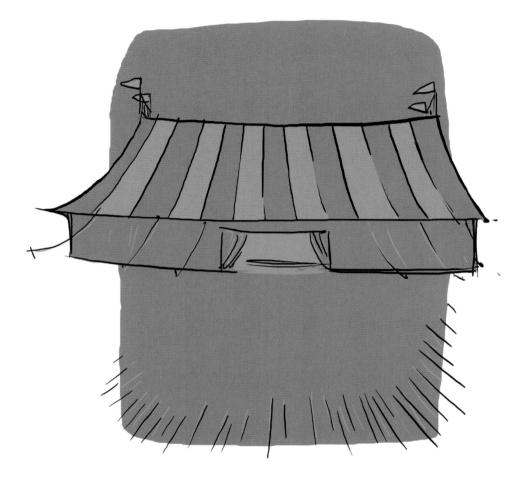

THE CIRCUS

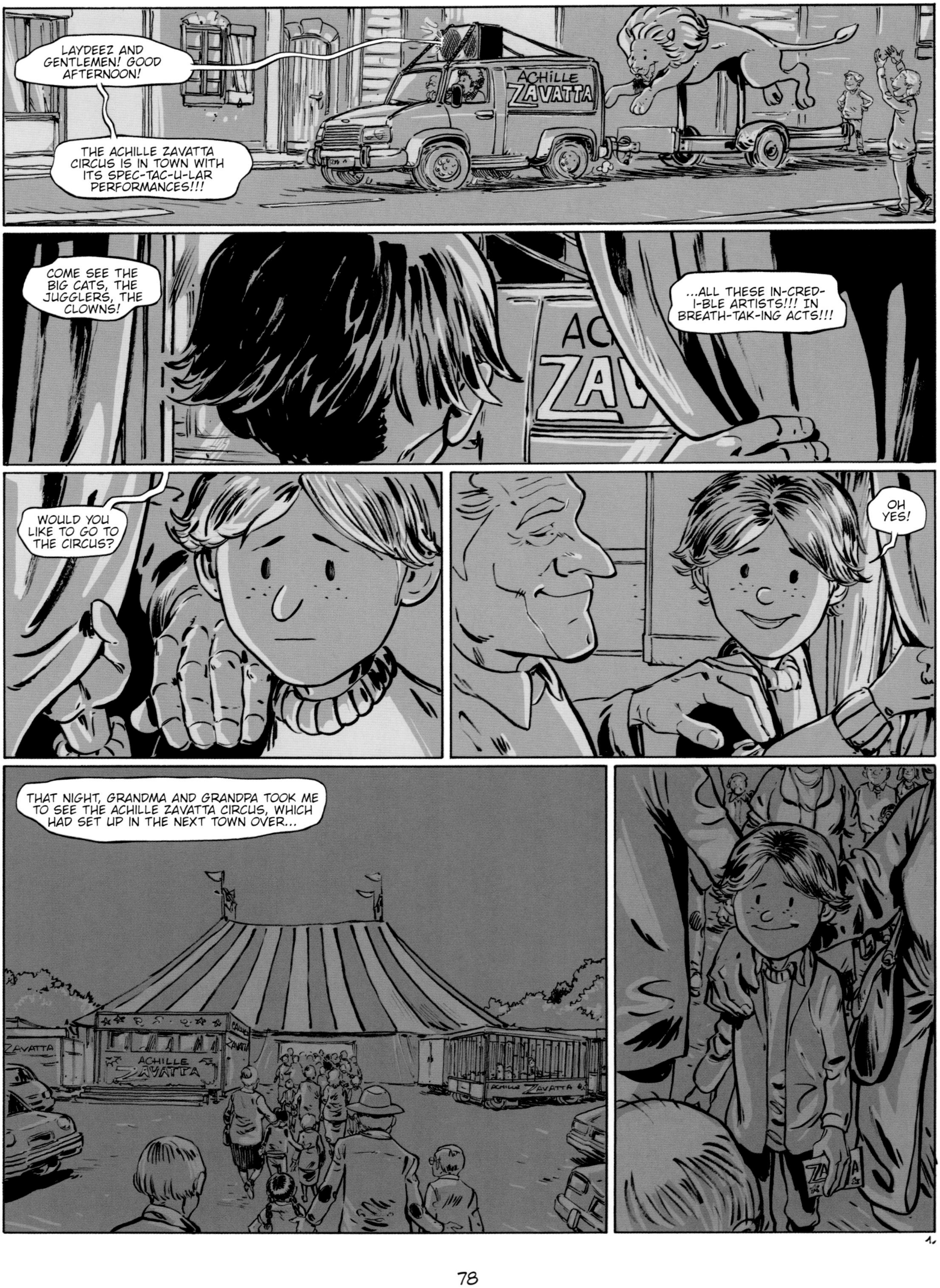
LAYDEEZ AND GENTLEMEN! GOOD AFTERNOON!
THE ACHILLE ZAVATTA CIRCUS IS IN TOWN WITH ITS SPEC-TAC-U-LAR PERFORMANCES!!!
ACHILLE ZAVATTA
COME SEE THE BIG CATS, THE JUGGLERS, THE CLOWNS!
...ALL THESE IN-CRED-I-BLE ARTISTS!!! IN BREATH-TAK-ING ACTS!!!
WOULD YOU LIKE TO GO TO THE CIRCUS?
OH YES!
THAT NIGHT, GRANDMA AND GRANDPA TOOK ME TO SEE THE ACHILLE ZAVATTA CIRCUS, WHICH HAD SET UP IN THE NEXT TOWN OVER...
ACHILLE ZAVATTA

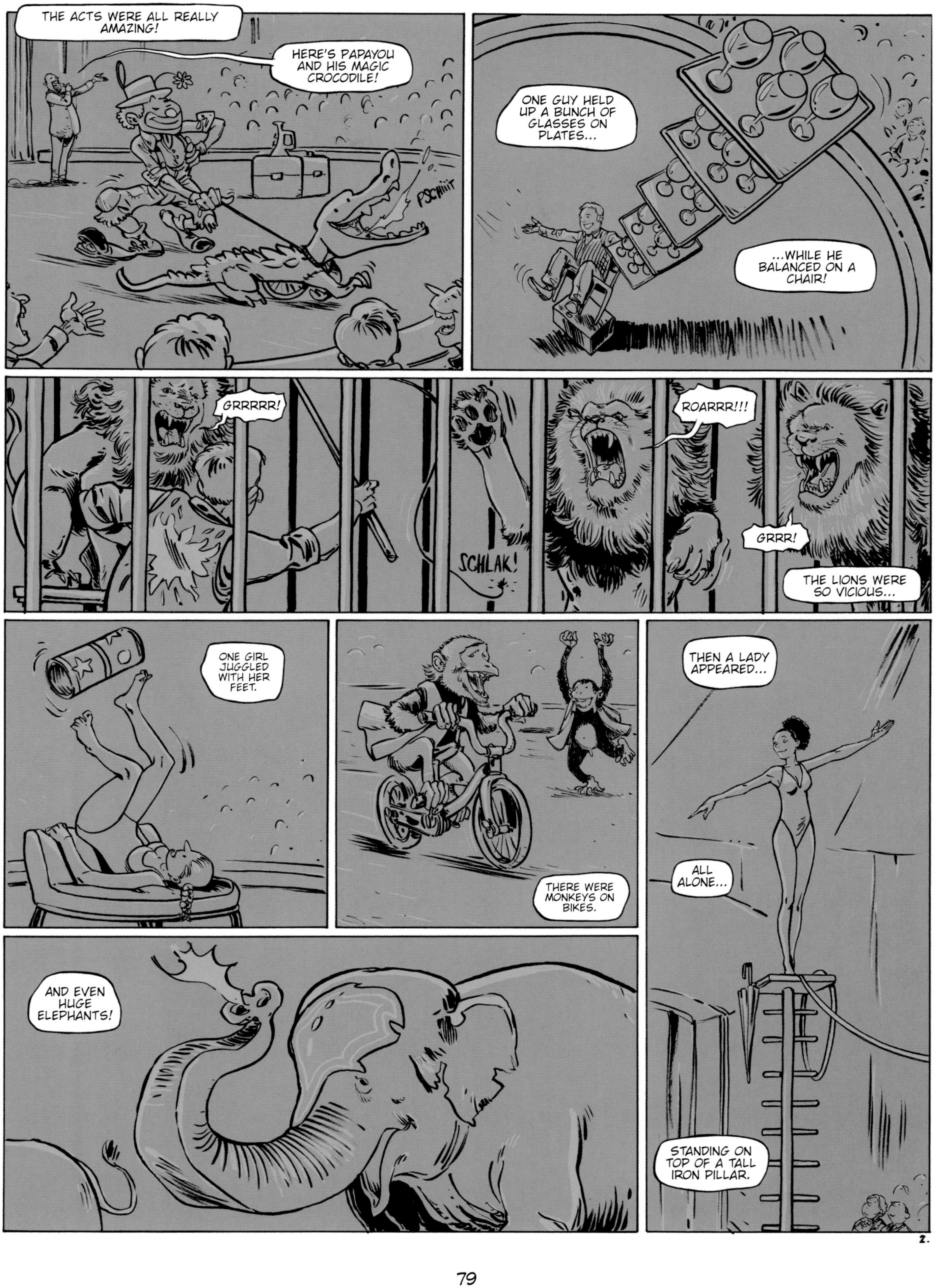
THE ACTS WERE ALL REALLY AMAZING!
HERE'S PAPAYOU AND HIS MAGIC CROCODILE!
PSCHIIIT
ONE GUY HELD UP A BUNCH OF GLASSES ON PLATES...
...WHILE HE BALANCED ON A CHAIR!
GRRRRR!
ROARRR!!!
SCHLAK!
GRRR!
THE LIONS WERE SO VICIOUS...
ONE GIRL JUGGLED WITH HER FEET.
THERE WERE MONKEYS ON BIKES.
THEN A LADY APPEARED...
ALL ALONE...
AND EVEN HUGE ELEPHANTS!
STANDING ON TOP OF A TALL IRON PILLAR.
2.

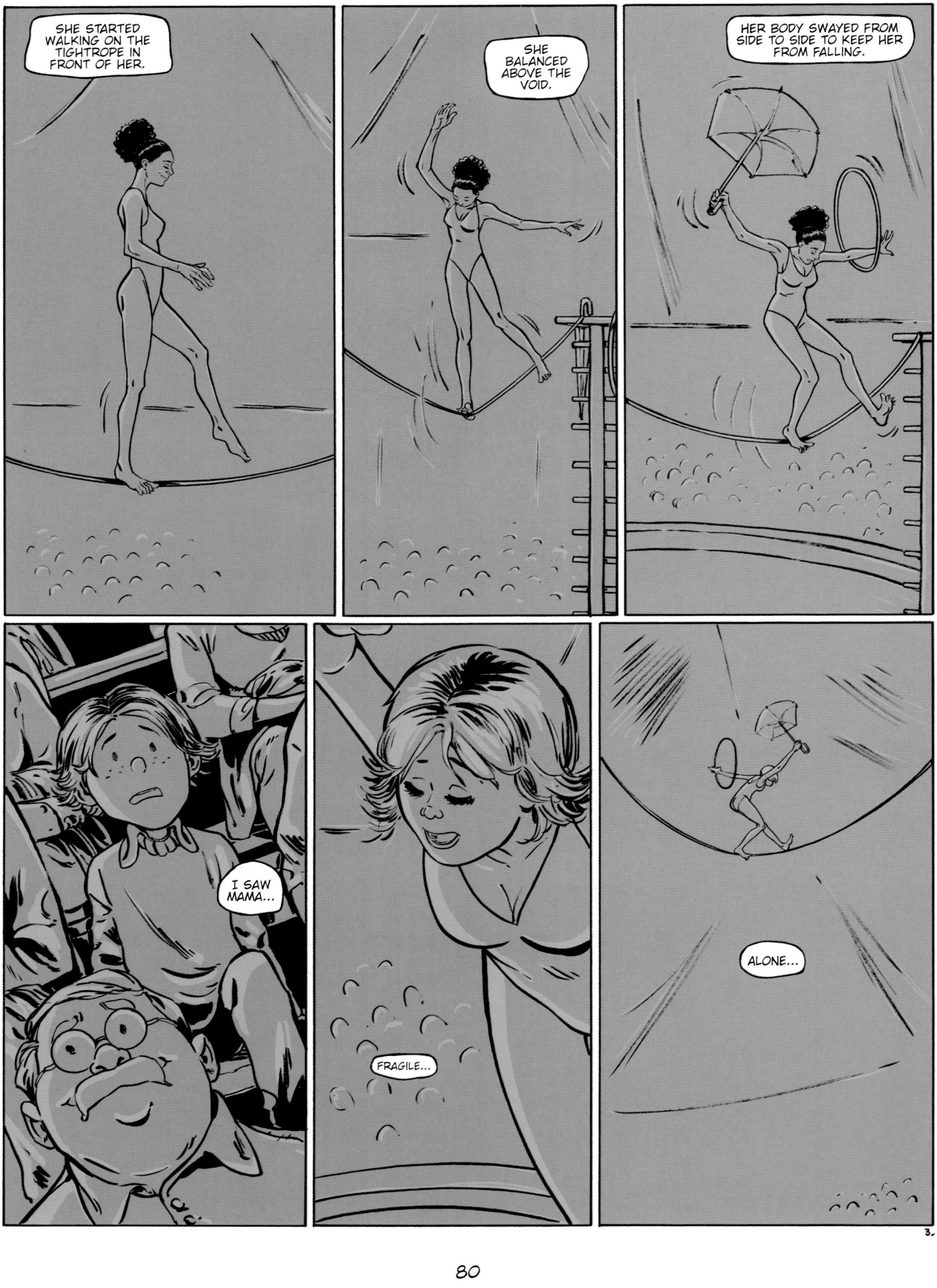
SHE STARTED WALKING ON THE TIGHTROPE IN FRONT OF HER.
SHE BALANCED ABOVE THE VOID.
HER BODY SWAYED FROM SIDE TO SIDE TO KEEP HER FROM FALLING.
I SAW MAMA...
FRAGILE...
ALONE...

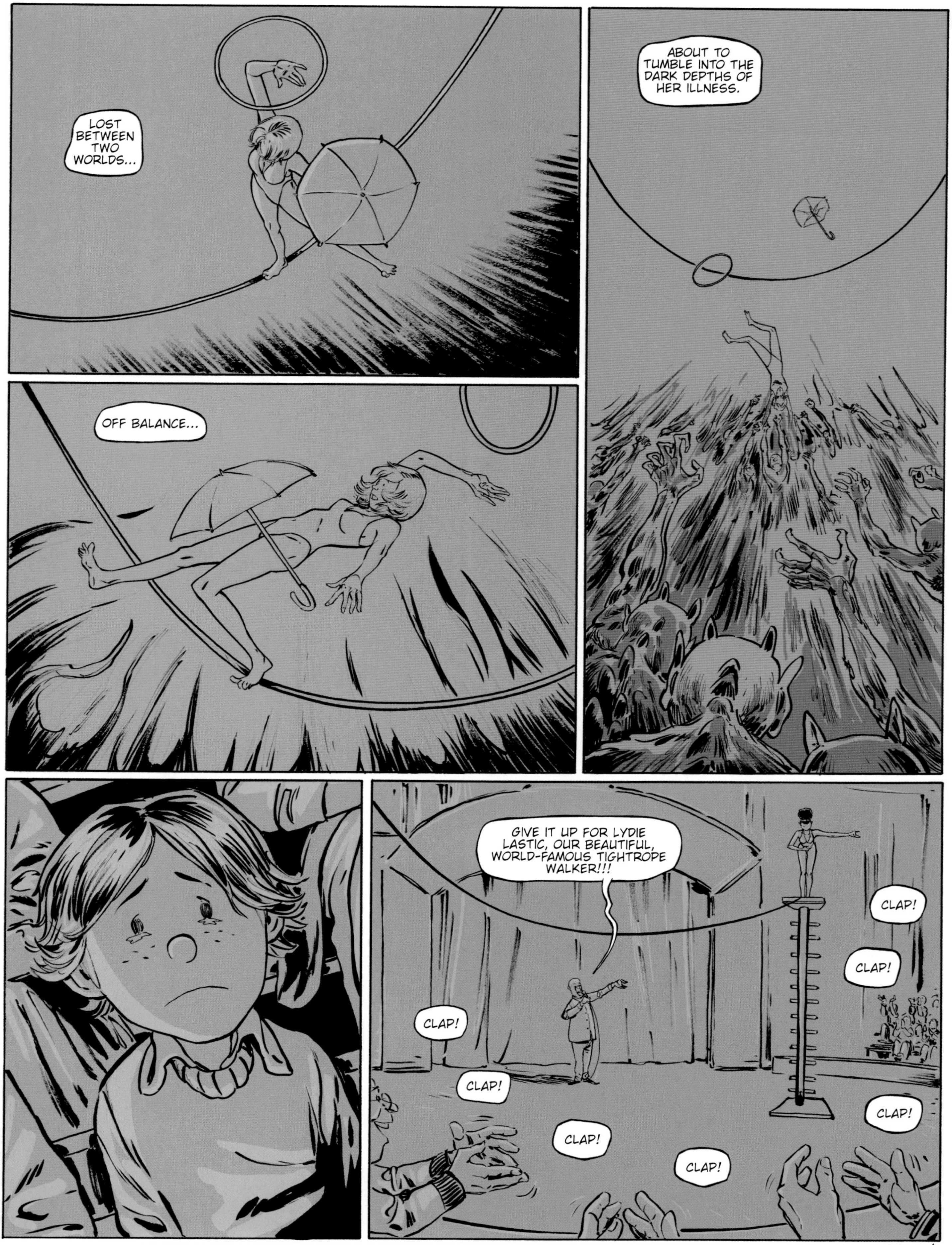
LOST BETWEEN TWO WORLDS...
ABOUT TO TUMBLE INTO THE DARK DEPTHS OF HER ILLNESS.
OFF BALANCE...
GIVE IT UP FOR LYDIE LASTIC, OUR BEAUTIFUL, WORLD-FAMOUS TIGHTROPE WALKER!!!
CLAP!
CLAP!
CLAP!
CLAP!
CLAP!
CLAP!
CLAP!
4.

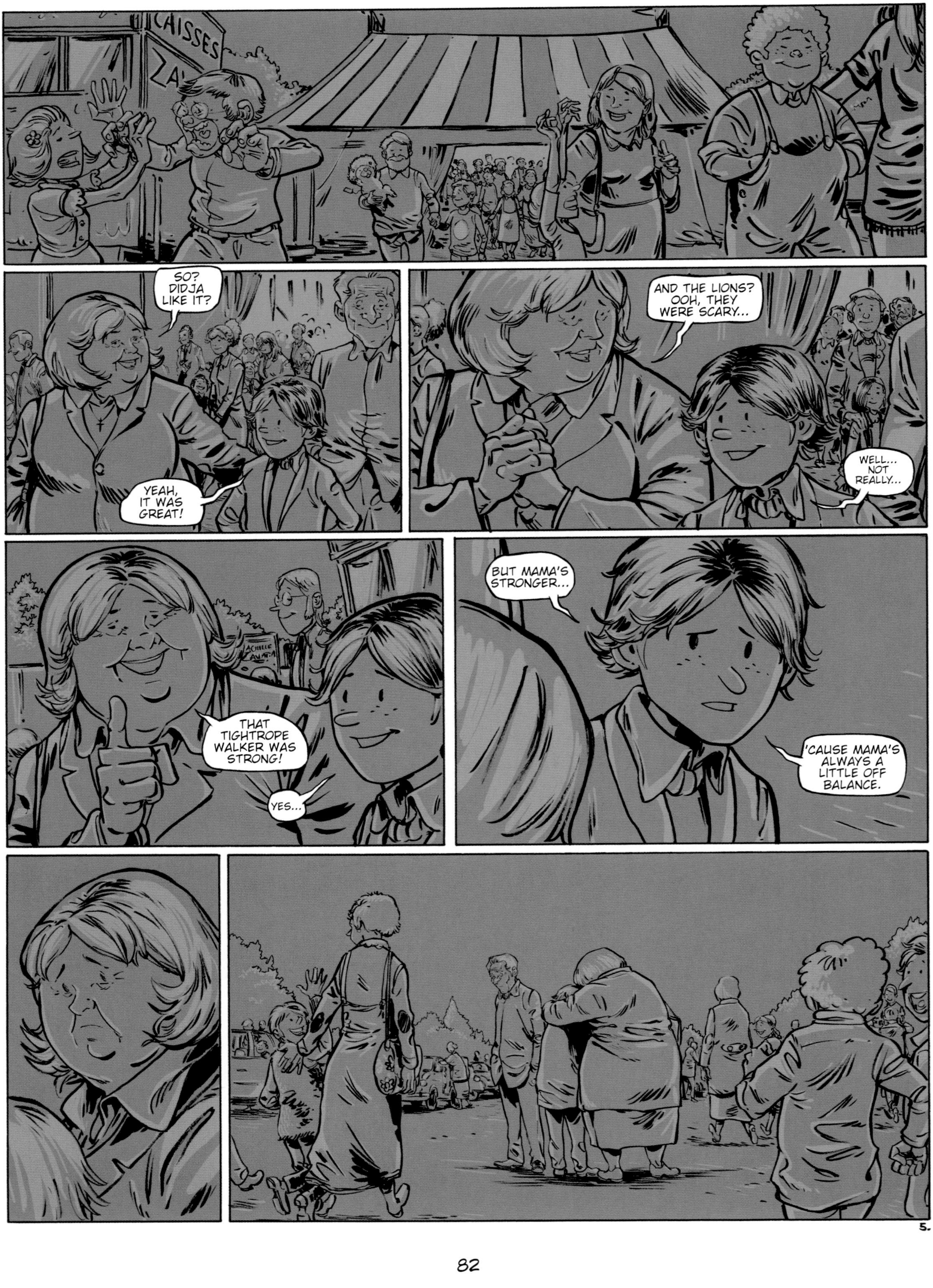
CAISSES
SO? DIDJA LIKE IT?
YEAH, IT WAS GREAT!
AND THE LIONS? OOH, THEY WERE SCARY...
WELL... NOT REALLY...
THAT TIGHTROPE WALKER WAS STRONG!
YES...
BUT MAMA'S STRONGER...
'CAUSE MAMA'S ALWAYS A LITTLE OFF BALANCE.
5.

WALLPAPER

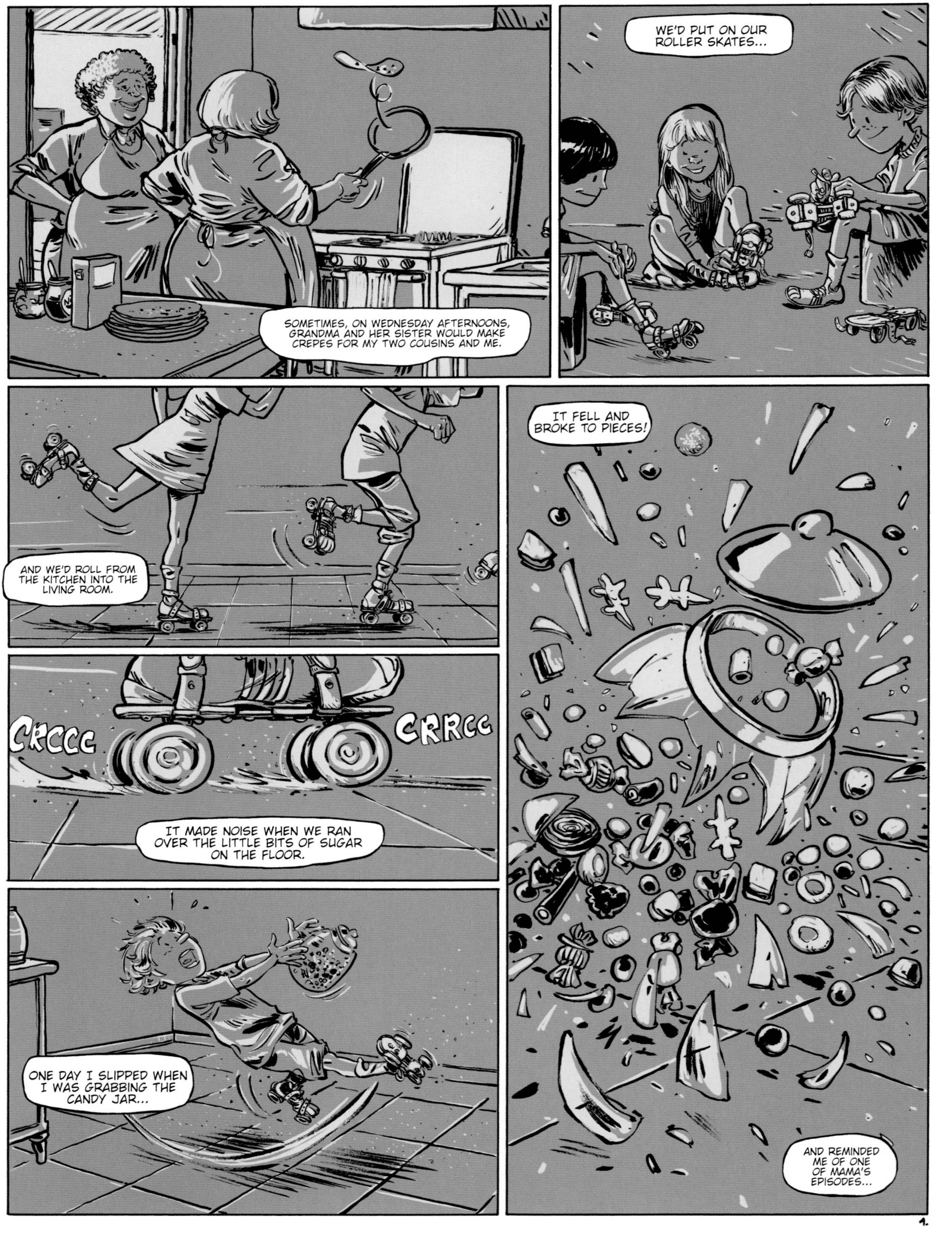

SOMETIMES, ON WEDNESDAY AFTERNOONS, GRANDMA AND HER SISTER WOULD MAKE CREPES FOR MY TWO COUSINS AND ME.
WE'D PUT ON OUR ROLLER SKATES...
AND WE'D ROLL FROM THE KITCHEN INTO THE LIVING ROOM.
CRCCC
CRRCC
IT MADE NOISE WHEN WE RAN OVER THE LITTLE BITS OF SUGAR ON THE FLOOR.
ONE DAY I SLIPPED WHEN I WAS GRABBING THE CANDY JAR...
IT FELL AND BROKE TO PIECES!
AND REMINDED ME OF ONE OF MAMA'S EPISODES...

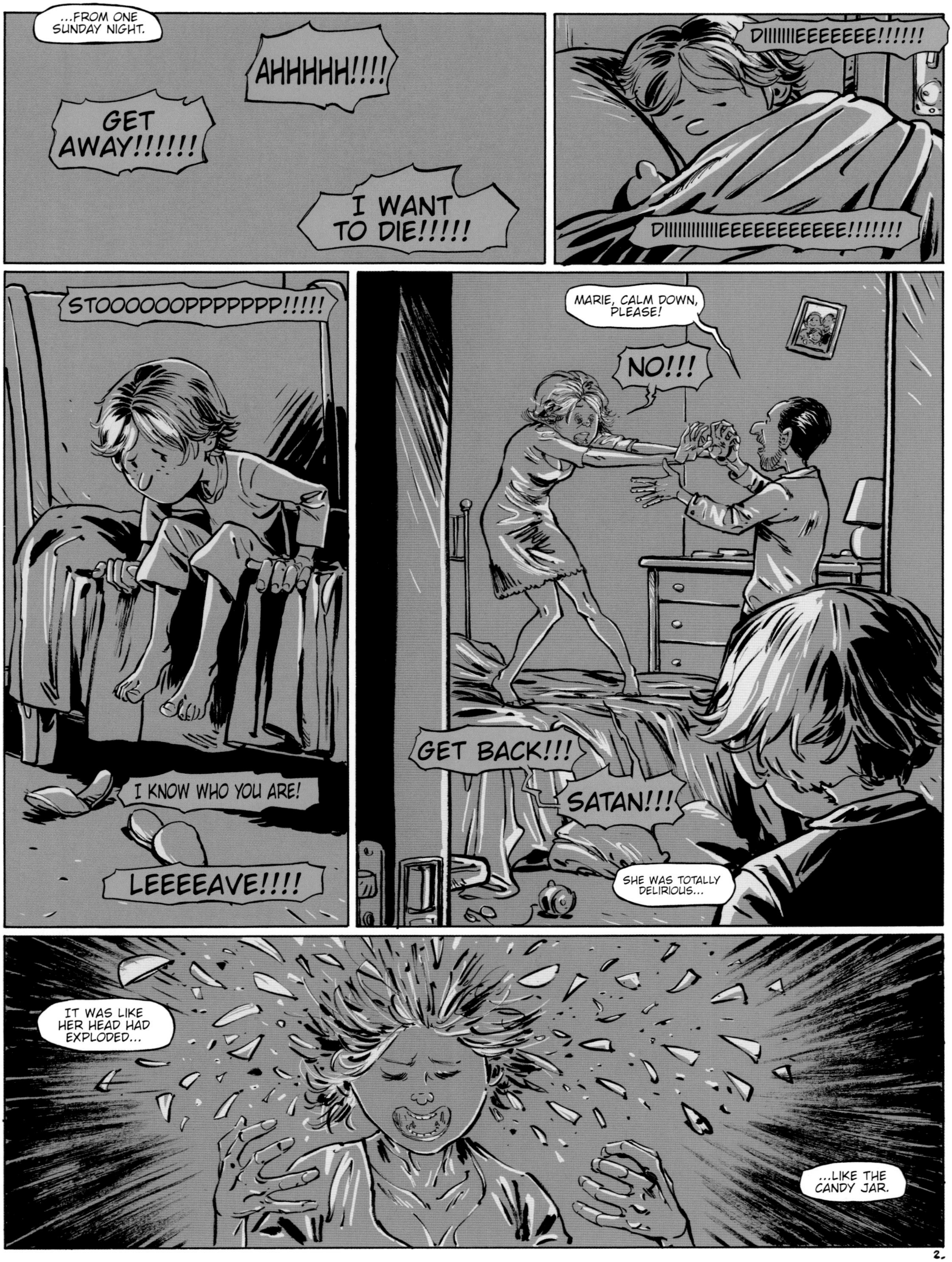
...FROM ONE SUNDAY NIGHT.
AHHHHH!!!!
GET AWAY!!!!!!
I WANT TO DIE!!!!!
DIIIIIIEEEEEEE!!!!!!
DIIIIIIIIIIIEEEEEEEEEE!!!!!!!
STOOOOOOPPPPPPP!!!!!
I KNOW WHO YOU ARE!
LEEEEAVE!!!!
MARIE, CALM DOWN, PLEASE!
NO!!!
GET BACK!!!
SATAN!!!
SHE WAS TOTALLY DELIRIOUS...
IT WAS LIKE HER HEAD HAD EXPLODED...
...LIKE THE CANDY JAR.

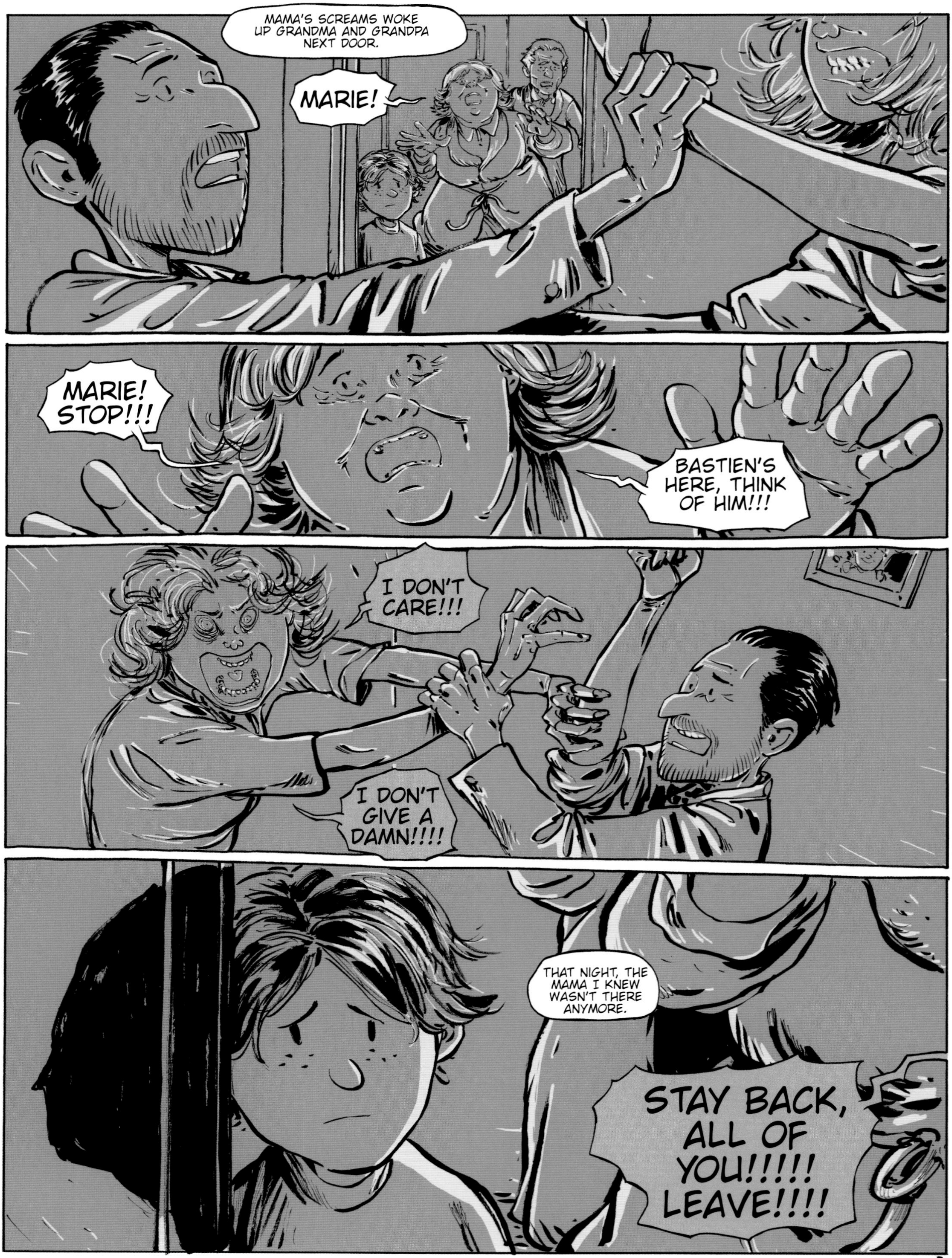
MAMA'S SCREAMS WOKE UP GRANDMA AND GRANDPA NEXT DOOR.
MARIE!
MARIE! STOP!!!
BASTIEN'S HERE, THINK OF HIM!!!
I DON'T CARE!!!
I DON'T GIVE A DAMN!!!!
THAT NIGHT, THE MAMA I KNEW WASN'T THERE ANYMORE.
STAY BACK, ALL OF YOU!!!!! LEAVE!!!!
3.

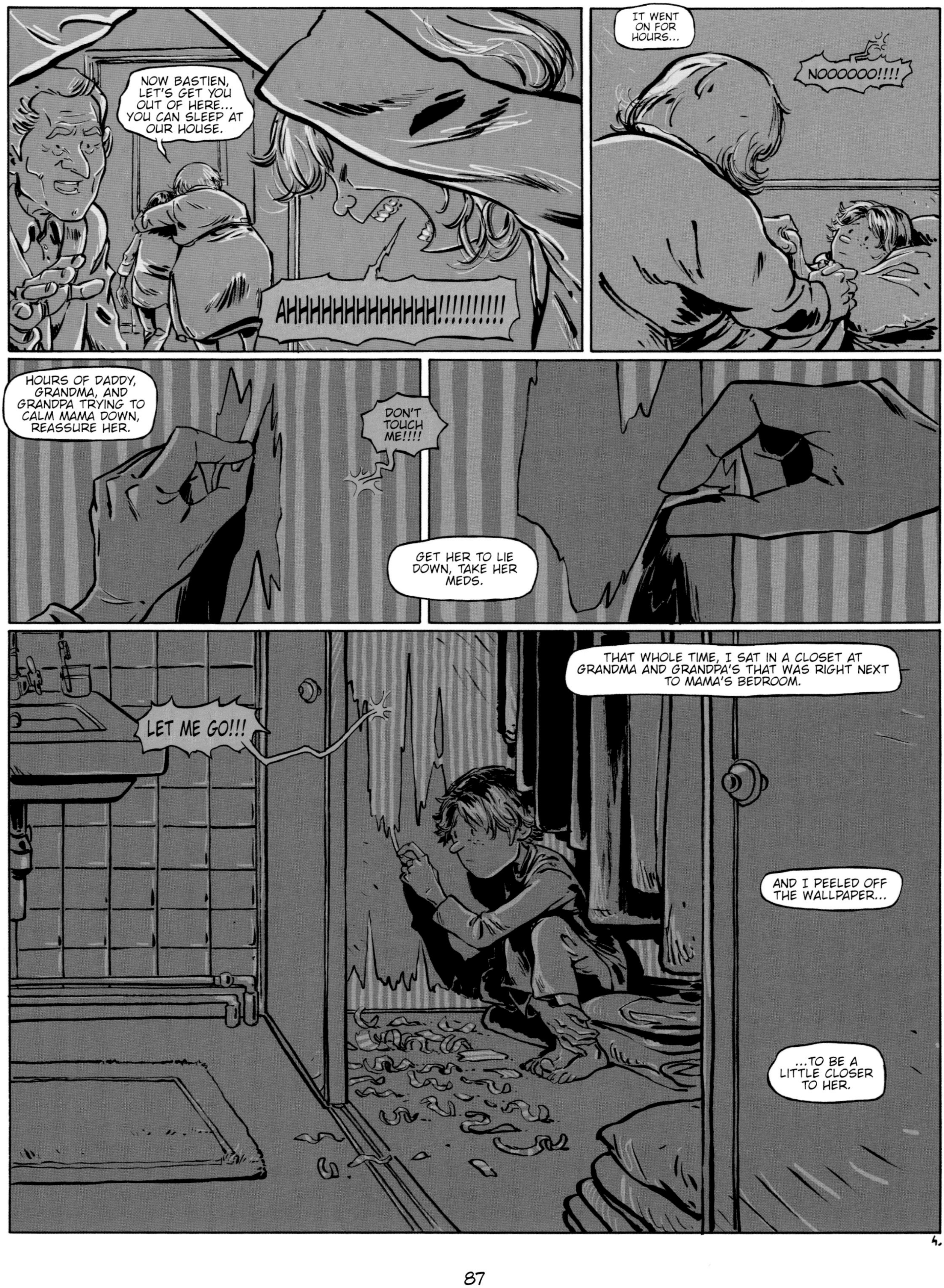
NOW BASTIEN, LET'S GET YOU OUT OF HERE... YOU CAN SLEEP AT OUR HOUSE.
AHHHHHHHHHHHHH!!!!!!!!!!
IT WENT ON FOR HOURS...
NOOOOOO!!!!
HOURS OF DADDY, GRANDMA, AND GRANDPA TRYING TO CALM MAMA DOWN, REASSURE HER.
DON'T TOUCH ME!!!!
GET HER TO LIE DOWN, TAKE HER MEDS.
THAT WHOLE TIME, I SAT IN A CLOSET AT GRANDMA AND GRANDPA'S THAT WAS RIGHT NEXT TO MAMA'S BEDROOM.
LET ME GO!!!
AND I PEELED OFF THE WALLPAPER...
...TO BE A LITTLE CLOSER TO HER.

CUSHIONS

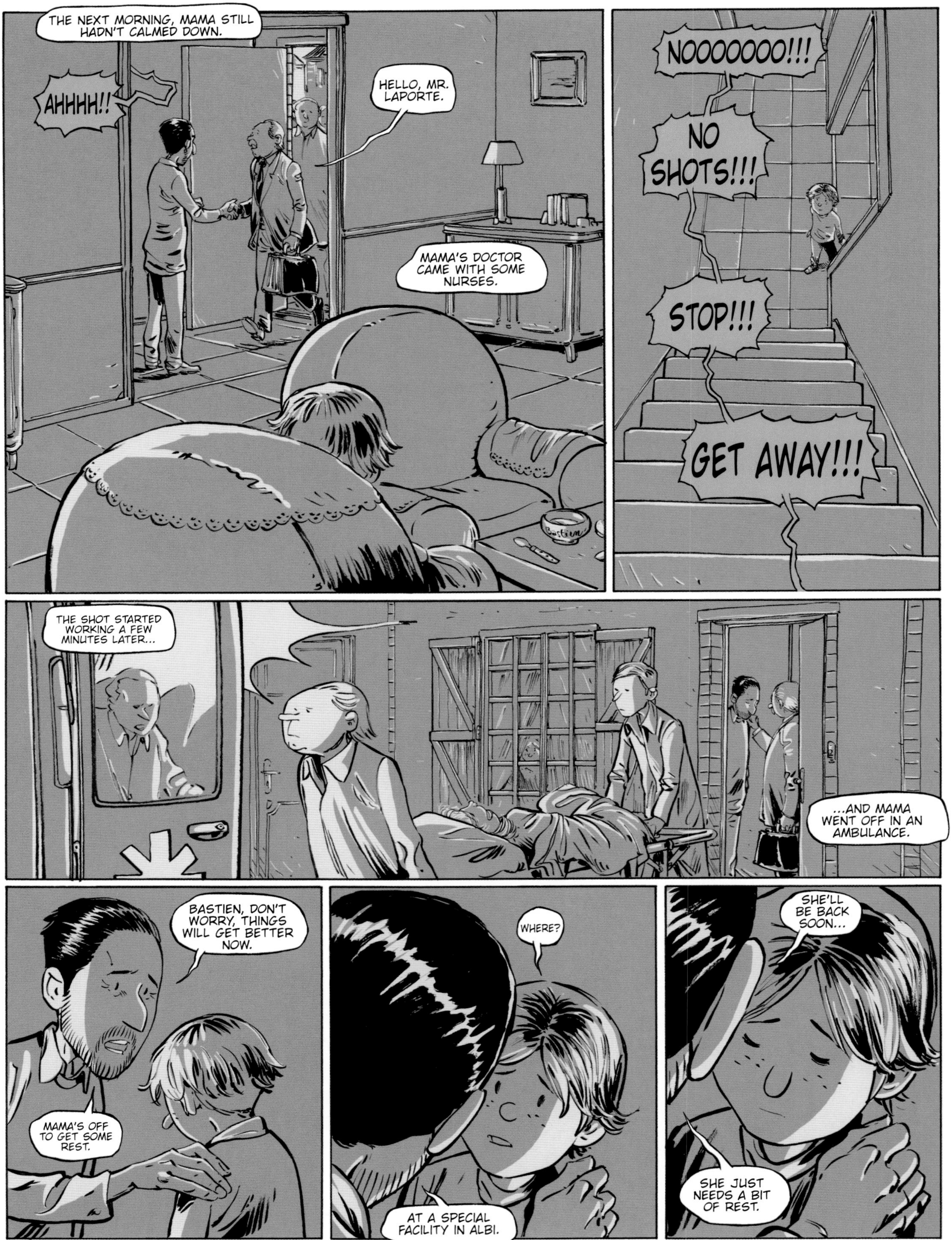
THE NEXT MORNING, MAMA STILL HADN'T CALMED DOWN.
AHHHH!!
HELLO, MR. LAPORTE.
MAMA'S DOCTOR CAME WITH SOME NURSES.
NOOOOOOO!!!
NO SHOTS!!!
STOP!!!
GET AWAY!!!
THE SHOT STARTED WORKING A FEW MINUTES LATER...
...AND MAMA WENT OFF IN AN AMBULANCE.
BASTIEN, DON'T WORRY, THINGS WILL GET BETTER NOW.
MAMA'S OFF TO GET SOME REST.
WHERE?
AT A SPECIAL FACILITY IN ALBI.
SHE'LL BE BACK SOON...
SHE JUST NEEDS A BIT OF REST.

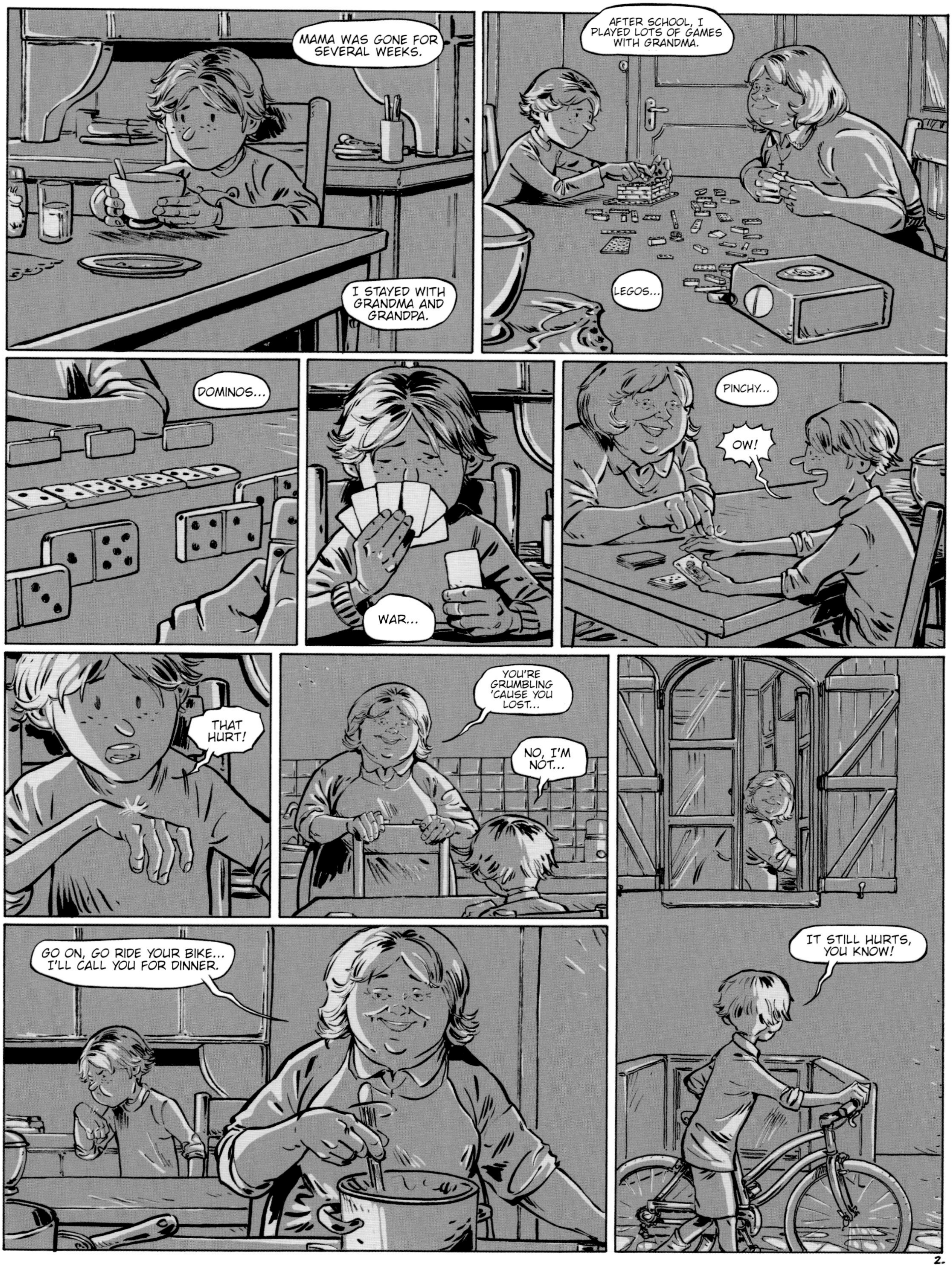
MAMA WAS GONE FOR SEVERAL WEEKS.
I STAYED WITH GRANDMA AND GRANDPA.
AFTER SCHOOL, I PLAYED LOTS OF GAMES WITH GRANDMA.
LEGOS...
DOMINOS...
WAR...
PINCHY...
OW!
THAT HURT!
YOU'RE GRUMBLING 'CAUSE YOU LOST...
NO, I'M NOT...
GO ON, GO RIDE YOUR BIKE... I'LL CALL YOU FOR DINNER.
IT STILL HURTS, YOU KNOW!
2.

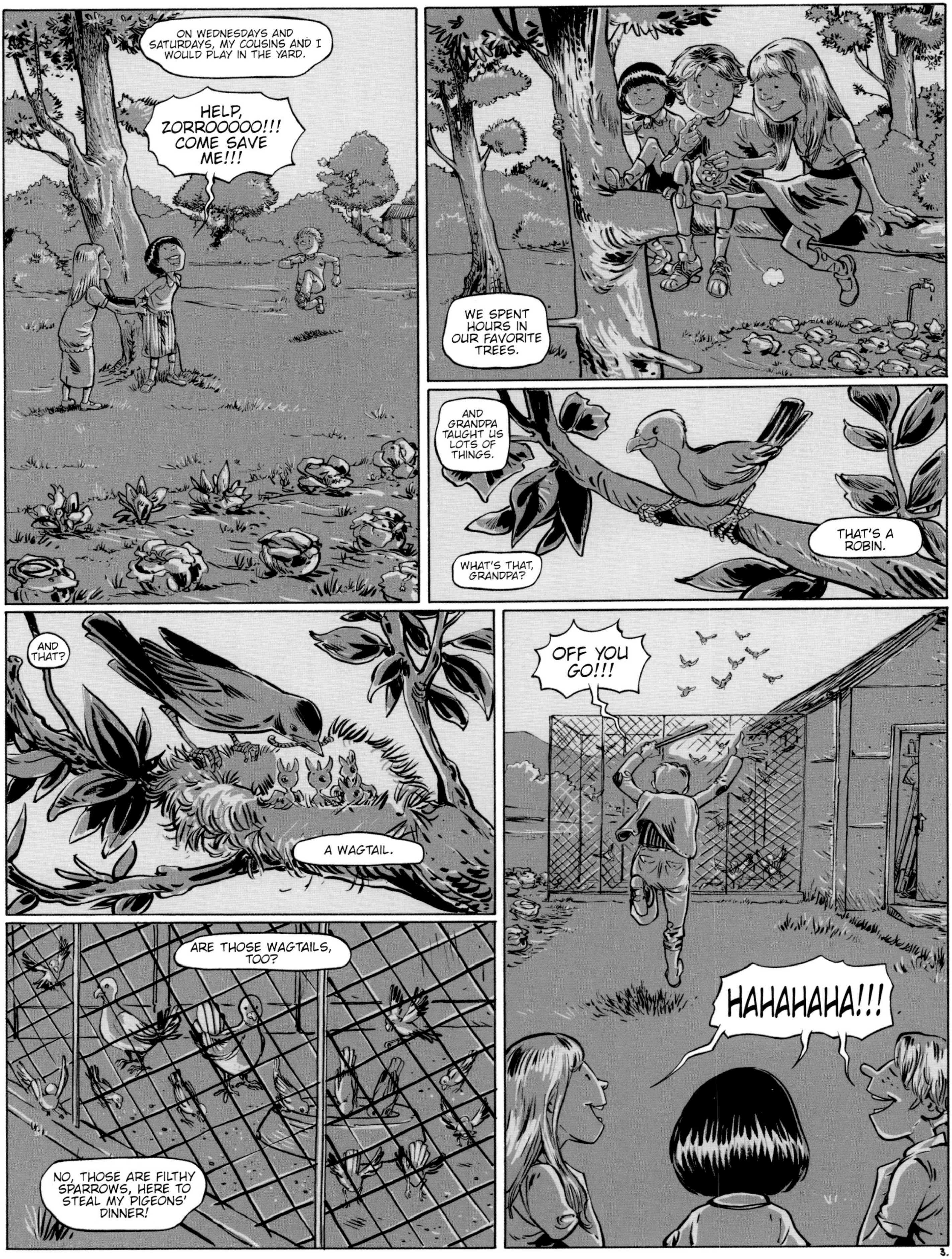
ON WEDNESDAYS AND SATURDAYS, MY COUSINS AND I WOULD PLAY IN THE YARD.
HELP, ZORROOOOO!!! COME SAVE ME!!!
WE SPENT HOURS IN OUR FAVORITE TREES.
AND GRANDPA TAUGHT US LOTS OF THINGS.
WHAT'S THAT, GRANDPA?
THAT'S A ROBIN.
AND THAT?
A WAGTAIL.
ARE THOSE WAGTAILS, TOO?
NO, THOSE ARE FILTHY SPARROWS, HERE TO STEAL MY PIGEONS' DINNER!
OFF YOU GO!!!
HAHAHAHA!!!
3.

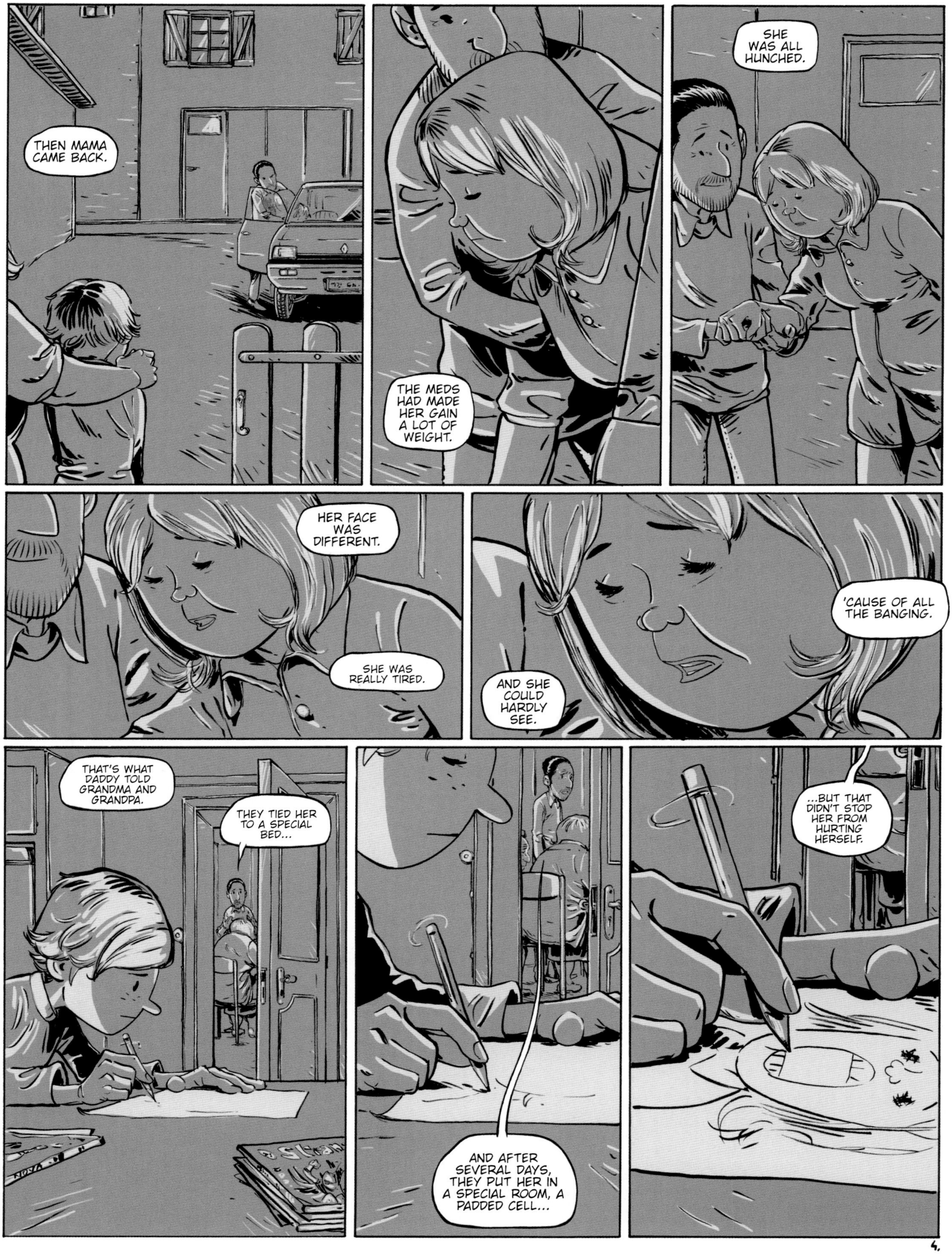

THEN MAMA CAME BACK.
THE MEDS HAD MADE HER GAIN A LOT OF WEIGHT.
SHE WAS ALL HUNCHED.
HER FACE WAS DIFFERENT.
SHE WAS REALLY TIRED.
AND SHE COULD HARDLY SEE.
'CAUSE OF ALL THE BANGING.
THAT'S WHAT DADDY TOLD GRANDMA AND GRANDPA.
THEY TIED HER TO A SPECIAL BED...
AND AFTER SEVERAL DAYS, THEY PUT HER IN A SPECIAL ROOM, A PADDED CELL...
...BUT THAT DIDN'T STOP HER FROM HURTING HERSELF.
4.

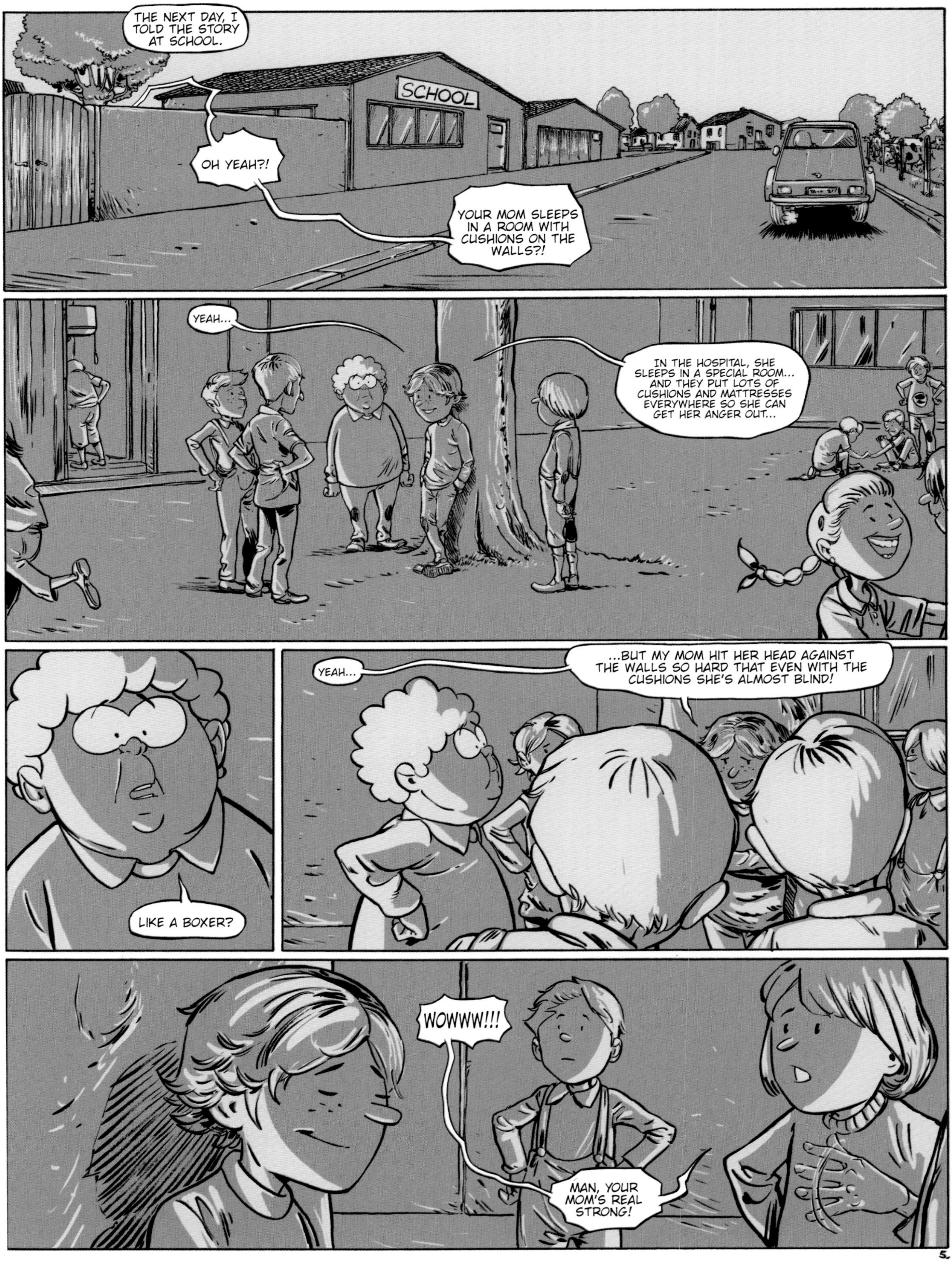
THE NEXT DAY, I TOLD THE STORY AT SCHOOL.
SCHOOL
OH YEAH?!
YOUR MOM SLEEPS IN A ROOM WITH CUSHIONS ON THE WALLS?!
YEAH...
IN THE HOSPITAL, SHE SLEEPS IN A SPECIAL ROOM... AND THEY PUT LOTS OF CUSHIONS AND MATTRESSES EVERYWHERE SO SHE CAN GET HER ANGER OUT...
LIKE A BOXER?
YEAH...
...BUT MY MOM HIT HER HEAD AGAINST THE WALLS SO HARD THAT EVEN WITH THE CUSHIONS SHE'S ALMOST BLIND!
WOWWW!!!
MAN, YOUR MOM'S REAL STRONG!
5.

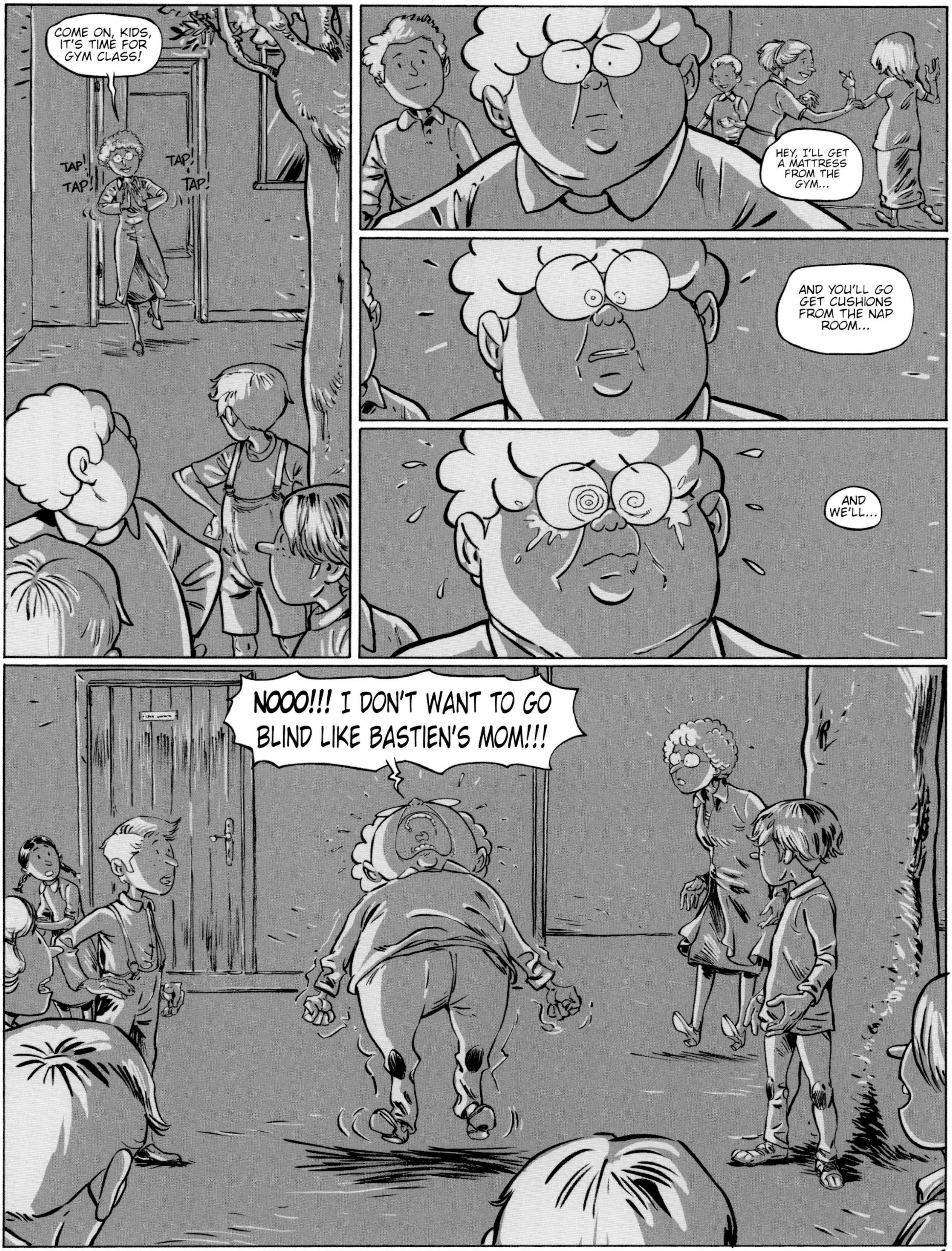
COME ON, KIDS, IT'S TIME FOR GYM CLASS!
TAP! TAP! TAP! TAP!
HEY, I'LL GET A MATTRESS FROM THE GYM...
AND YOU'LL GO GET CUSHIONS FROM THE NAP ROOM...
AND WE'LL...
NOOO!!! I DON'T WANT TO GO BLIND LIKE BASTIEN'S MOM!!!
6.

SPRING BREAK

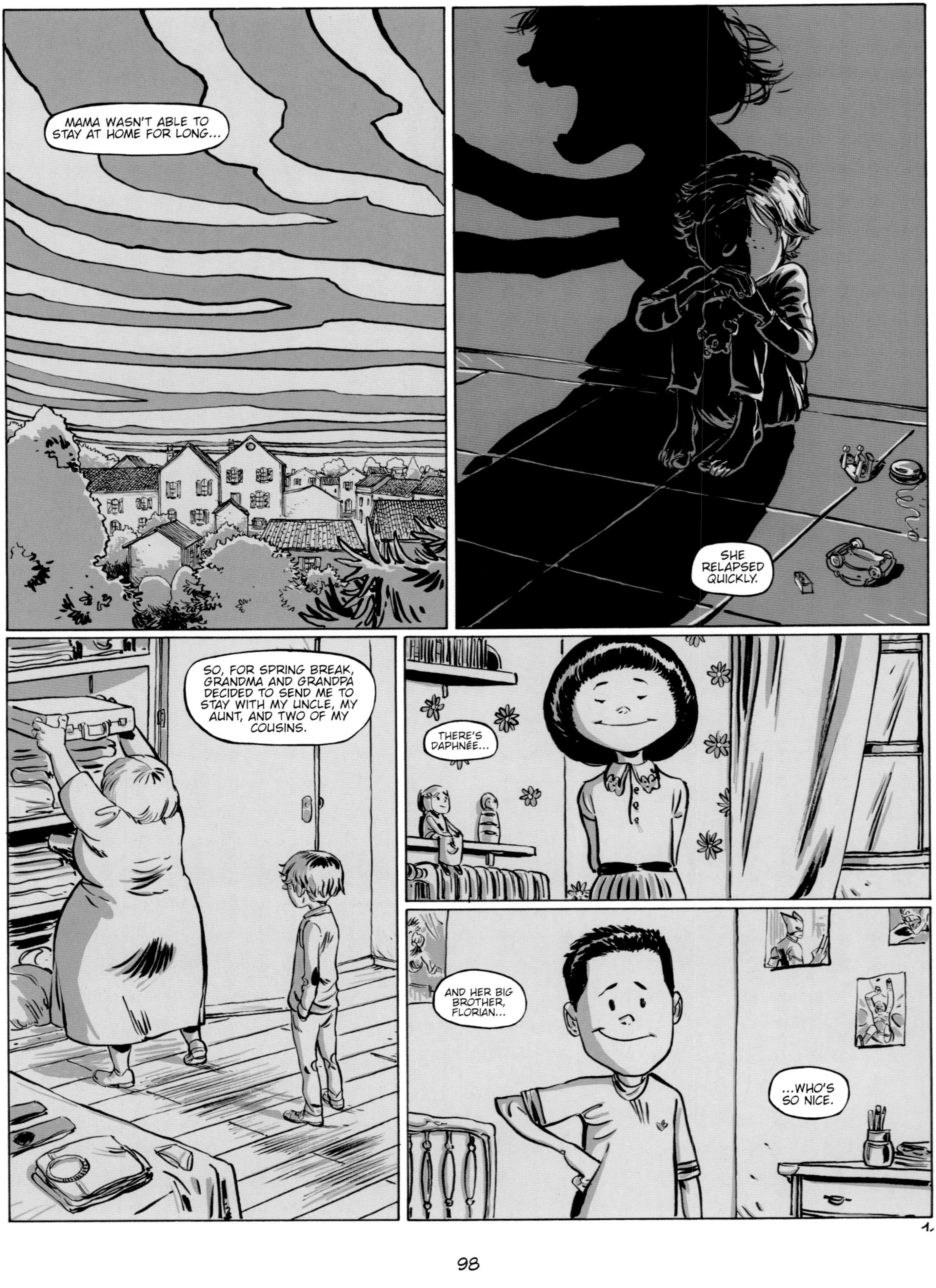
MAMA WASN'T ABLE TO STAY AT HOME FOR LONG...
SHE RELAPSED QUICKLY.
SO, FOR SPRING BREAK, GRANDMA AND GRANDPA DECIDED TO SEND ME TO STAY WITH MY UNCLE, MY AUNT, AND TWO OF MY COUSINS.
THERE'S DAPHNÉE...
AND HER BIG BROTHER, FLORIAN...
...WHO'S SO NICE.

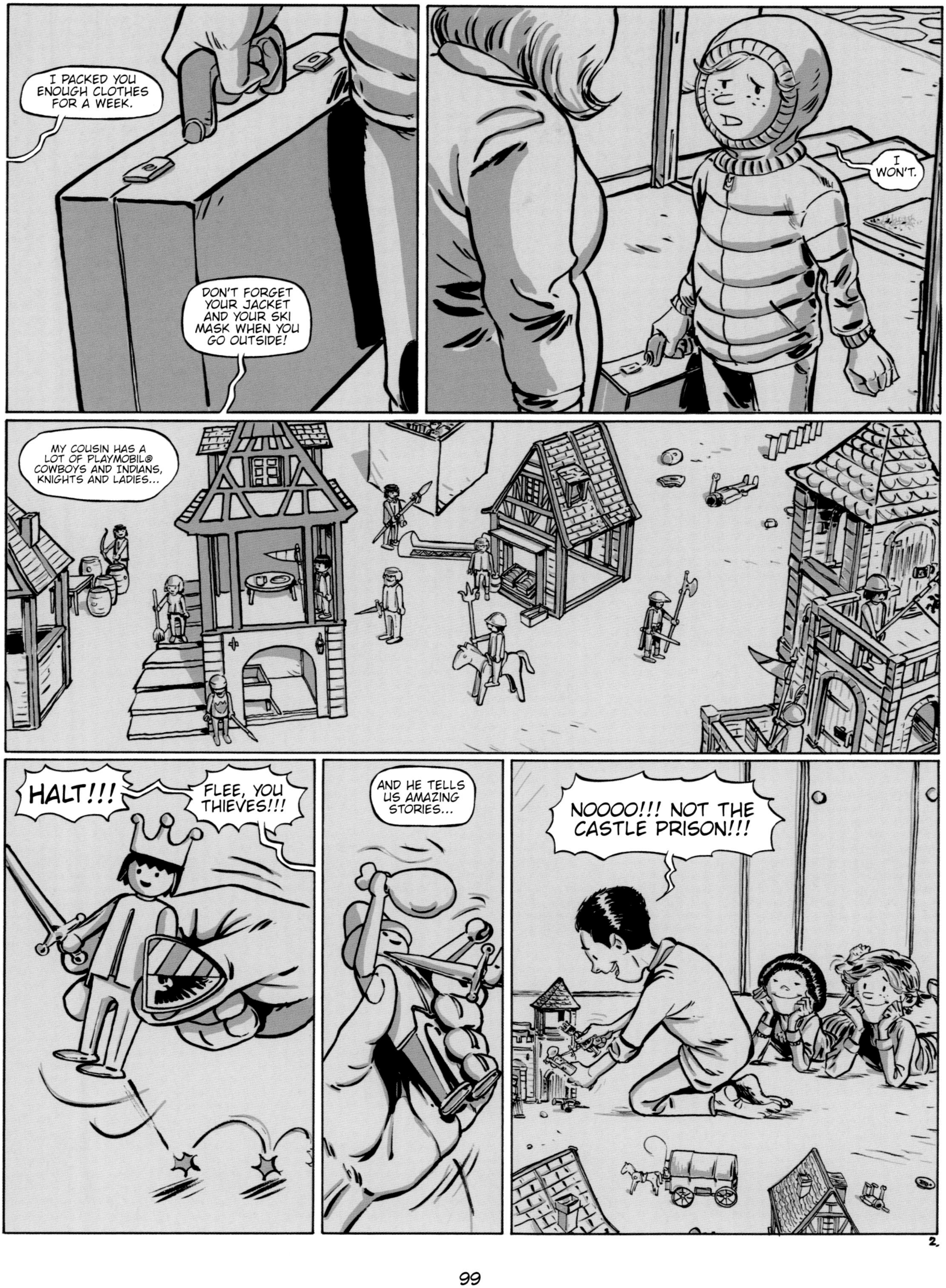
I PACKED YOU ENOUGH CLOTHES FOR A WEEK.
DON'T FORGET YOUR JACKET AND YOUR SKI MASK WHEN YOU GO OUTSIDE!
I WON'T.
MY COUSIN HAS A LOT OF PLAYMOBIL® COWBOYS AND INDIANS, KNIGHTS AND LADIES...
HALT!!!
FLEE, YOU THIEVES!!!
AND HE TELLS US AMAZING STORIES...
NOOOO!!! NOT THE CASTLE PRISON!!!
2.

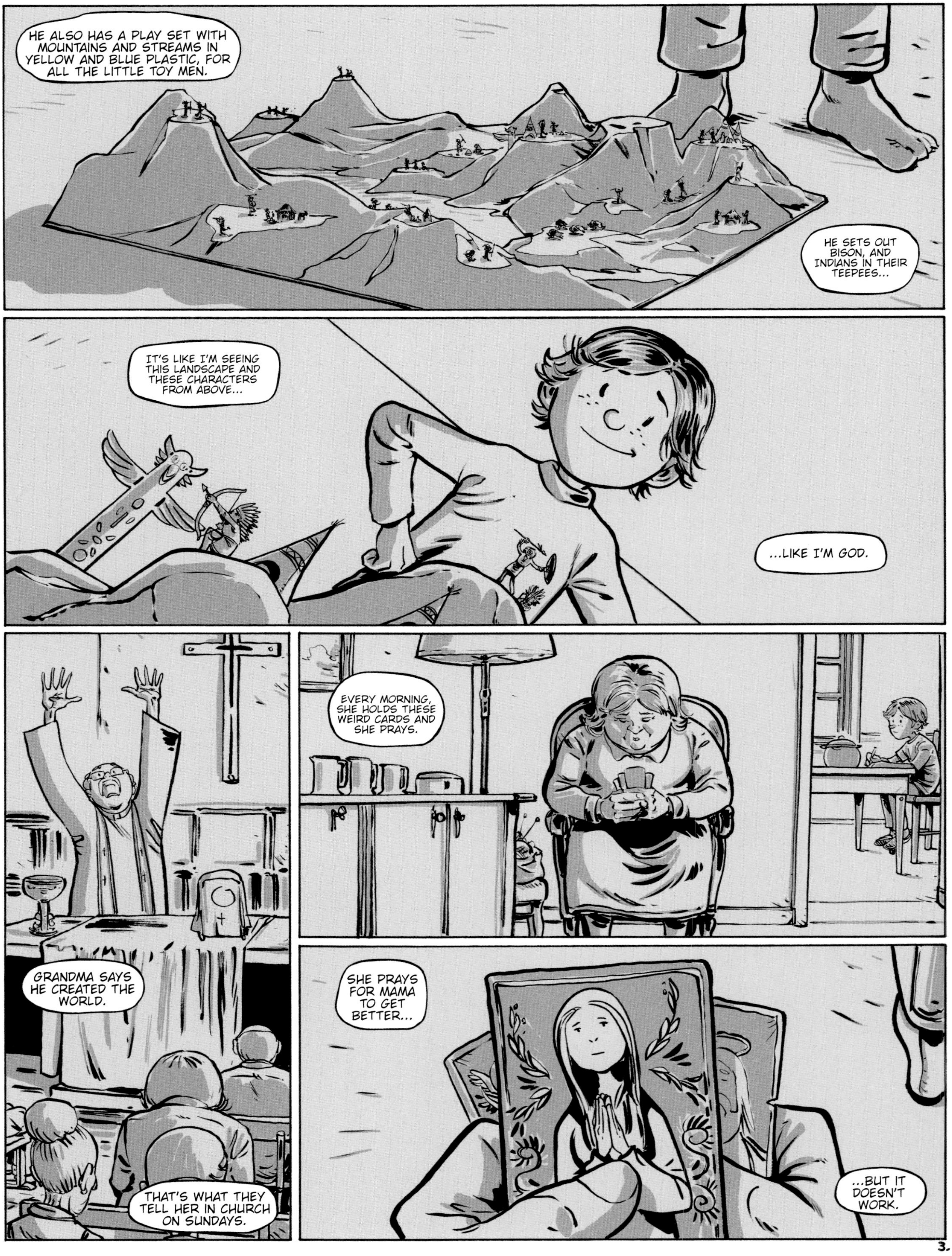
HE ALSO HAS A PLAY SET WITH MOUNTAINS AND STREAMS IN YELLOW AND BLUE PLASTIC, FOR ALL THE LITTLE TOY MEN.
HE SETS OUT BISON, AND INDIANS IN THEIR TEEPEES...
IT'S LIKE I'M SEEING THIS LANDSCAPE AND THESE CHARACTERS FROM ABOVE...
...LIKE I'M GOD.
GRANDMA SAYS HE CREATED THE WORLD.
THAT'S WHAT THEY TELL HER IN CHURCH ON SUNDAYS.
EVERY MORNING, SHE HOLDS THESE WEIRD CARDS AND SHE PRAYS.
SHE PRAYS FOR MAMA TO GET BETTER...
...BUT IT DOESN'T WORK.
3.

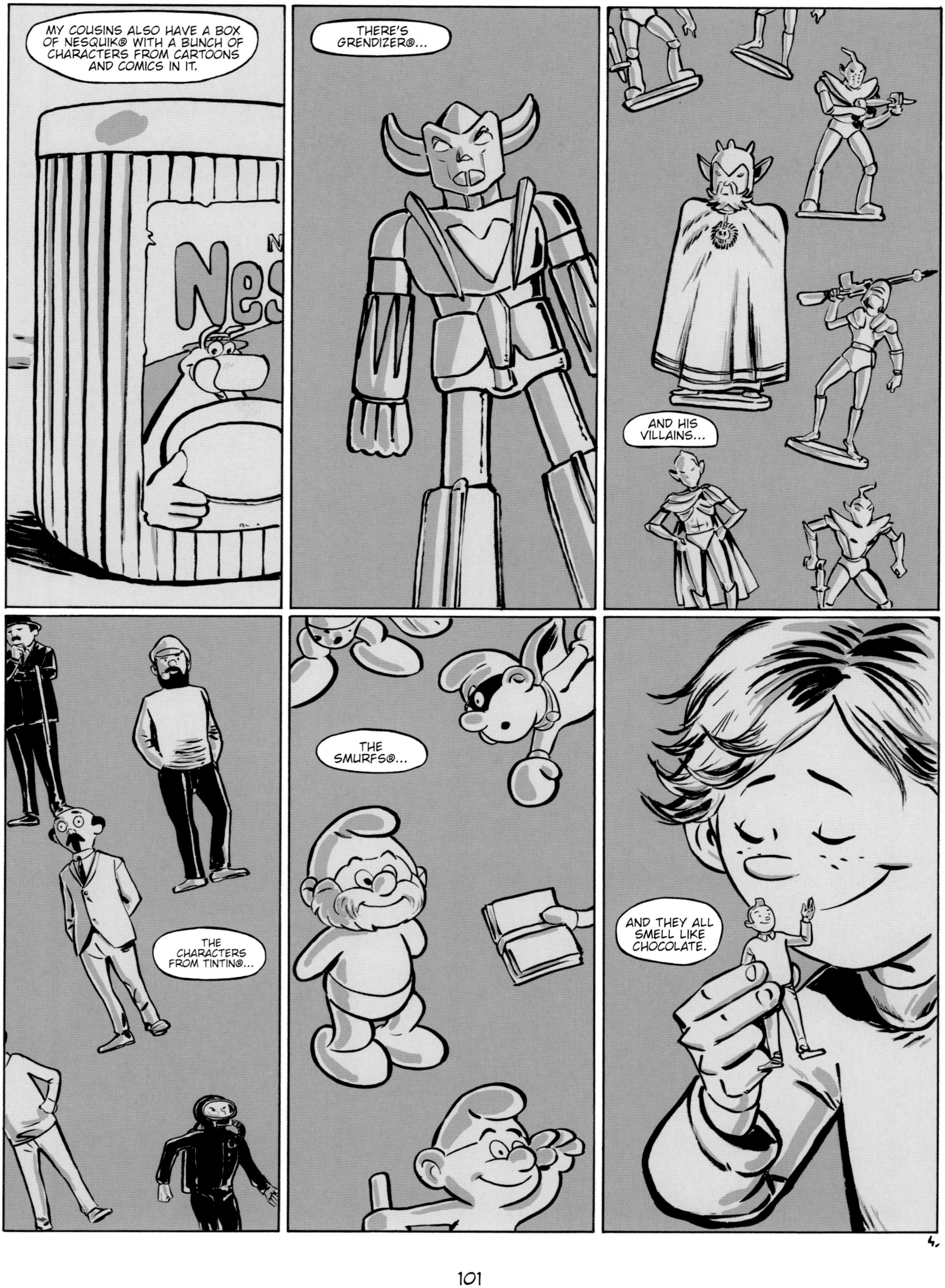
MY COUSINS ALSO HAVE A BOX OF NESQUIK® WITH A BUNCH OF CHARACTERS FROM CARTOONS AND COMICS IN IT.
THERE'S GRENDIZER®...
AND HIS VILLAINS...
THE CHARACTERS FROM TINTIN®...
THE SMURFS®...
AND THEY ALL SMELL LIKE CHOCOLATE.

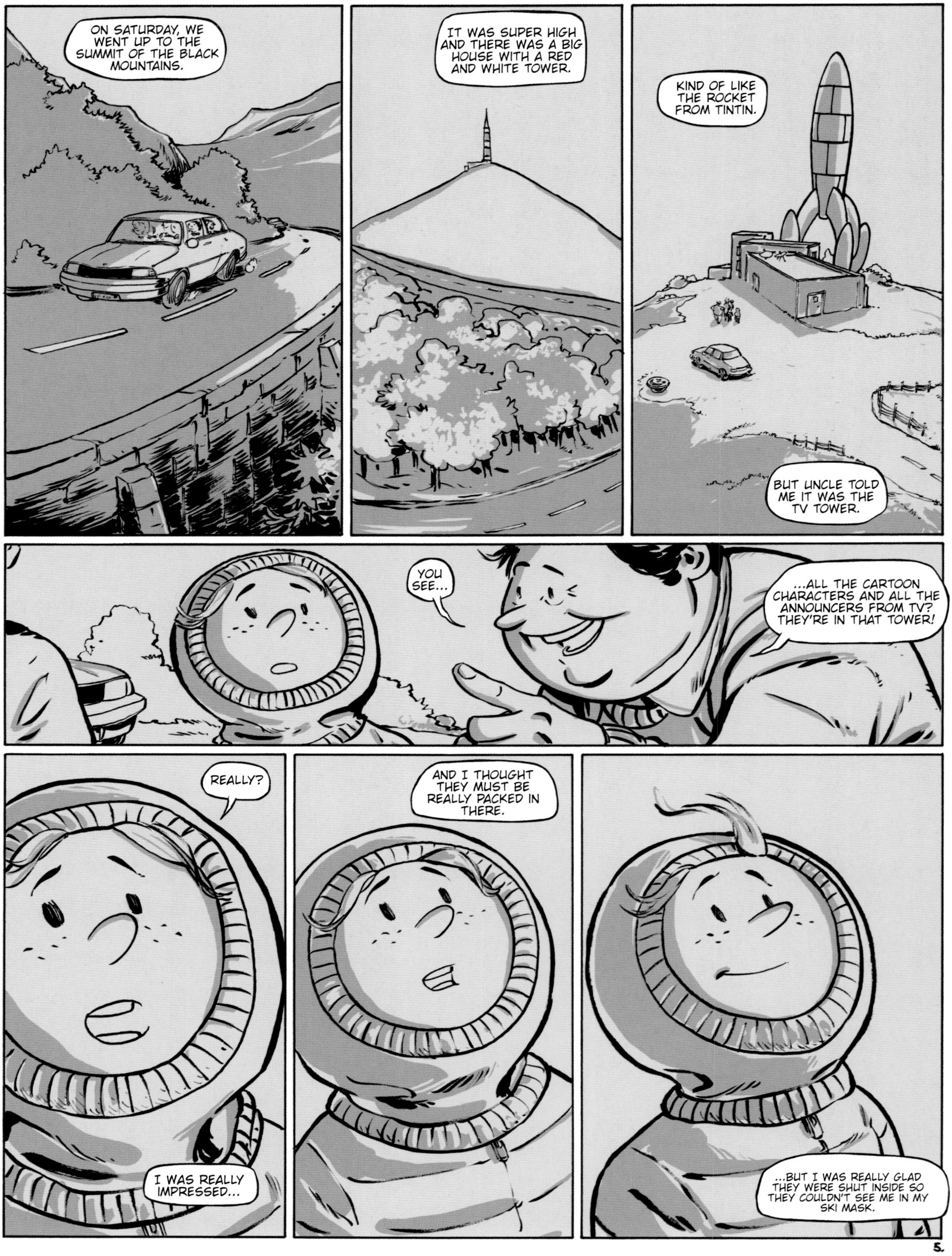

ON SATURDAY, WE WENT UP TO THE SUMMIT OF THE BLACK MOUNTAINS.
IT WAS SUPER HIGH AND THERE WAS A BIG HOUSE WITH A RED AND WHITE TOWER.
KIND OF LIKE THE ROCKET FROM TINTIN.
BUT UNCLE TOLD ME IT WAS THE TV TOWER.
YOU SEE...
...ALL THE CARTOON CHARACTERS AND ALL THE ANNOUNCERS FROM TV? THEY'RE IN THAT TOWER!
REALLY?
I WAS REALLY IMPRESSED...
AND I THOUGHT THEY MUST BE REALLY PACKED IN THERE.
...BUT I WAS REALLY GLAD THEY WERE SHUT INSIDE SO THEY COULDN'T SEE ME IN MY SKI MASK.
5.

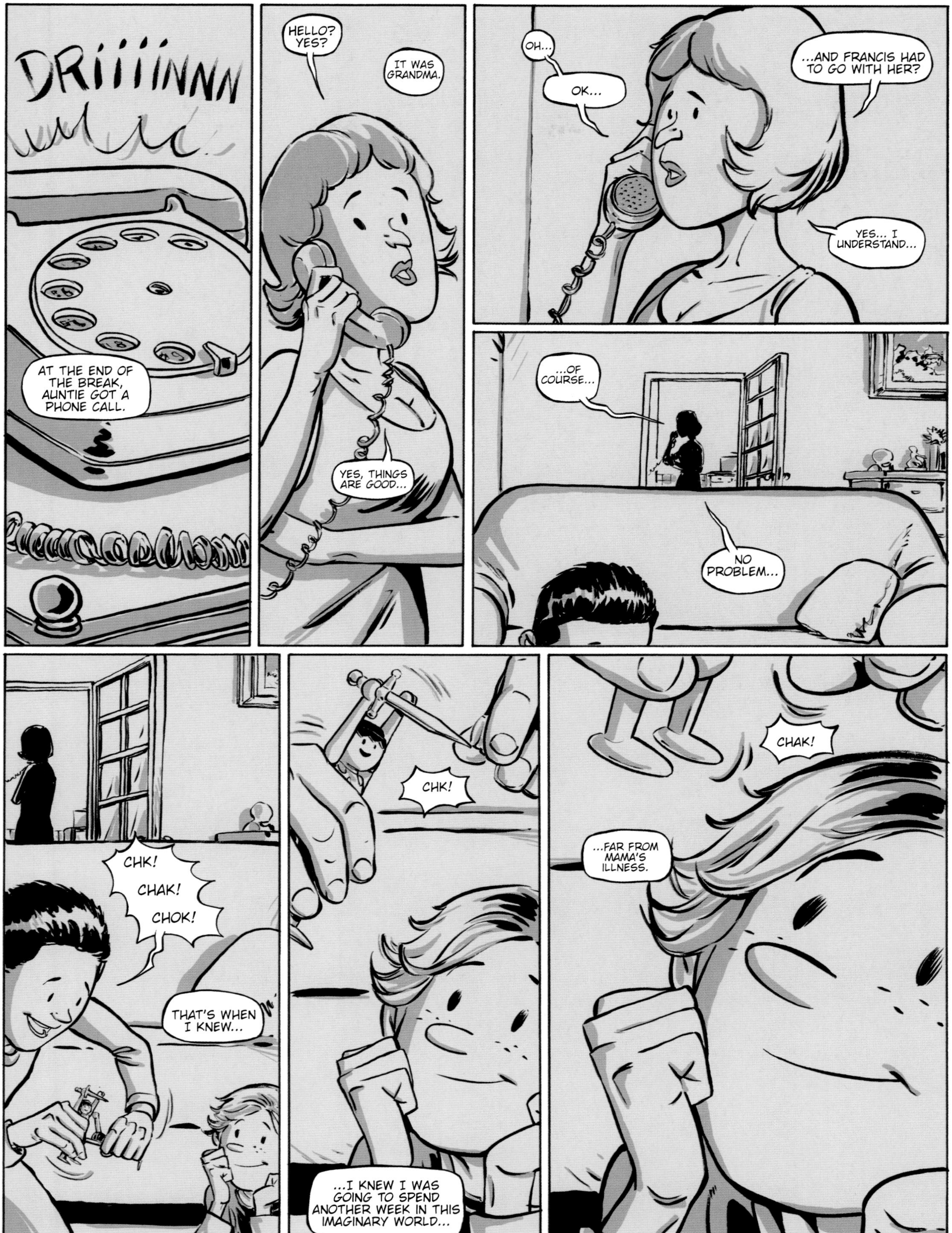
DRiiiiNNN
AT THE END OF THE BREAK, AUNTIE GOT A PHONE CALL.
HELLO? YES?
IT WAS GRANDMA.
YES, THINGS ARE GOOD...
OH...
OK...
...AND FRANCIS HAD TO GO WITH HER?
YES... I UNDERSTAND...
...OF COURSE...
NO PROBLEM...
CHK!
CHAK!
CHOK!
THAT'S WHEN I KNEW...
CHK!
...I KNEW I WAS GOING TO SPEND ANOTHER WEEK IN THIS IMAGINARY WORLD...
CHAK!
...FAR FROM MAMA'S ILLNESS.
6.

THE VISIT

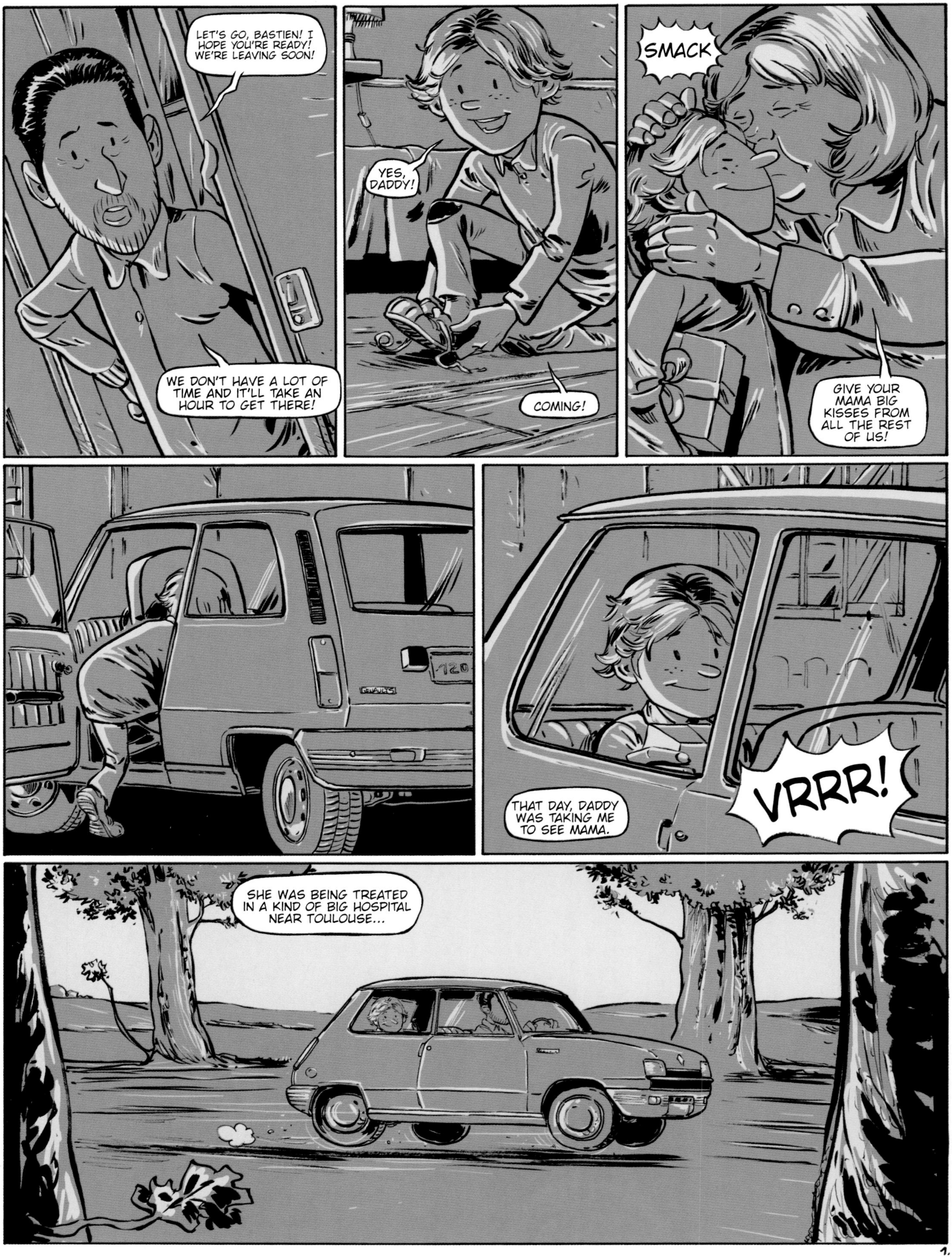
LET'S GO, BASTIEN! I HOPE YOU'RE READY! WE'RE LEAVING SOON!
WE DON'T HAVE A LOT OF TIME AND IT'LL TAKE AN HOUR TO GET THERE!
YES, DADDY!
COMING!
SMACK
GIVE YOUR MAMA BIG KISSES FROM ALL THE REST OF US!
THAT DAY, DADDY WAS TAKING ME TO SEE MAMA.
VRRR!
SHE WAS BEING TREATED IN A KIND OF BIG HOSPITAL NEAR TOULOUSE...

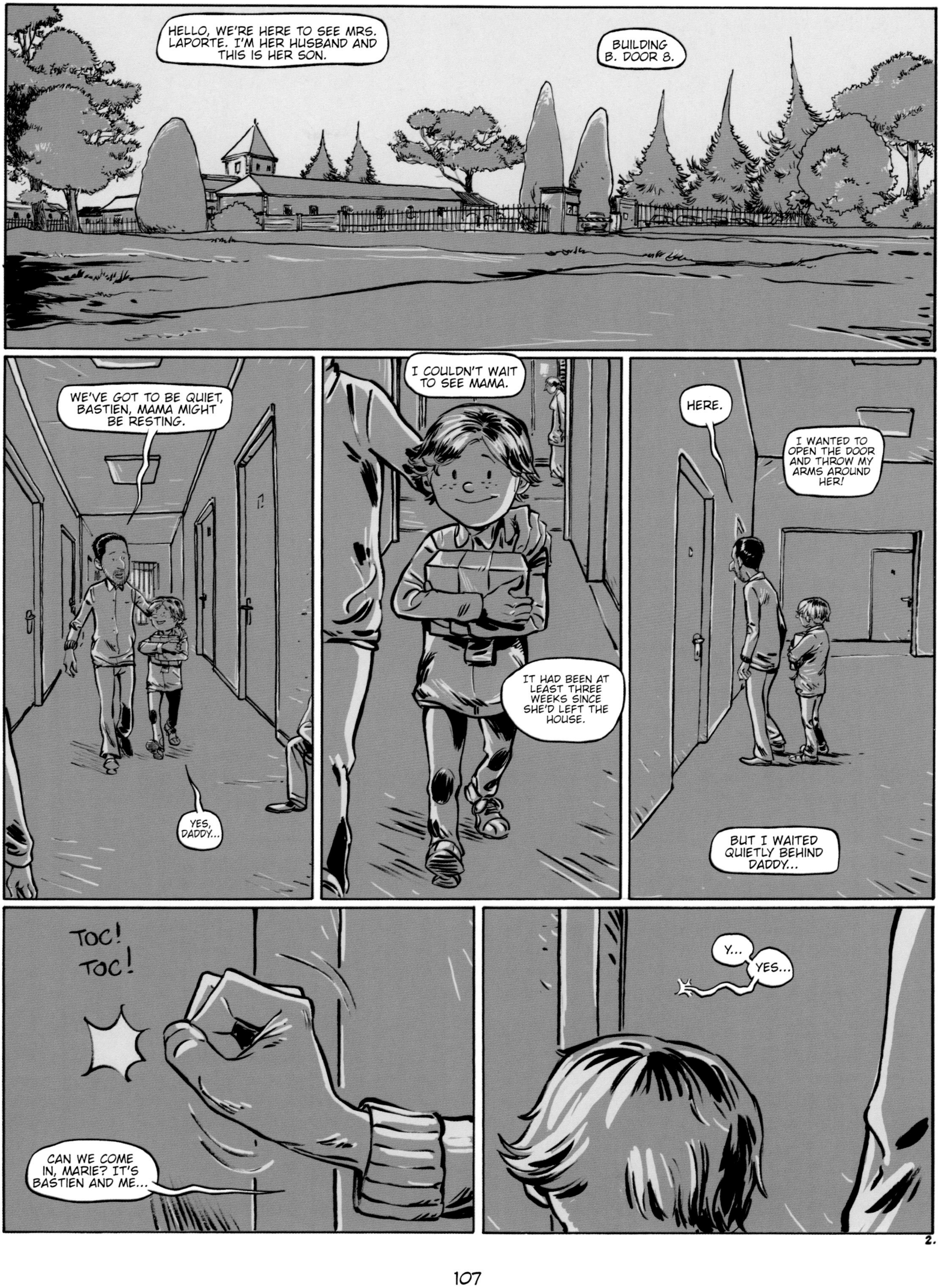
HELLO, WE'RE HERE TO SEE MRS. LAPORTE. I'M HER HUSBAND AND THIS IS HER SON.
BUILDING B. DOOR 8.
WE'VE GOT TO BE QUIET, BASTIEN, MAMA MIGHT BE RESTING.
YES, DADDY...
I COULDN'T WAIT TO SEE MAMA.
IT HAD BEEN AT LEAST THREE WEEKS SINCE SHE'D LEFT THE HOUSE.
HERE.
I WANTED TO OPEN THE DOOR AND THROW MY ARMS AROUND HER!
BUT I WAITED QUIETLY BEHIND DADDY...
TOC! TOC!
CAN WE COME IN, MARIE? IT'S BASTIEN AND ME...
Y...
YES...
2.

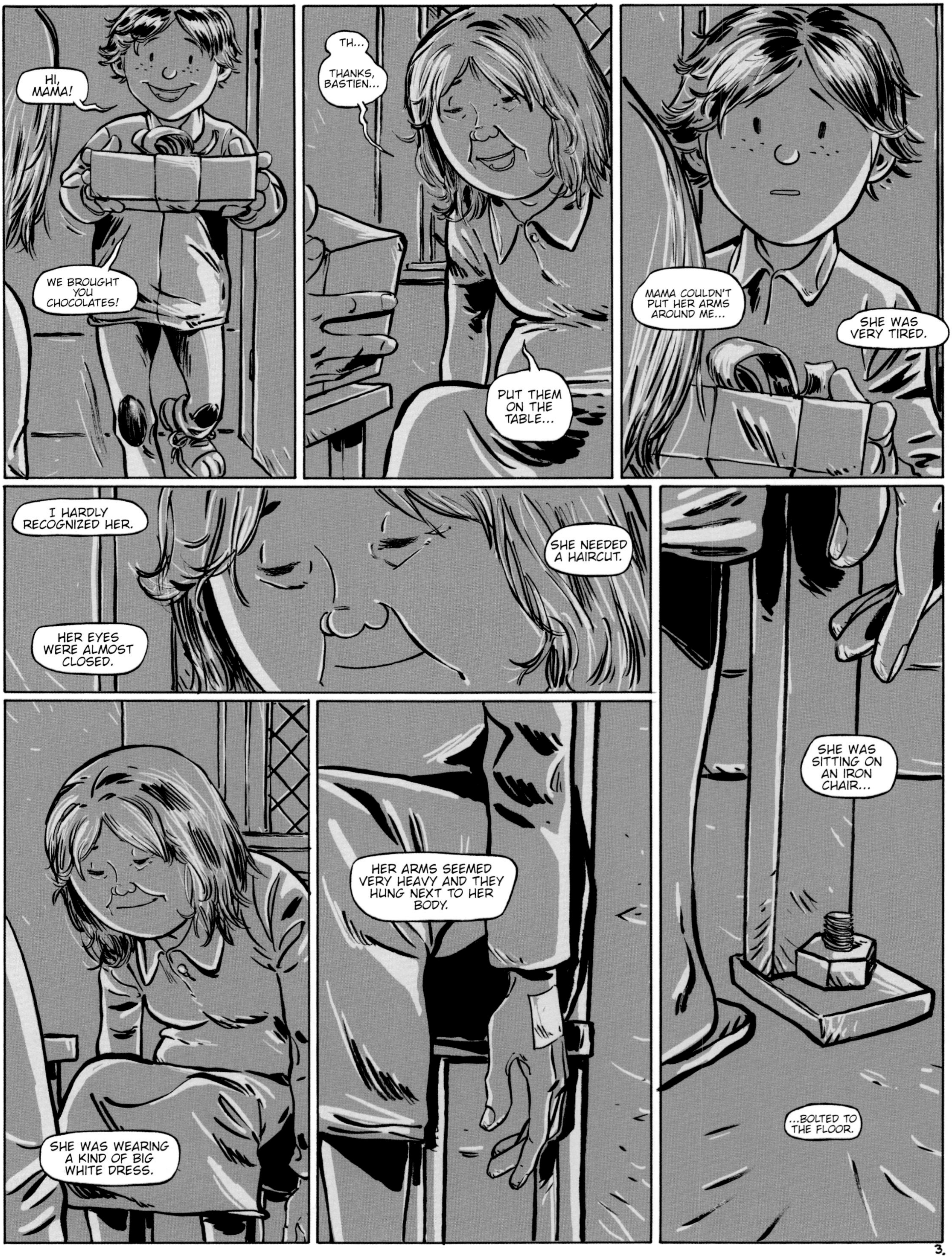
HI, MAMA!
WE BROUGHT YOU CHOCOLATES!
TH...
THANKS, BASTIEN...
PUT THEM ON THE TABLE...
MAMA COULDN'T PUT HER ARMS AROUND ME...
SHE WAS VERY TIRED.
I HARDLY RECOGNIZED HER.
SHE NEEDED A HAIRCUT.
HER EYES WERE ALMOST CLOSED.
SHE WAS WEARING A KIND OF BIG WHITE DRESS.
HER ARMS SEEMED VERY HEAVY AND THEY HUNG NEXT TO HER BODY.
SHE WAS SITTING ON AN IRON CHAIR...
...BOLTED TO THE FLOOR.
3.

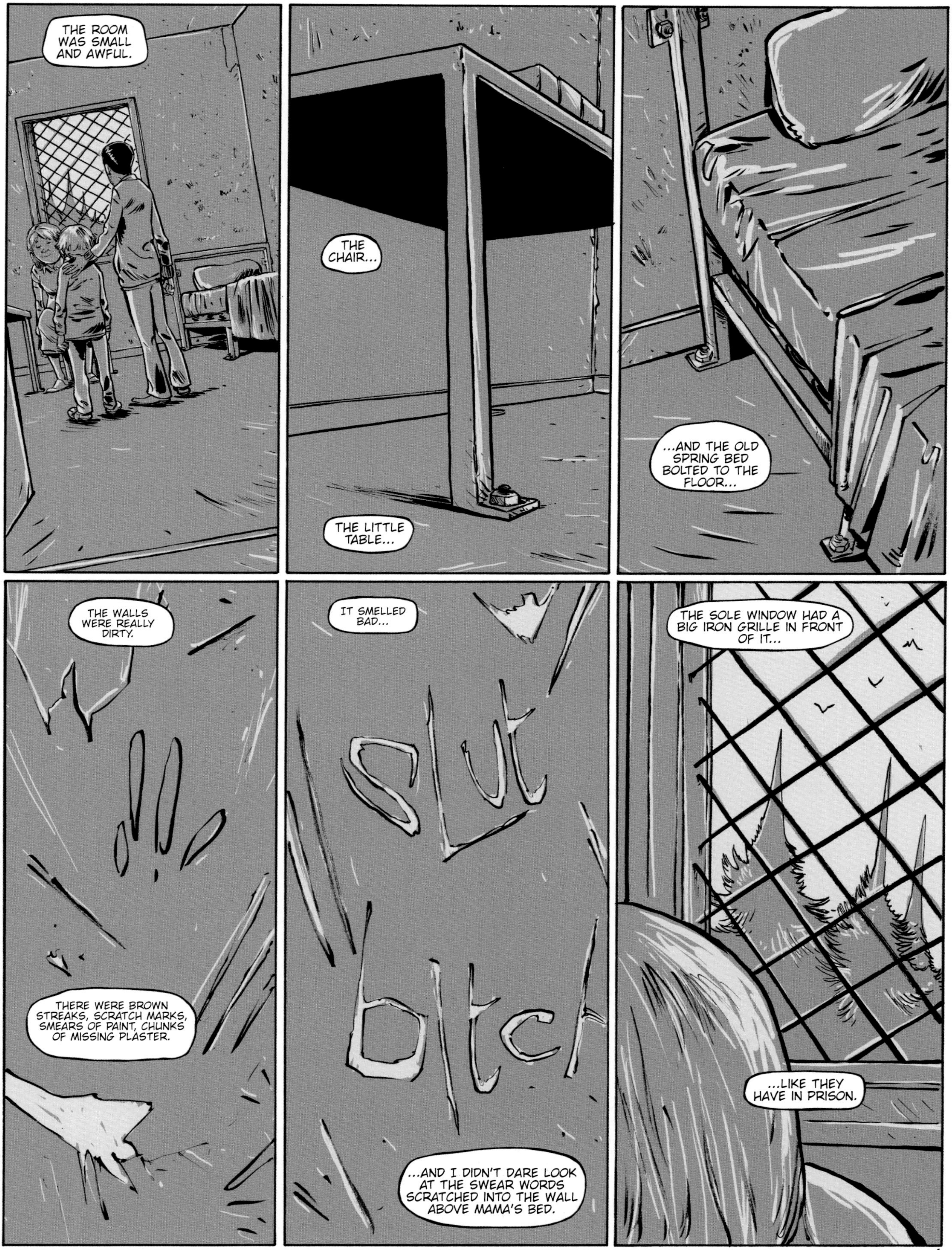
THE ROOM WAS SMALL AND AWFUL.
THE CHAIR...
THE LITTLE TABLE...
...AND THE OLD SPRING BED BOLTED TO THE FLOOR...
THE WALLS WERE REALLY DIRTY.
THERE WERE BROWN STREAKS, SCRATCH MARKS, SMEARS OF PAINT, CHUNKS OF MISSING PLASTER.
IT SMELLED BAD...
slut
bitch
...AND I DIDN'T DARE LOOK AT THE SWEAR WORDS SCRATCHED INTO THE WALL ABOVE MAMA'S BED.
THE SOLE WINDOW HAD A BIG IRON GRILLE IN FRONT OF IT...
...LIKE THEY HAVE IN PRISON.

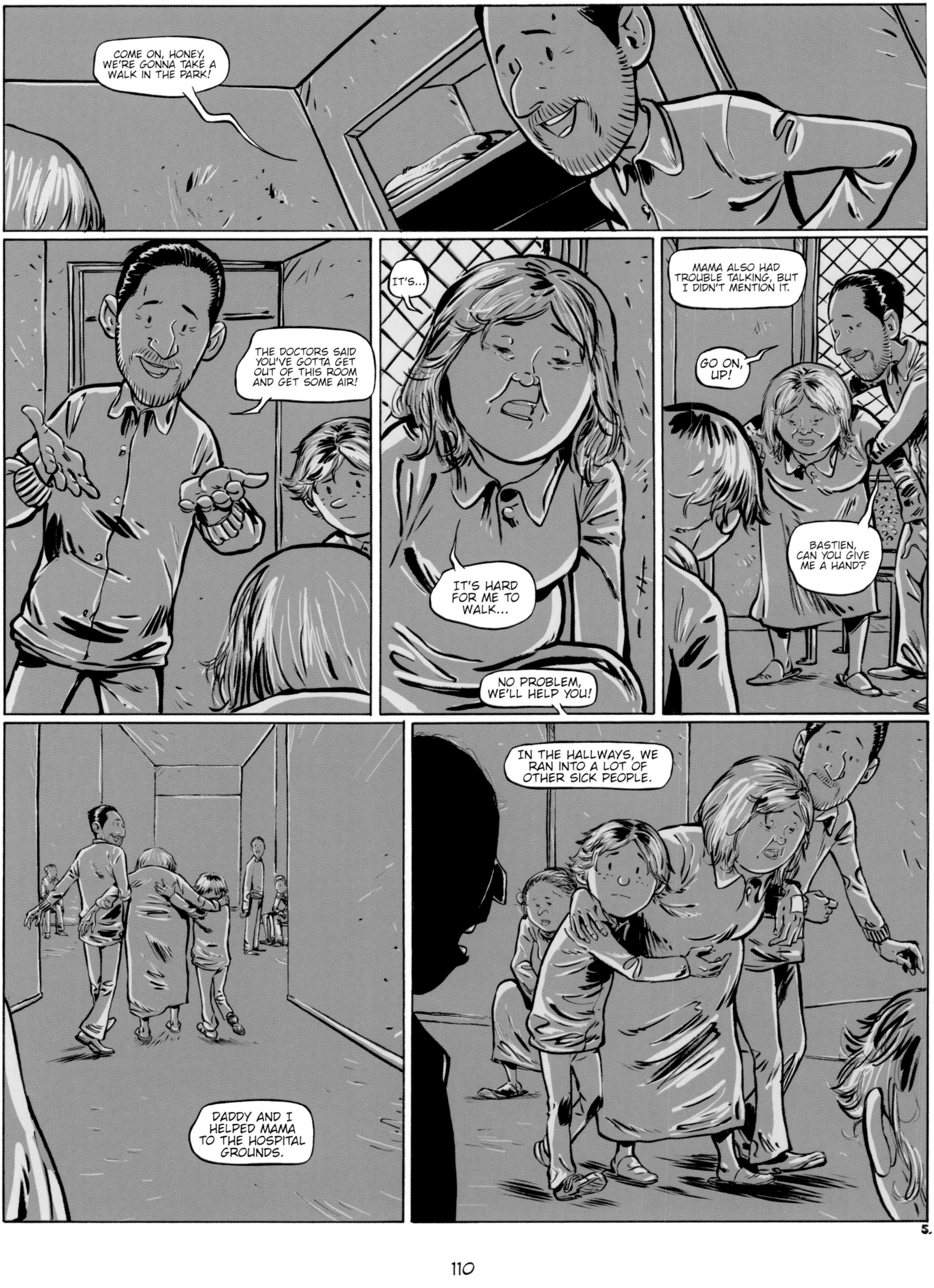
COME ON, HONEY, WE'RE GONNA TAKE A WALK IN THE PARK!
THE DOCTORS SAID YOU'VE GOTTA GET OUT OF THIS ROOM AND GET SOME AIR!
IT'S...
IT'S HARD FOR ME TO WALK...
NO PROBLEM, WE'LL HELP YOU!
MAMA ALSO HAD TROUBLE TALKING, BUT I DIDN'T MENTION IT.
GO ON, UP!
BASTIEN, CAN YOU GIVE ME A HAND?
DADDY AND I HELPED MAMA TO THE HOSPITAL GROUNDS.
IN THE HALLWAYS, WE RAN INTO A LOT OF OTHER SICK PEOPLE.
5.

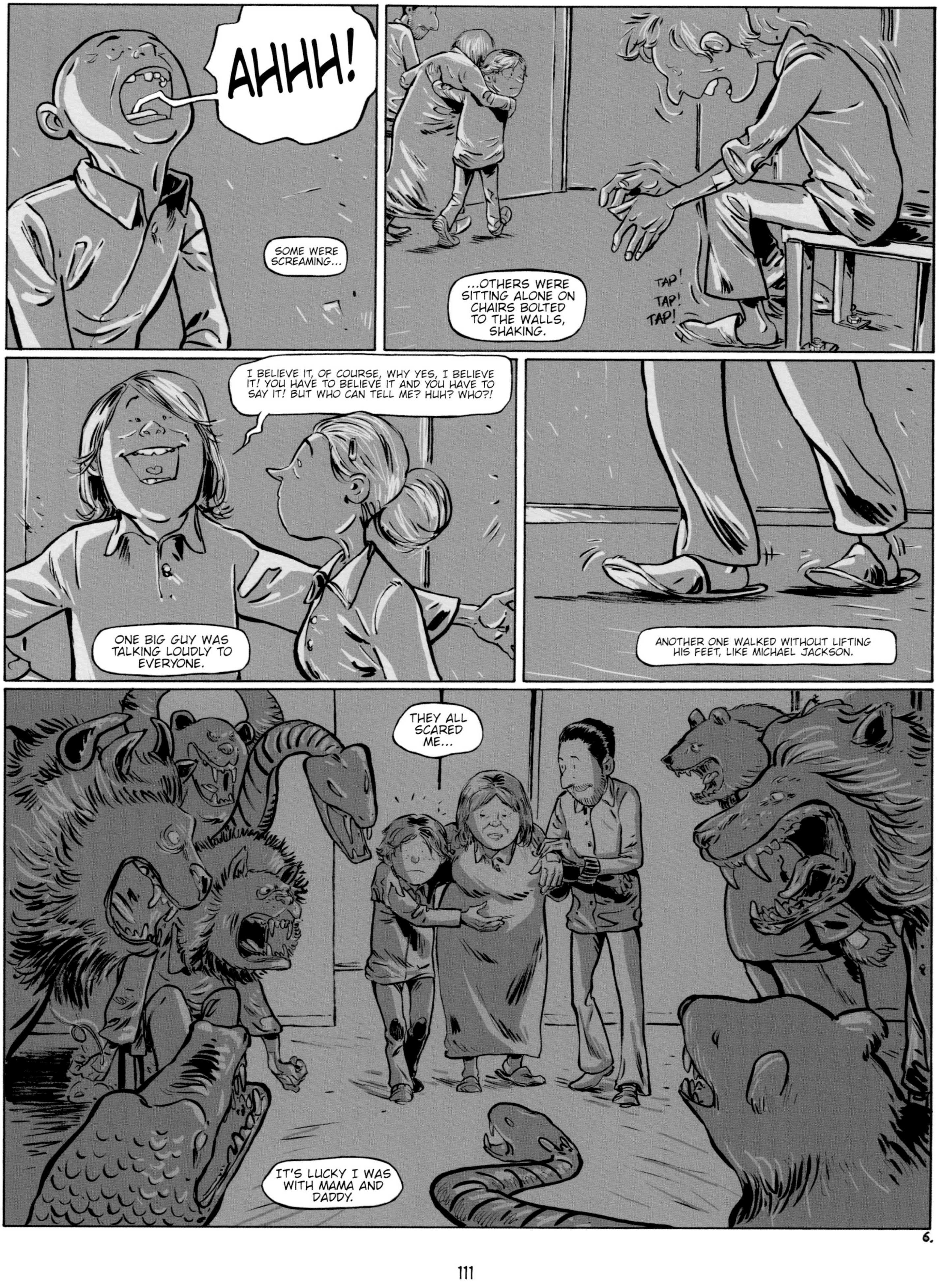
AHHH!
SOME WERE SCREAMING...
...OTHERS WERE SITTING ALONE ON CHAIRS BOLTED TO THE WALLS, SHAKING.
TAP! TAP! TAP!
I BELIEVE IT, OF COURSE, WHY YES, I BELIEVE IT! YOU HAVE TO BELIEVE IT AND YOU HAVE TO SAY IT! BUT WHO CAN TELL ME? HUH? WHO?!
ONE BIG GUY WAS TALKING LOUDLY TO EVERYONE.
ANOTHER ONE WALKED WITHOUT LIFTING HIS FEET, LIKE MICHAEL JACKSON.
THEY ALL SCARED ME...
IT'S LUCKY I WAS WITH MAMA AND DADDY.
6.

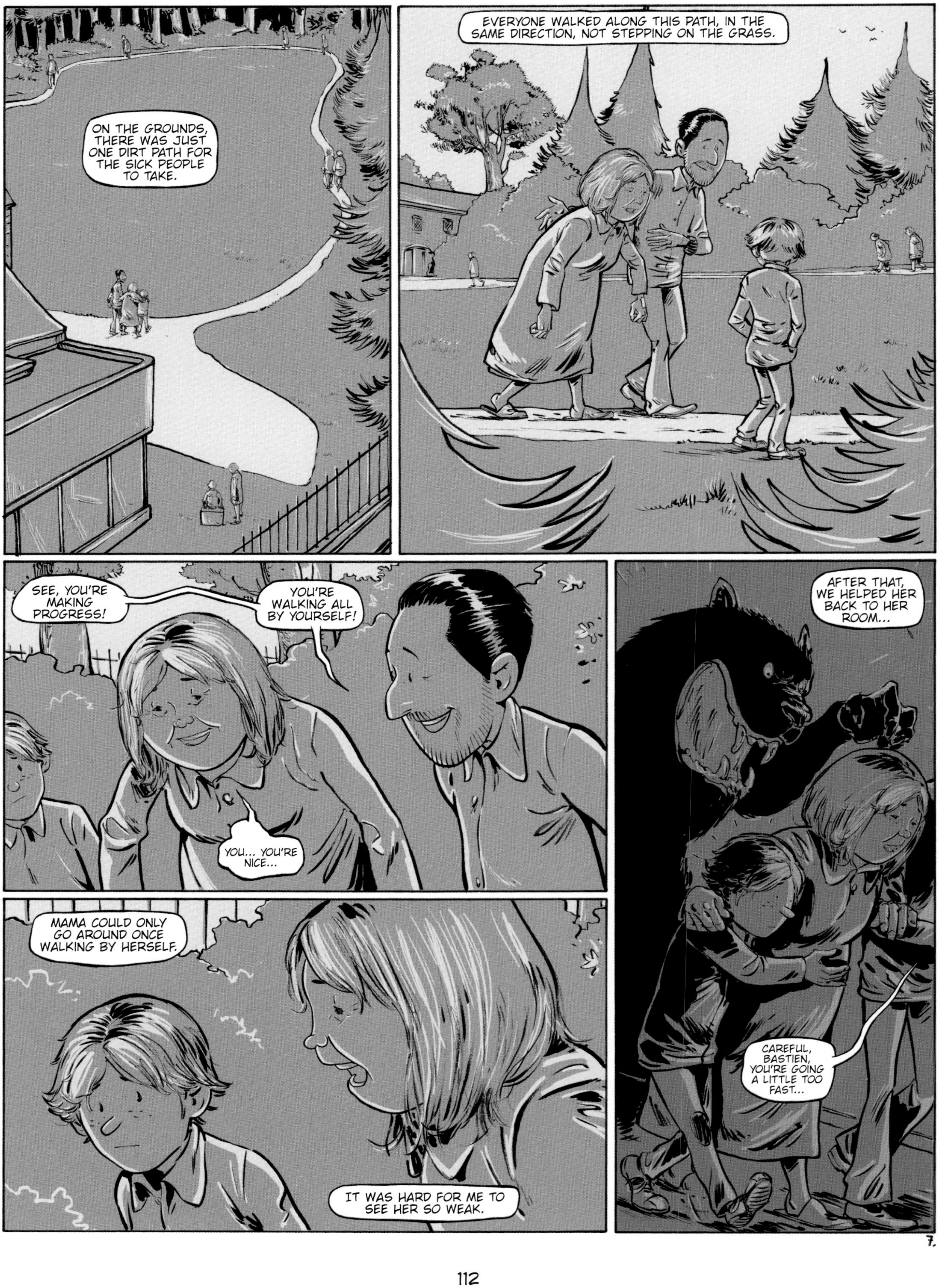
ON THE GROUNDS, THERE WAS JUST ONE DIRT PATH FOR THE SICK PEOPLE TO TAKE.
EVERYONE WALKED ALONG THIS PATH, IN THE SAME DIRECTION, NOT STEPPING ON THE GRASS.
SEE, YOU'RE MAKING PROGRESS!
YOU'RE WALKING ALL BY YOURSELF!
YOU... YOU'RE NICE...
AFTER THAT, WE HELPED HER BACK TO HER ROOM...
CAREFUL, BASTIEN, YOU'RE GOING A LITTLE TOO FAST...
MAMA COULD ONLY GO AROUND ONCE WALKING BY HERSELF.
IT WAS HARD FOR ME TO SEE HER SO WEAK.
7.

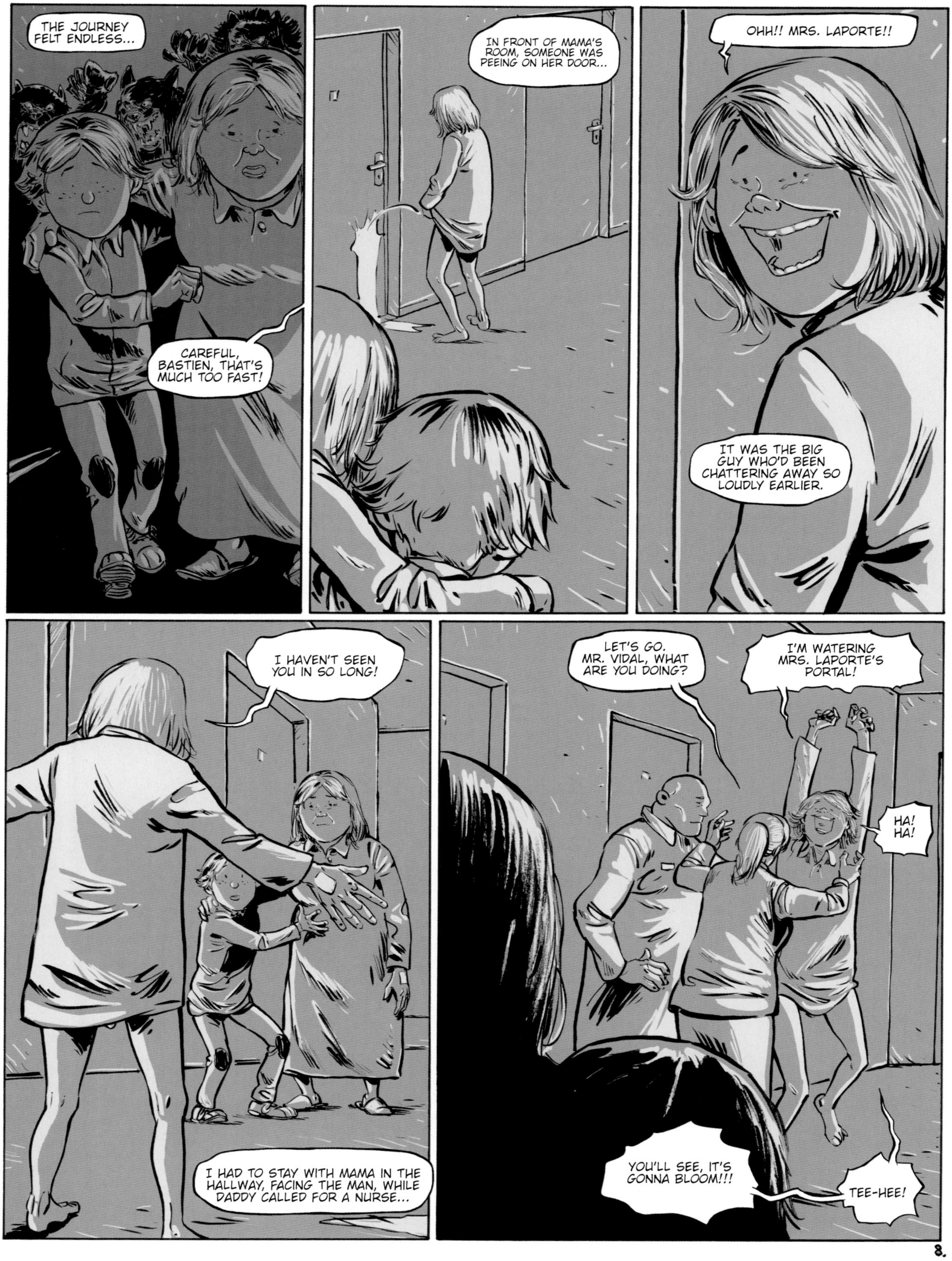
THE JOURNEY FELT ENDLESS...
CAREFUL, BASTIEN, THAT'S MUCH TOO FAST!
IN FRONT OF MAMA'S ROOM, SOMEONE WAS PEEING ON HER DOOR...
OHH!! MRS. LAPORTE!!
IT WAS THE BIG GUY WHO'D BEEN CHATTERING AWAY SO LOUDLY EARLIER.
I HAVEN'T SEEN YOU IN SO LONG!
I HAD TO STAY WITH MAMA IN THE HALLWAY, FACING THE MAN, WHILE DADDY CALLED FOR A NURSE...
LET'S GO. MR. VIDAL, WHAT ARE YOU DOING?
I'M WATERING MRS. LAPORTE'S PORTAL!
HA! HA!
YOU'LL SEE, IT'S GONNA BLOOM!!!
TEE-HEE!
8.

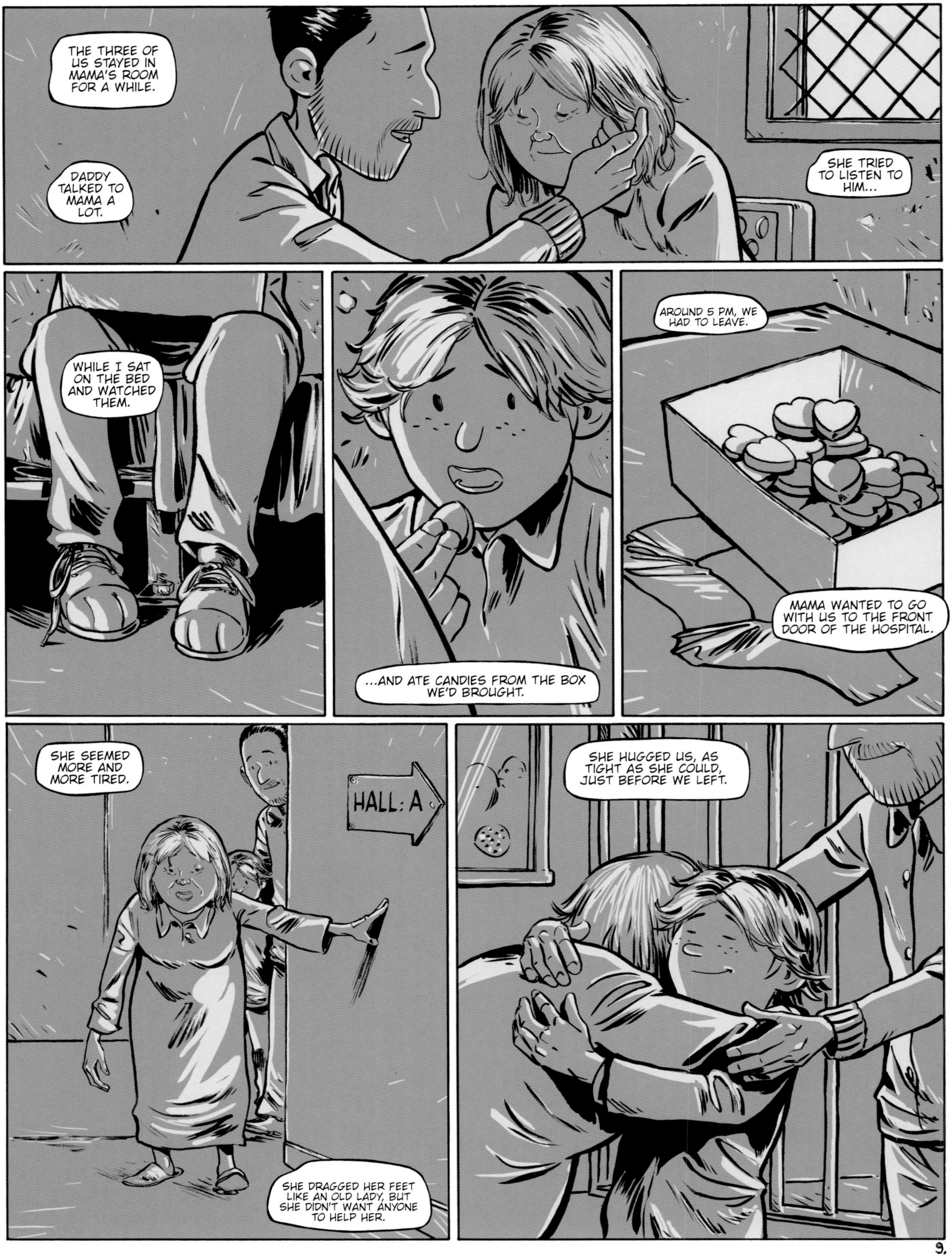
THE THREE OF US STAYED IN MAMA'S ROOM FOR A WHILE.
DADDY TALKED TO MAMA A LOT.
SHE TRIED TO LISTEN TO HIM...
WHILE I SAT ON THE BED AND WATCHED THEM.
...AND ATE CANDIES FROM THE BOX WE'D BROUGHT.
AROUND 5 PM, WE HAD TO LEAVE.
MAMA WANTED TO GO WITH US TO THE FRONT DOOR OF THE HOSPITAL.
SHE SEEMED MORE AND MORE TIRED.
HALL: A
SHE DRAGGED HER FEET LIKE AN OLD LADY, BUT SHE DIDN'T WANT ANYONE TO HELP HER.
SHE HUGGED US, AS TIGHT AS SHE COULD, JUST BEFORE WE LEFT.
9.

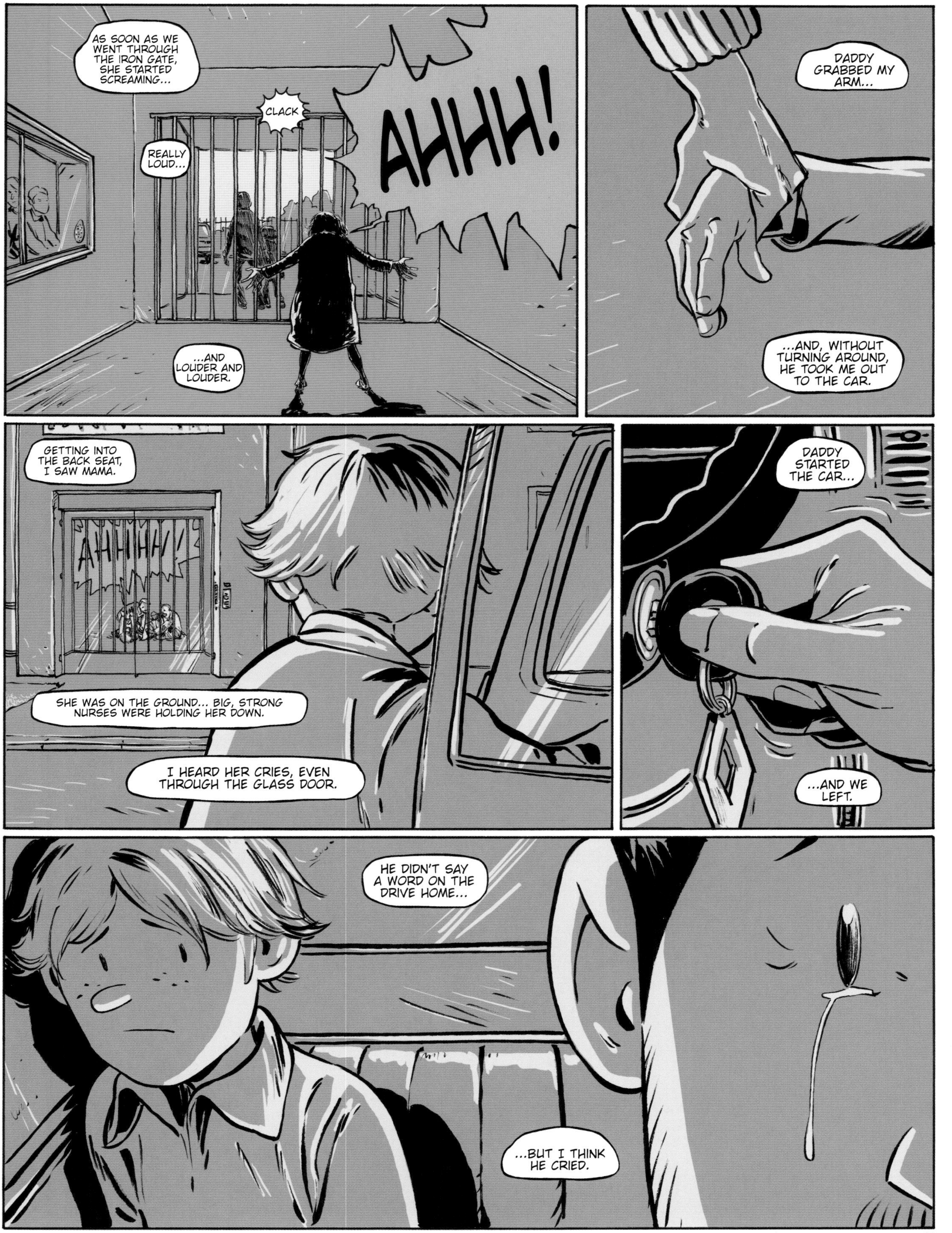
AS SOON AS WE WENT THROUGH THE IRON GATE, SHE STARTED SCREAMING...
CLACK
REALLY LOUD...
AHHH!
...AND LOUDER AND LOUDER.
DADDY GRABBED MY ARM...
...AND, WITHOUT TURNING AROUND, HE TOOK ME OUT TO THE CAR.
GETTING INTO THE BACK SEAT, I SAW MAMA.
AHHHHH!
SHE WAS ON THE GROUND... BIG, STRONG NURSES WERE HOLDING HER DOWN.
I HEARD HER CRIES, EVEN THROUGH THE GLASS DOOR.
DADDY STARTED THE CAR...
...AND WE LEFT.
HE DIDN'T SAY A WORD ON THE DRIVE HOME...
...BUT I THINK HE CRIED.
10.

DADDY

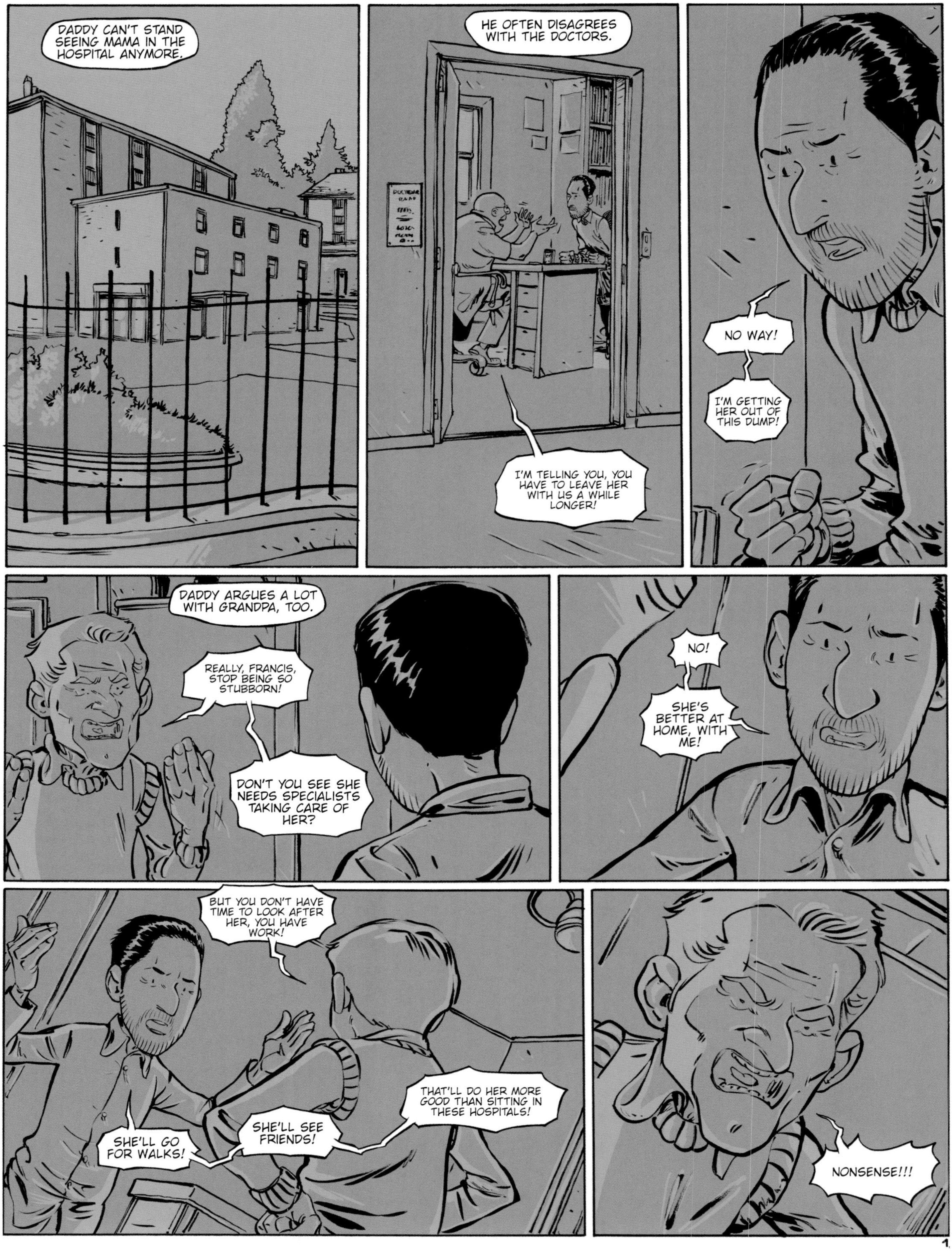
DADDY CAN'T STAND SEEING MAMA IN THE HOSPITAL ANYMORE.
HE OFTEN DISAGREES WITH THE DOCTORS.
I'M TELLING YOU, YOU HAVE TO LEAVE HER WITH US A WHILE LONGER!
NO WAY!
I'M GETTING HER OUT OF THIS DUMP!
DADDY ARGUES A LOT WITH GRANDPA, TOO.
REALLY, FRANCIS, STOP BEING SO STUBBORN!
DON'T YOU SEE SHE NEEDS SPECIALISTS TAKING CARE OF HER?
NO!
SHE'S BETTER AT HOME, WITH ME!
BUT YOU DON'T HAVE TIME TO LOOK AFTER HER, YOU HAVE WORK!
SHE'LL GO FOR WALKS!
SHE'LL SEE FRIENDS!
THAT'LL DO HER MORE GOOD THAN SITTING IN THESE HOSPITALS!
NONSENSE!!!

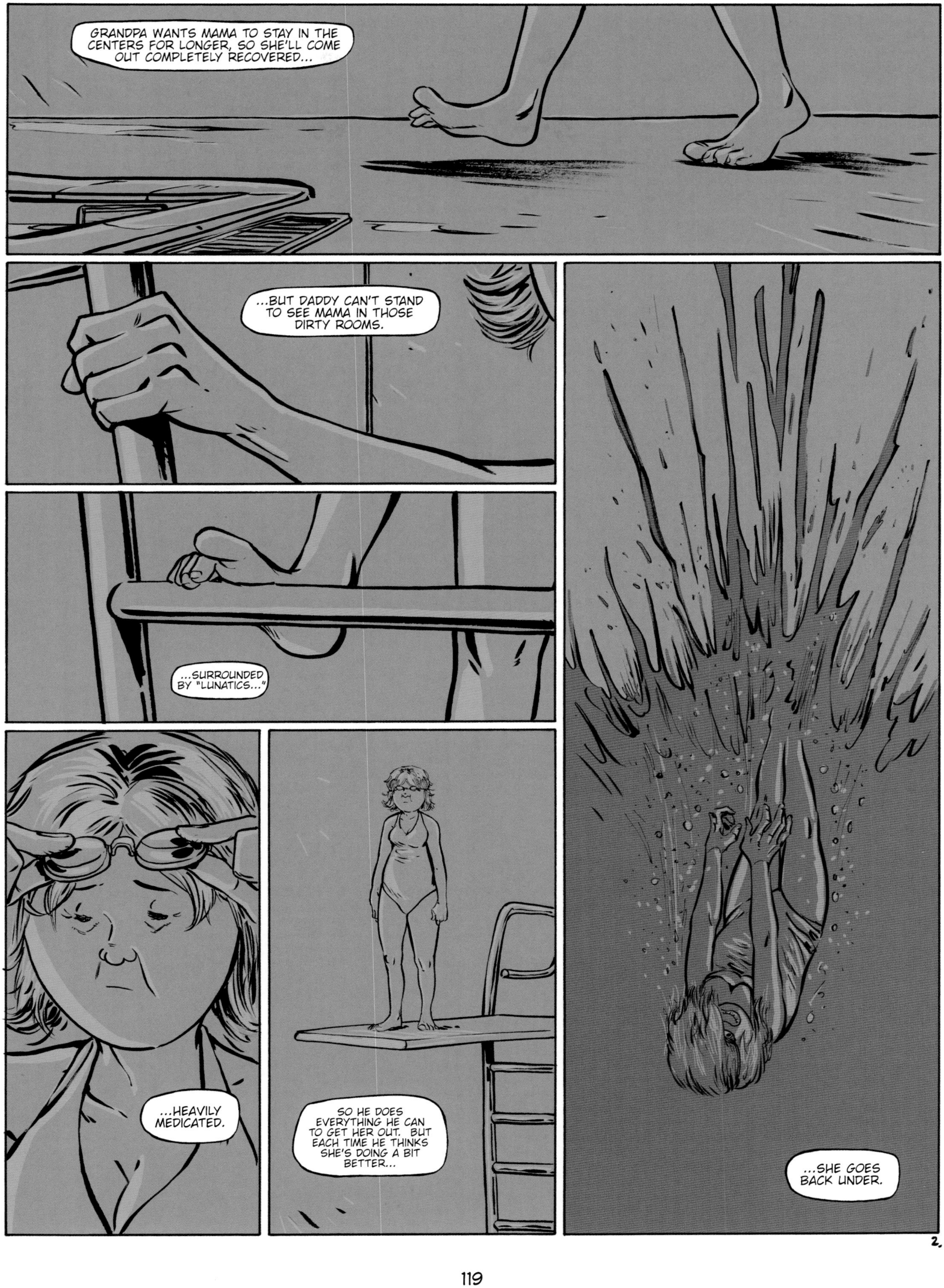
GRANDPA WANTS MAMA TO STAY IN THE CENTERS FOR LONGER, SO SHE'LL COME OUT COMPLETELY RECOVERED...
...BUT DADDY CAN'T STAND TO SEE MAMA IN THOSE DIRTY ROOMS.
...SURROUNDED BY "LUNATICS..."
...HEAVILY MEDICATED.
SO HE DOES EVERYTHING HE CAN TO GET HER OUT. BUT EACH TIME HE THINKS SHE'S DOING A BIT BETTER...
...SHE GOES BACK UNDER.
2.

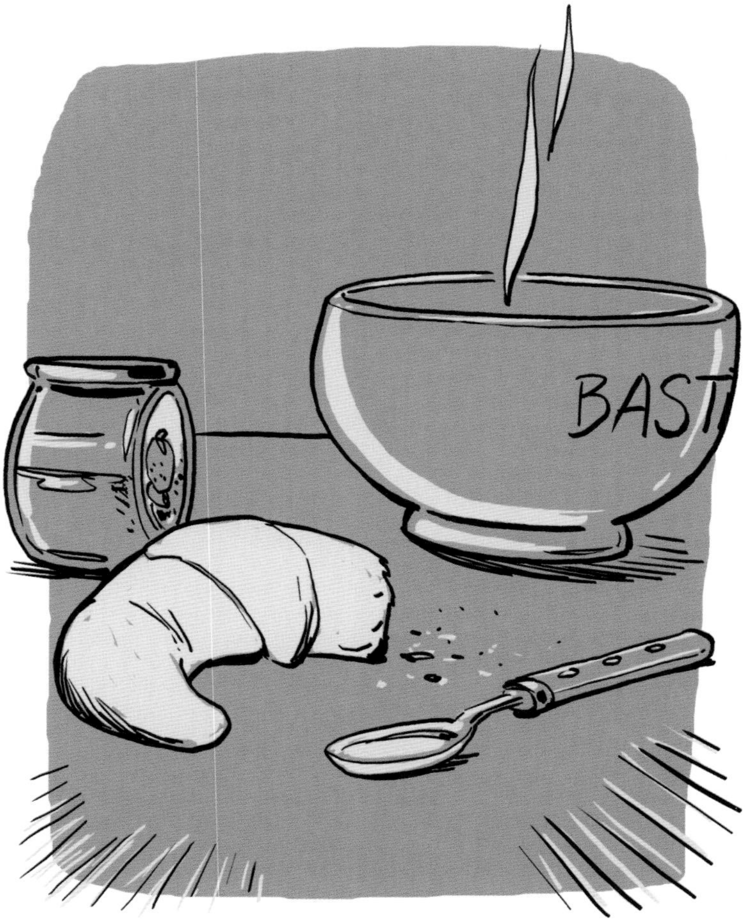
BAST

AT BREAKFAST

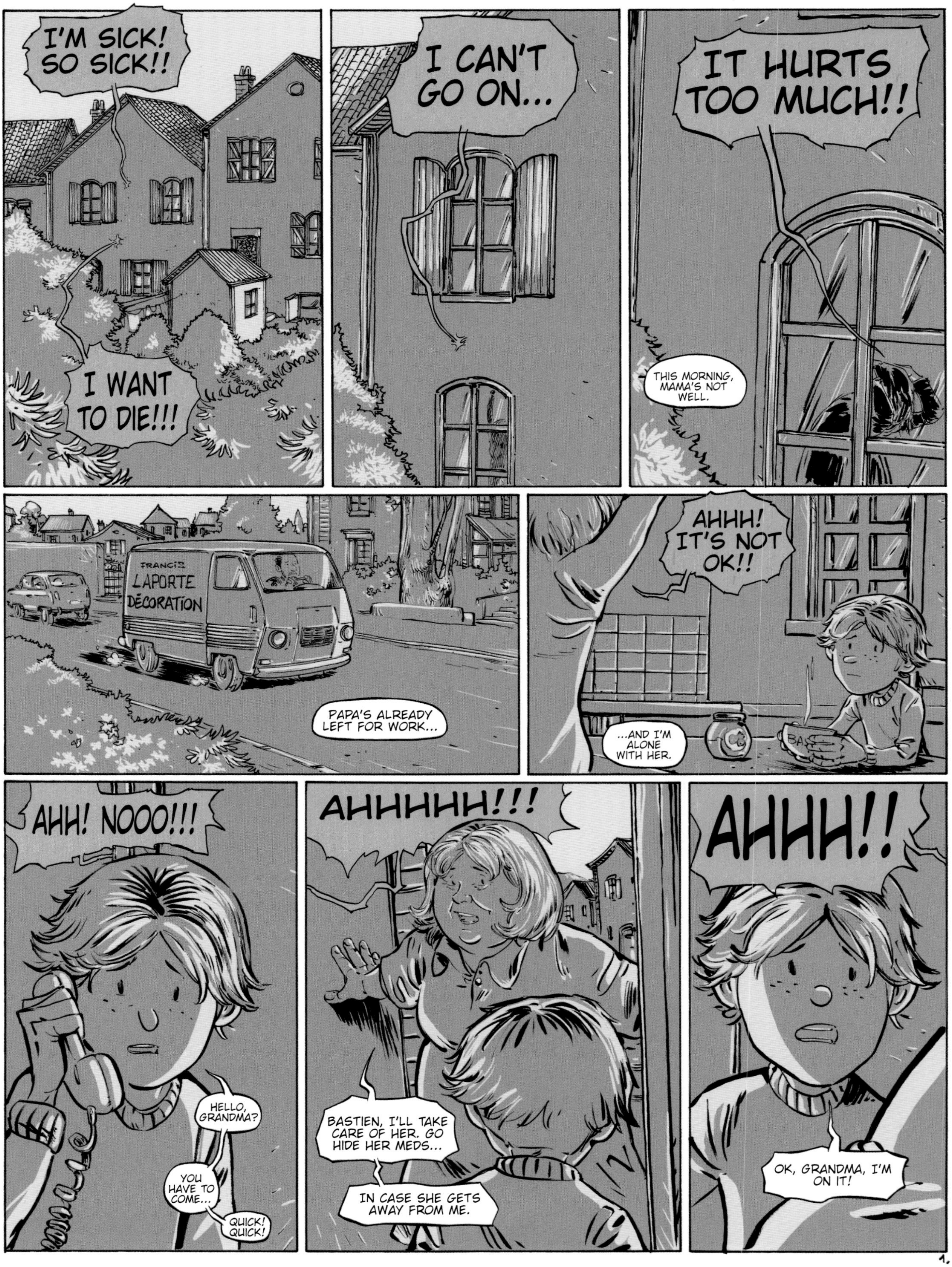
I'M SICK! SO SICK!!
I WANT TO DIE!!!
I CAN'T GO ON...
IT HURTS TOO MUCH!!
THIS MORNING, MAMA'S NOT WELL.
FRANCIS LAPORTE DÉCORATION
PAPA'S ALREADY LEFT FOR WORK...
AHHH! IT'S NOT OK!!
...AND I'M ALONE WITH HER.
AHH! NOOO!!!
HELLO, GRANDMA?
YOU HAVE TO COME...
QUICK! QUICK!
AHHHHH!!!
BASTIEN, I'LL TAKE CARE OF HER. GO HIDE HER MEDS...
IN CASE SHE GETS AWAY FROM ME.
AHHH!!
OK, GRANDMA, I'M ON IT!
1.

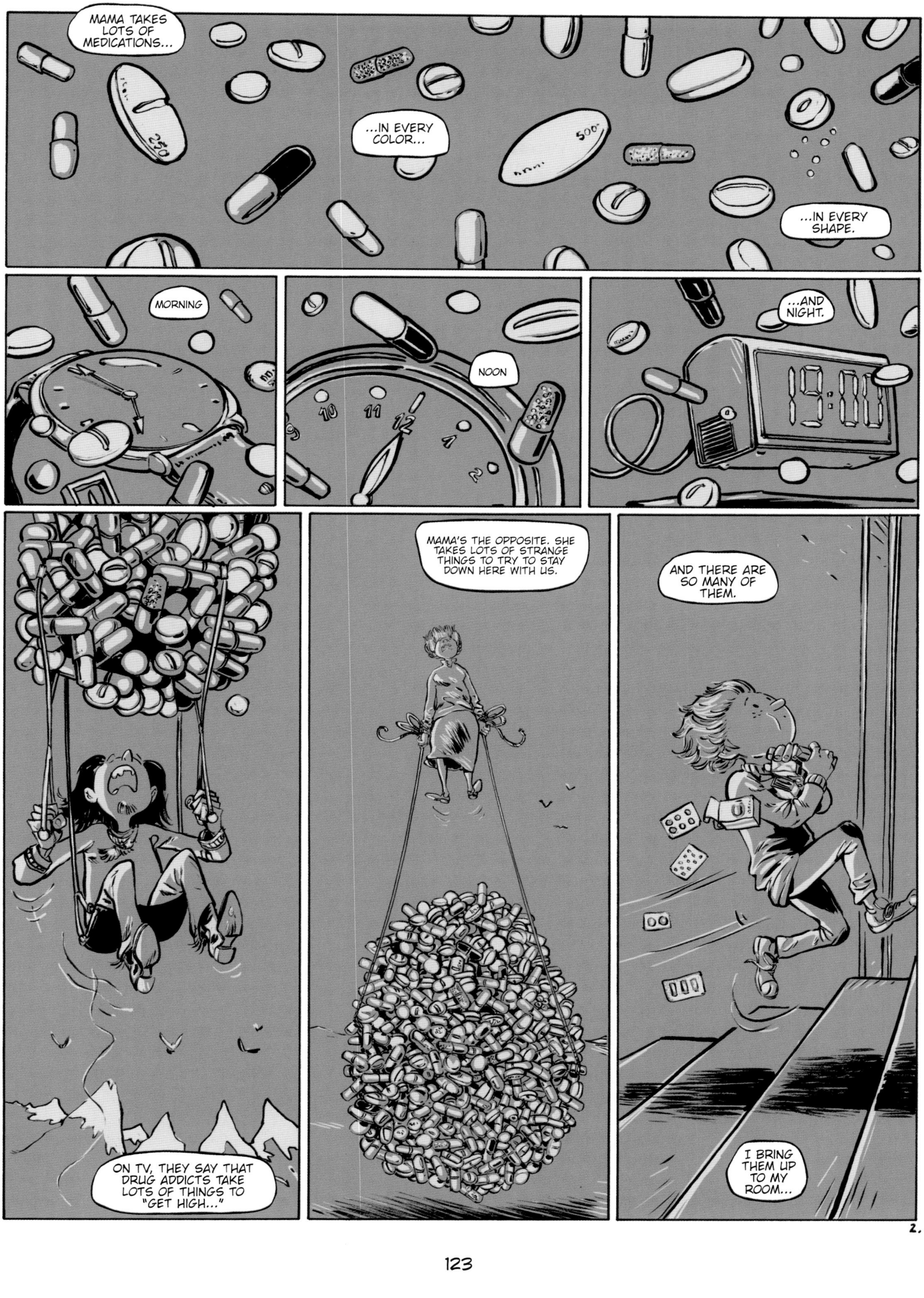
MAMA TAKES LOTS OF MEDICATIONS...
...IN EVERY COLOR...
...IN EVERY SHAPE.
MORNING
NOON
...AND NIGHT.
19:00
ON TV, THEY SAY THAT DRUG ADDICTS TAKE LOTS OF THINGS TO "GET HIGH..."
MAMA'S THE OPPOSITE. SHE TAKES LOTS OF STRANGE THINGS TO TRY TO STAY DOWN HERE WITH US.
AND THERE ARE SO MANY OF THEM.
I BRING THEM UP TO MY ROOM...
2.

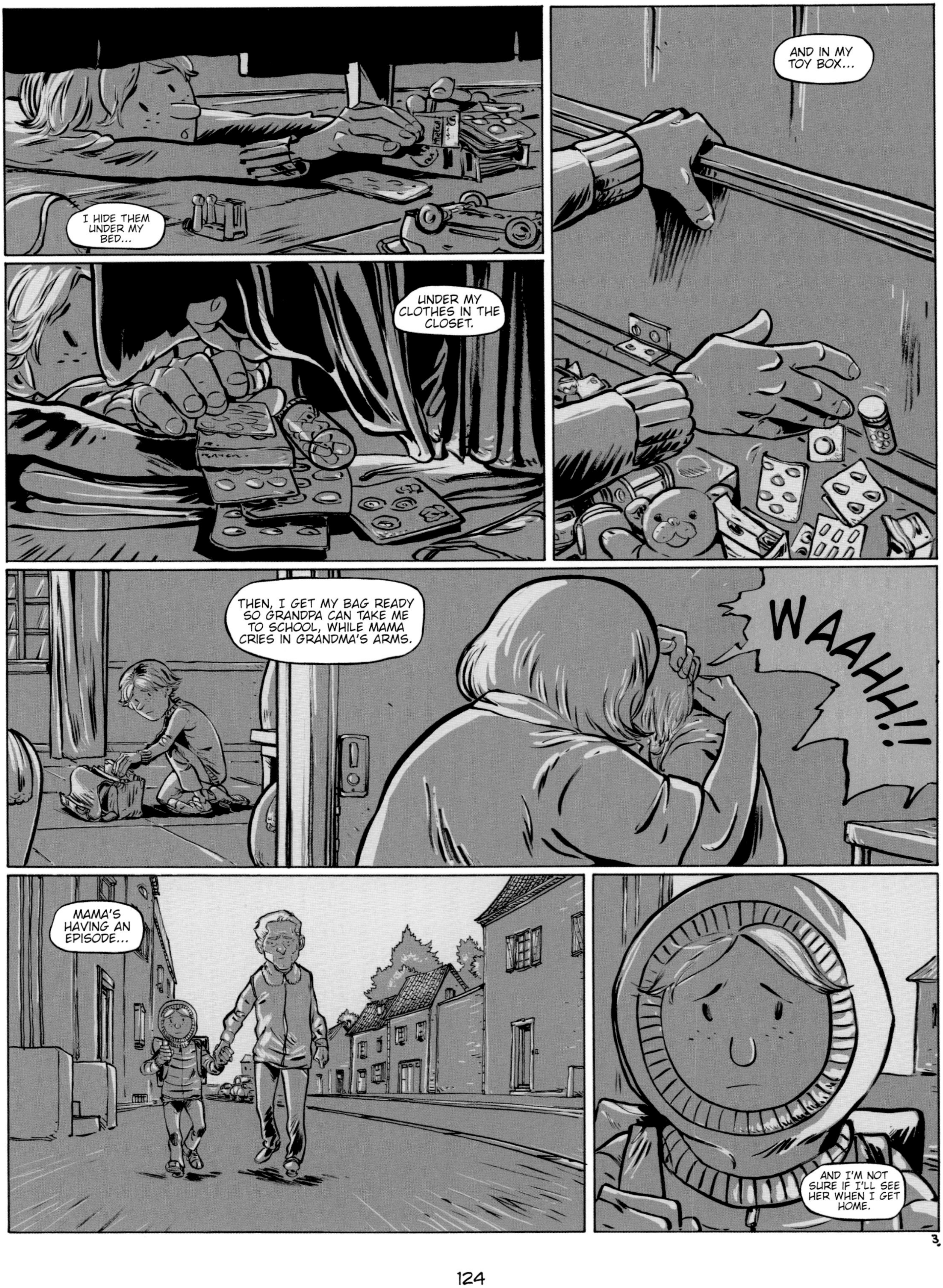
I HIDE THEM UNDER MY BED...
AND IN MY TOY BOX...
UNDER MY CLOTHES IN THE CLOSET.
THEN, I GET MY BAG READY SO GRANDPA CAN TAKE ME TO SCHOOL, WHILE MAMA CRIES IN GRANDMA'S ARMS.
WAAHH!!
MAMA'S HAVING AN EPISODE...
AND I'M NOT SURE IF I'LL SEE HER WHEN I GET HOME.
3.

THE PARAKEET

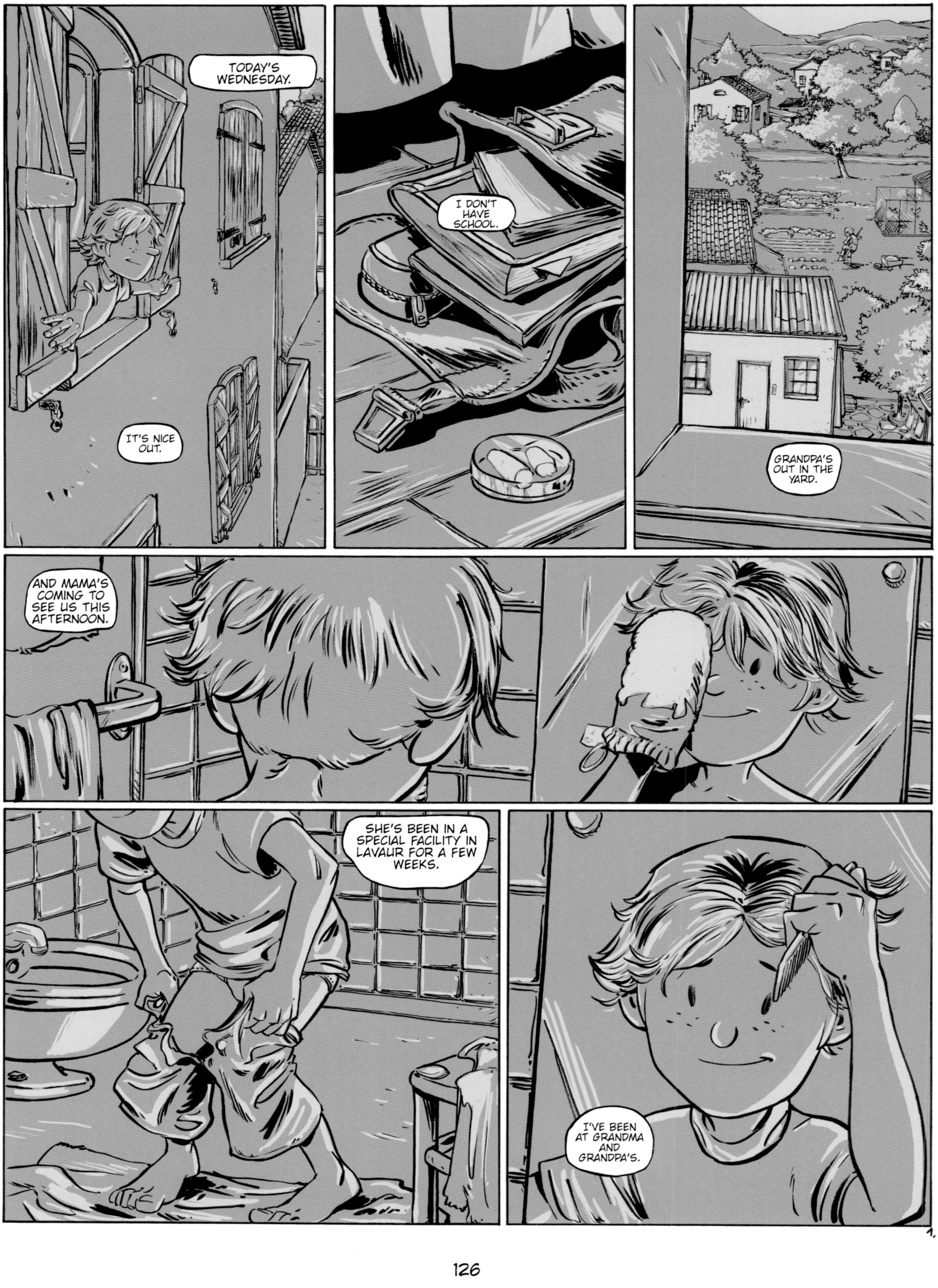
TODAY'S WEDNESDAY.
IT'S NICE OUT.
I DON'T HAVE SCHOOL.
GRANDPA'S OUT IN THE YARD.
AND MAMA'S COMING TO SEE US THIS AFTERNOON.
SHE'S BEEN IN A SPECIAL FACILITY IN LAVAUR FOR A FEW WEEKS.
I'VE BEEN AT GRANDMA AND GRANDPA'S.
1.

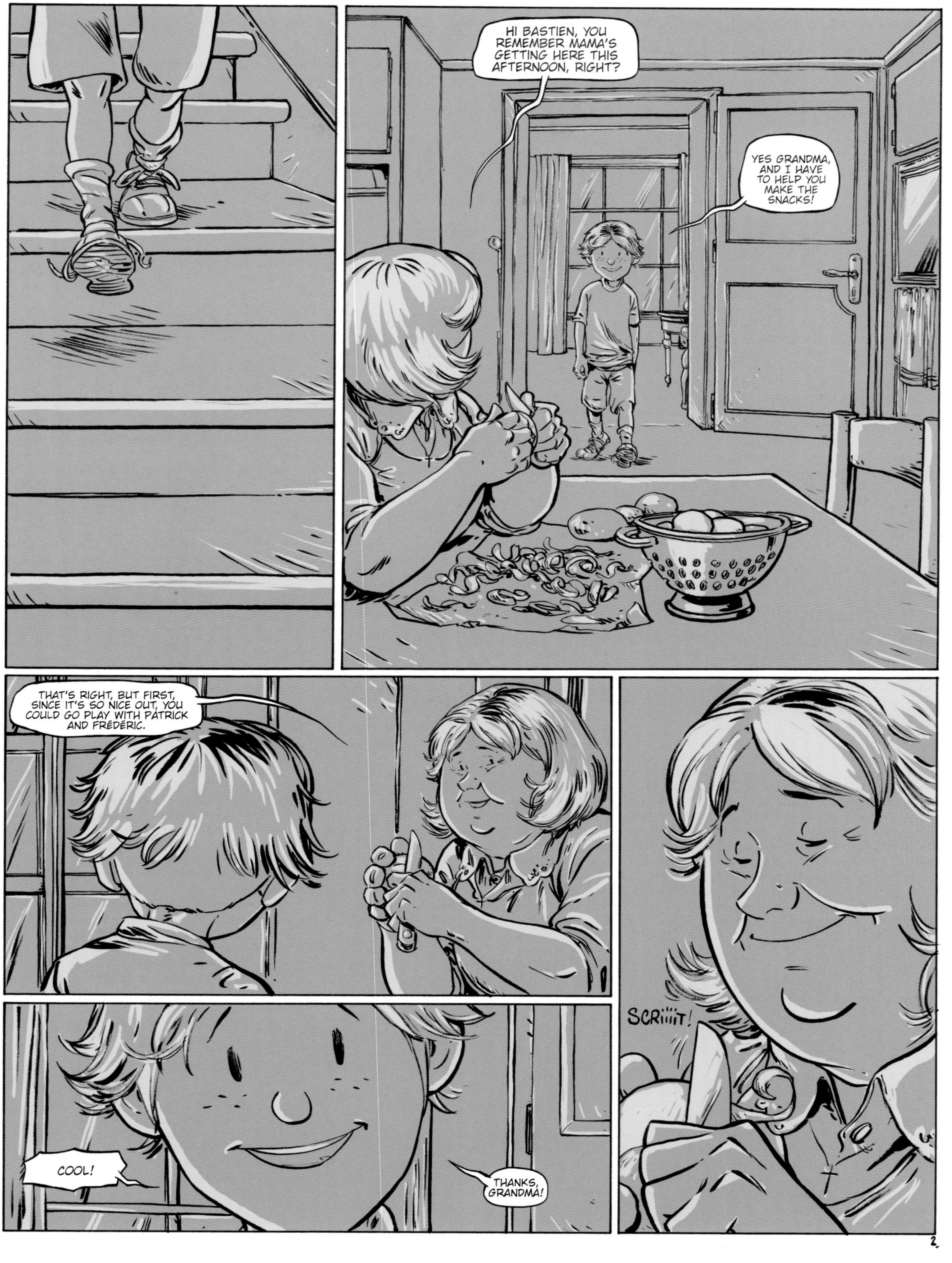
HI BASTIEN, YOU REMEMBER MAMA'S GETTING HERE THIS AFTERNOON, RIGHT?
YES GRANDMA, AND I HAVE TO HELP YOU MAKE THE SNACKS!
THAT'S RIGHT, BUT FIRST, SINCE IT'S SO NICE OUT, YOU COULD GO PLAY WITH PATRICK AND FRÉDÉRIC.
SCRiiiiT!
COOL!
THANKS, GRANDMA!
2

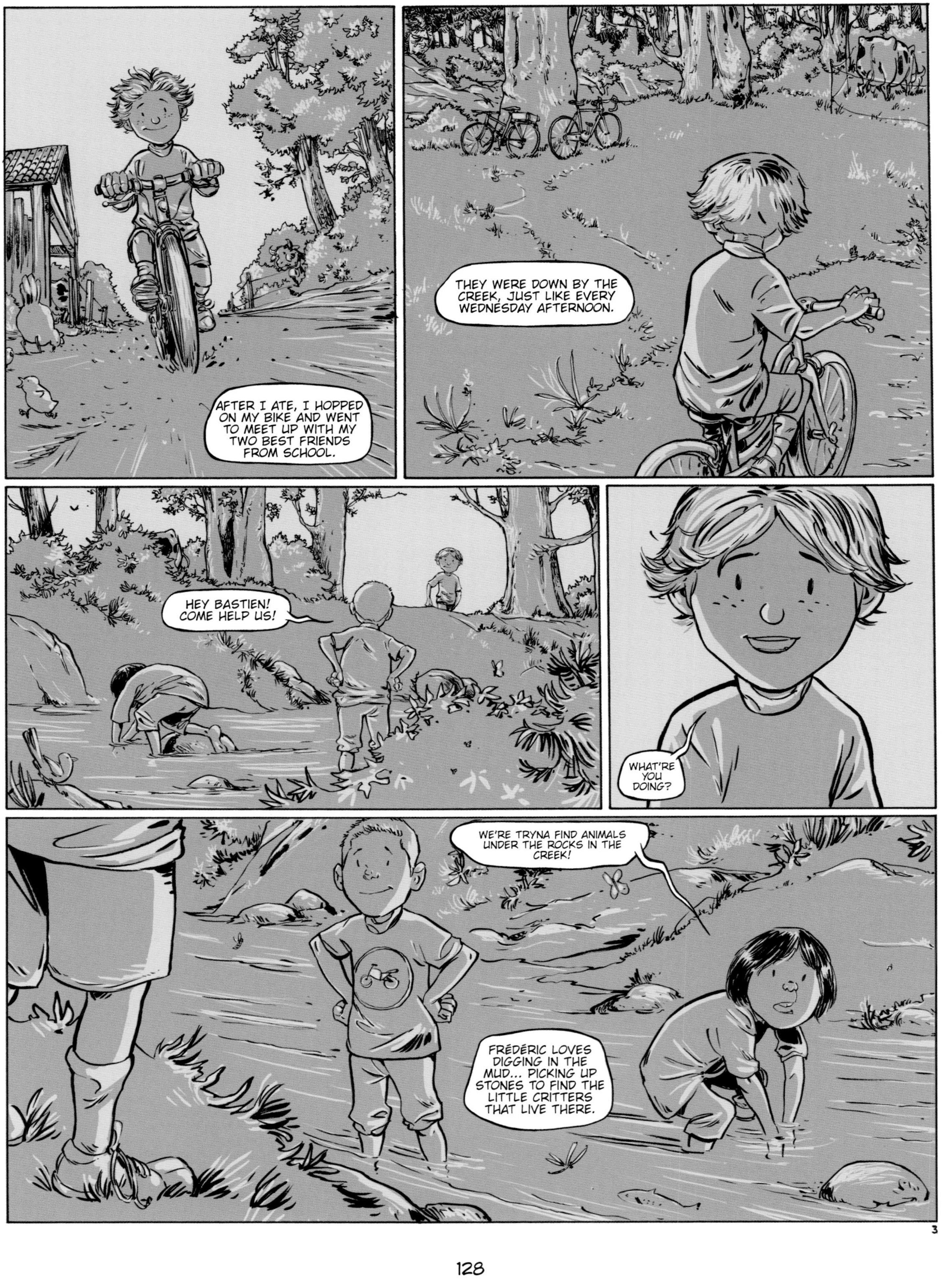
AFTER I ATE, I HOPPED ON MY BIKE AND WENT TO MEET UP WITH MY TWO BEST FRIENDS FROM SCHOOL.
THEY WERE DOWN BY THE CREEK, JUST LIKE EVERY WEDNESDAY AFTERNOON.
HEY BASTIEN! COME HELP US!
WHAT'RE YOU DOING?
WE'RE TRYNA FIND ANIMALS UNDER THE ROCKS IN THE CREEK!
FRÉDÉRIC LOVES DIGGING IN THE MUD… PICKING UP STONES TO FIND THE LITTLE CRITTERS THAT LIVE THERE.
3

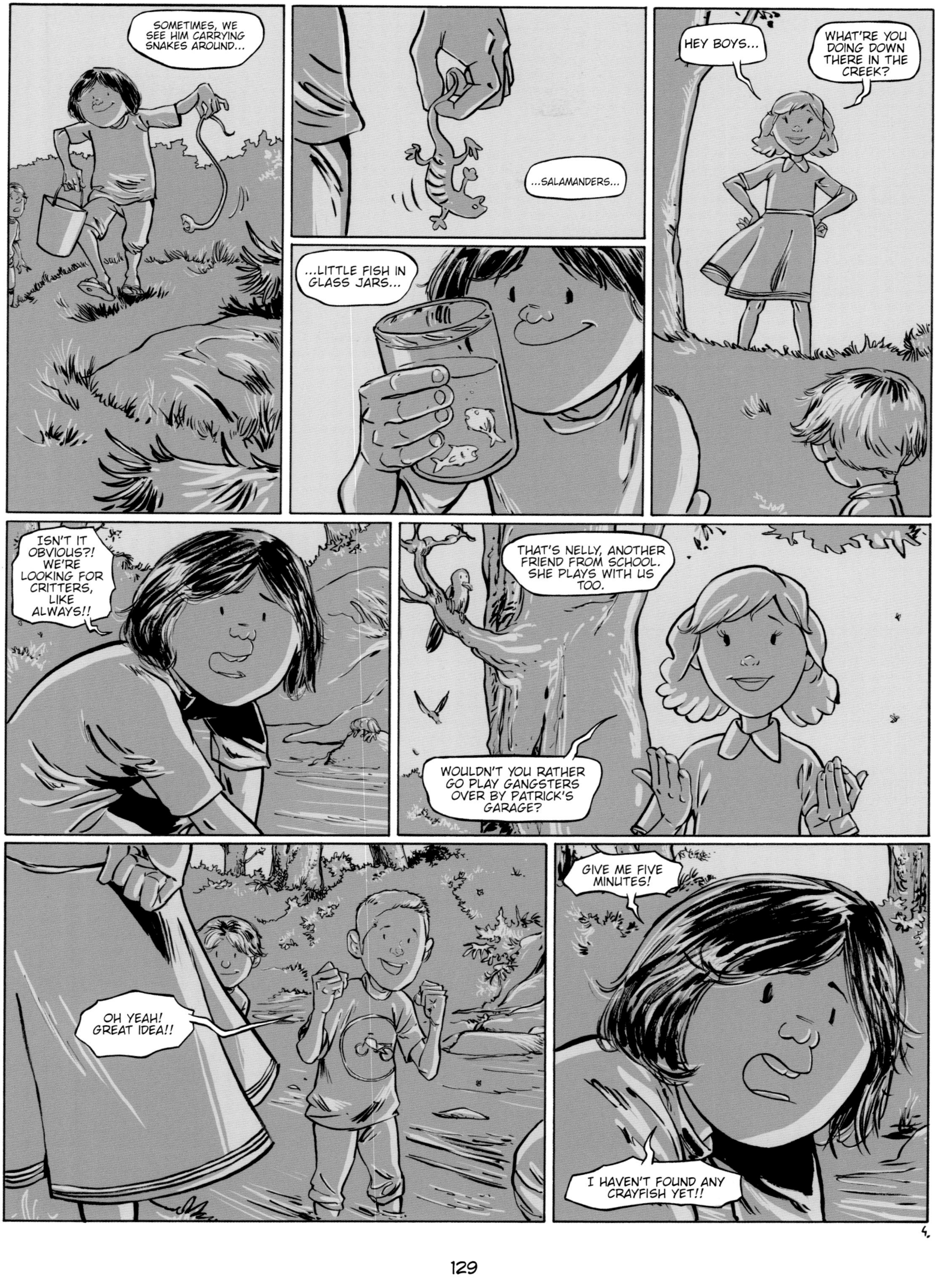
SOMETIMES, WE SEE HIM CARRYING SNAKES AROUND...
...SALAMANDERS...
...LITTLE FISH IN GLASS JARS...
HEY BOYS...
WHAT'RE YOU DOING DOWN THERE IN THE CREEK?
ISN'T IT OBVIOUS?! WE'RE LOOKING FOR CRITTERS, LIKE ALWAYS!!
THAT'S NELLY, ANOTHER FRIEND FROM SCHOOL. SHE PLAYS WITH US TOO.
WOULDN'T YOU RATHER GO PLAY GANGSTERS OVER BY PATRICK'S GARAGE?
OH YEAH! GREAT IDEA!!
GIVE ME FIVE MINUTES!
I HAVEN'T FOUND ANY CRAYFISH YET!!
4.

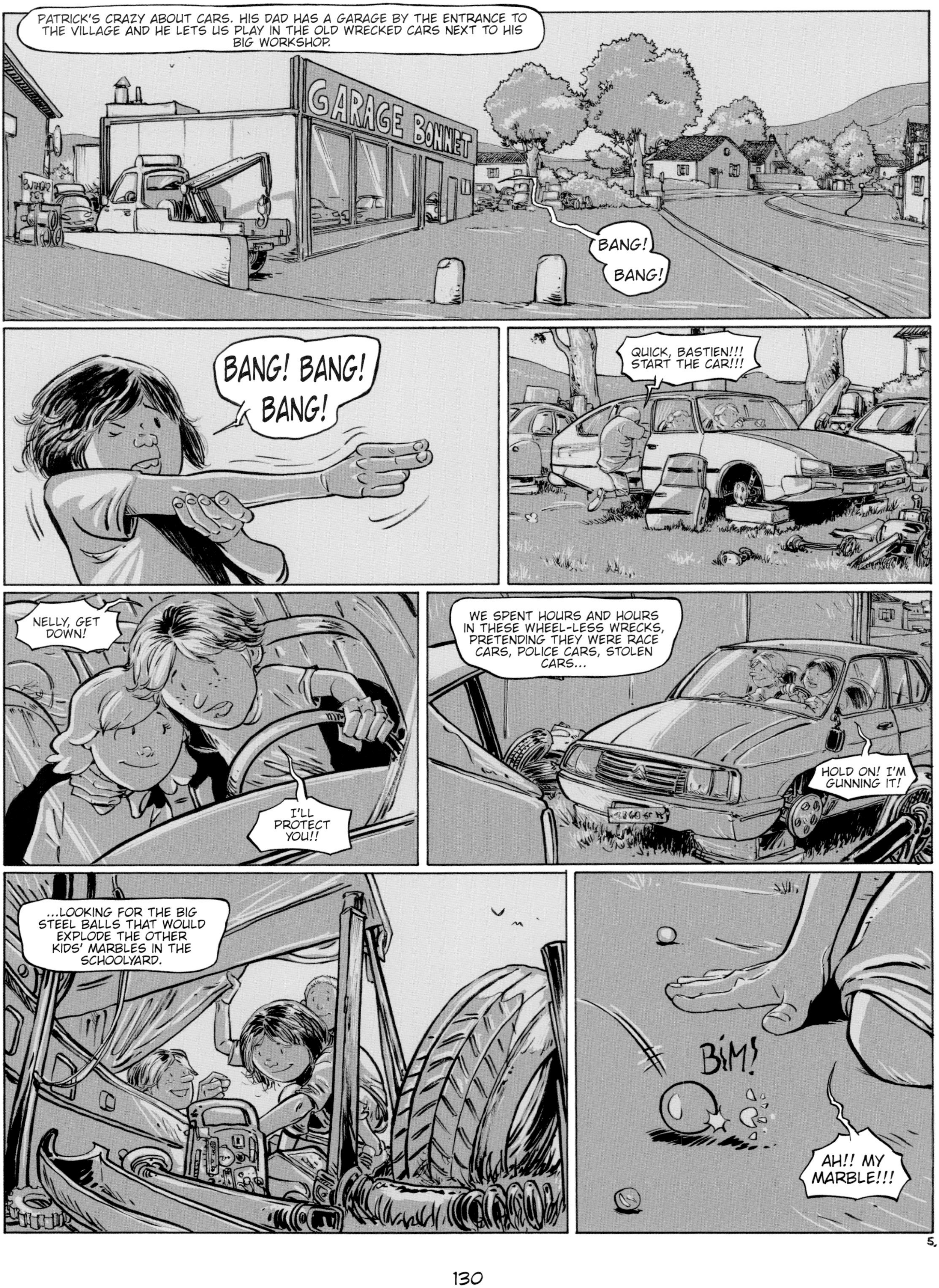
PATRICK'S CRAZY ABOUT CARS. HIS DAD HAS A GARAGE BY THE ENTRANCE TO THE VILLAGE AND HE LETS US PLAY IN THE OLD WRECKED CARS NEXT TO HIS BIG WORKSHOP.
GARAGE BONNET
BANG!
BANG!
BANG! BANG! BANG!
QUICK, BASTIEN!!! START THE CAR!!!
NELLY, GET DOWN!
I'LL PROTECT YOU!!
WE SPENT HOURS AND HOURS IN THESE WHEEL-LESS WRECKS, PRETENDING THEY WERE RACE CARS, POLICE CARS, STOLEN CARS...
HOLD ON! I'M GUNNING IT!
...LOOKING FOR THE BIG STEEL BALLS THAT WOULD EXPLODE THE OTHER KIDS' MARBLES IN THE SCHOOLYARD.
BIM!
AH!! MY MARBLE!!!

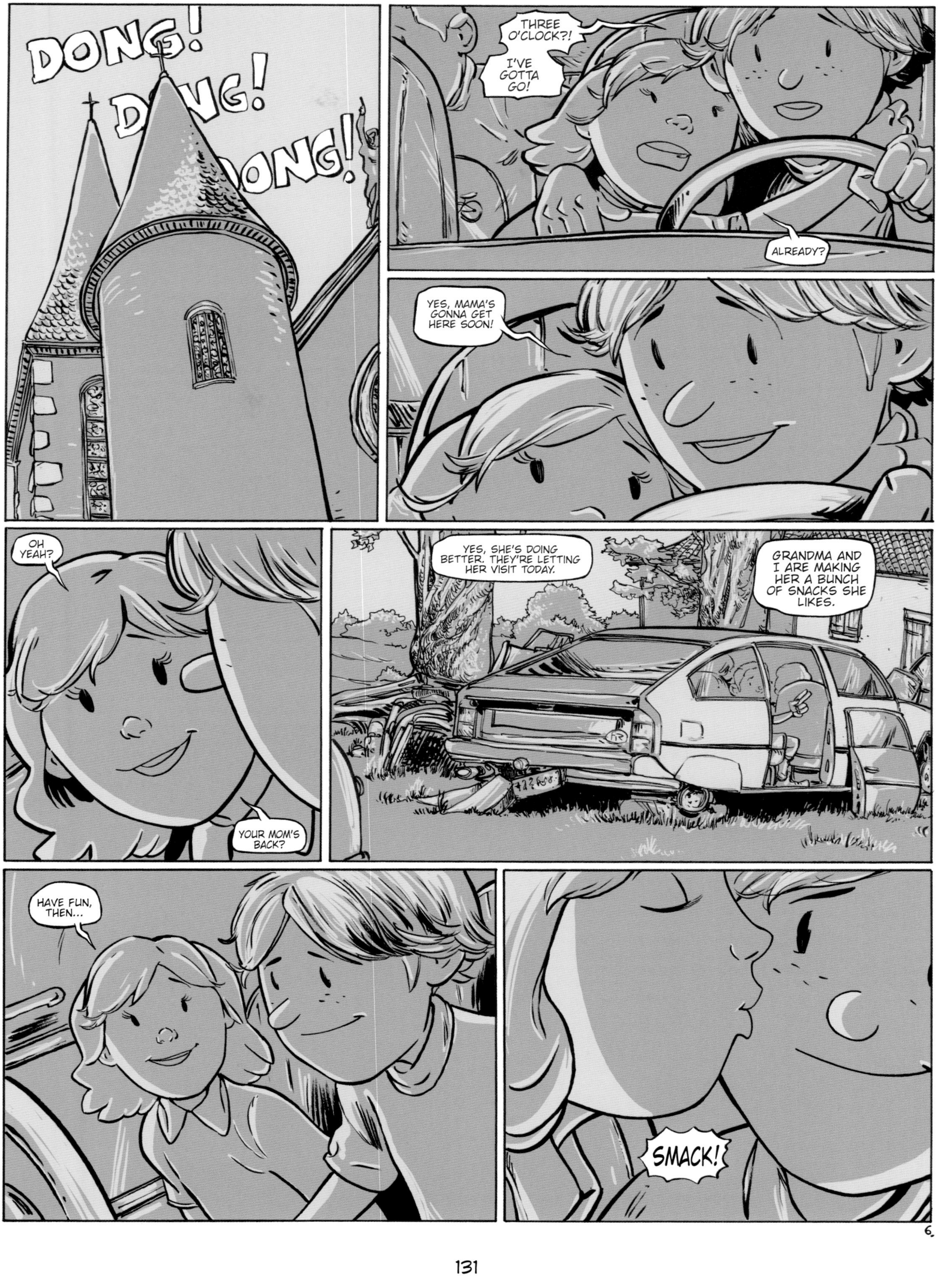
DONG! DONG! DONG!
THREE O'CLOCK?!
I'VE GOTTA GO!
ALREADY?
YES, MAMA'S GONNA GET HERE SOON!
OH YEAH?
YOUR MOM'S BACK?
YES, SHE'S DOING BETTER. THEY'RE LETTING HER VISIT TODAY.
GRANDMA AND I ARE MAKING HER A BUNCH OF SNACKS SHE LIKES.
HAVE FUN, THEN...
SMACK!
6.

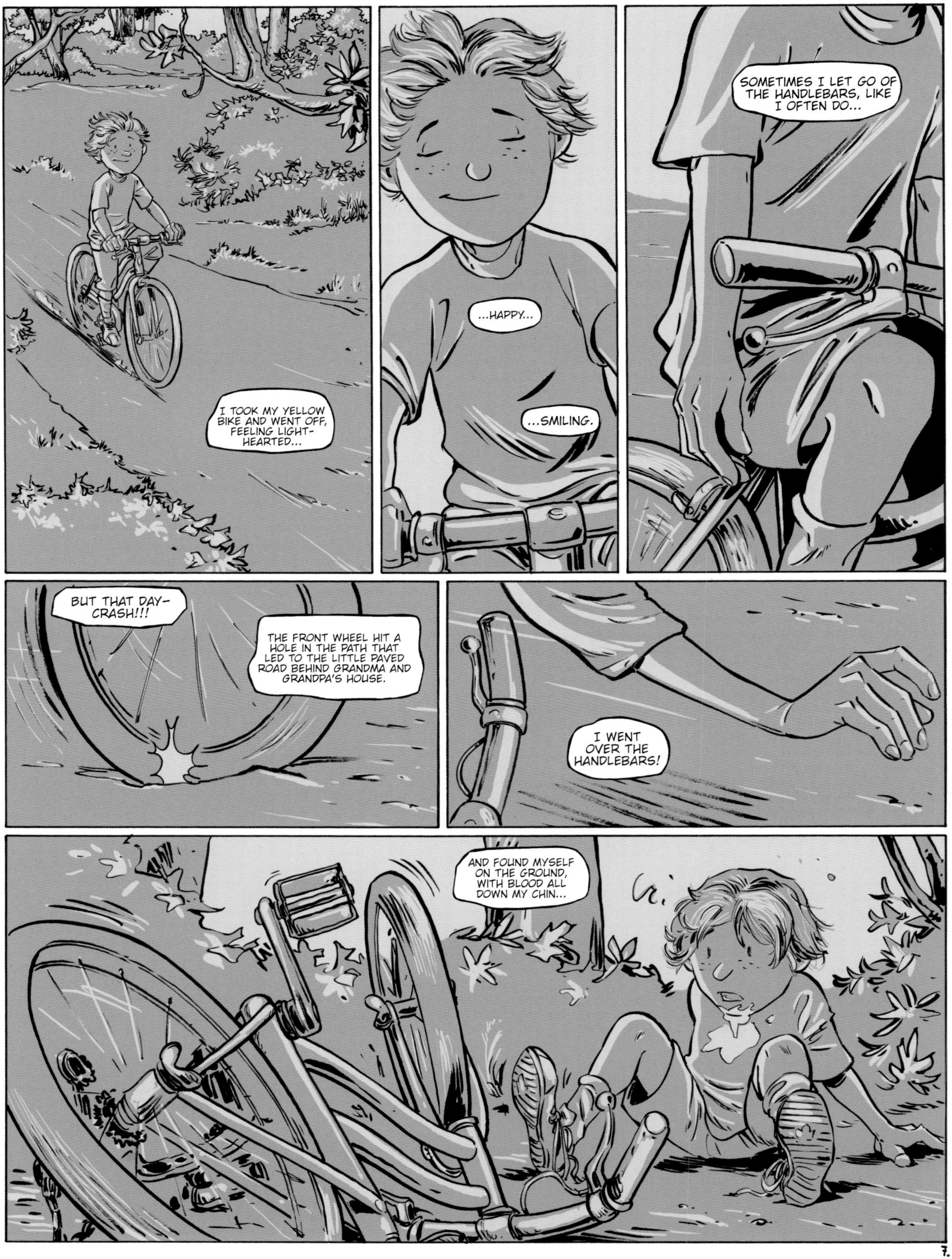
I TOOK MY YELLOW BIKE AND WENT OFF, FEELING LIGHT-HEARTED...
...HAPPY...
...SMILING.
SOMETIMES I LET GO OF THE HANDLEBARS, LIKE I OFTEN DO...
BUT THAT DAY–CRASH!!!
THE FRONT WHEEL HIT A HOLE IN THE PATH THAT LED TO THE LITTLE PAVED ROAD BEHIND GRANDMA AND GRANDPA'S HOUSE.
I WENT OVER THE HANDLEBARS!
AND FOUND MYSELF ON THE GROUND, WITH BLOOD ALL DOWN MY CHIN...
7.

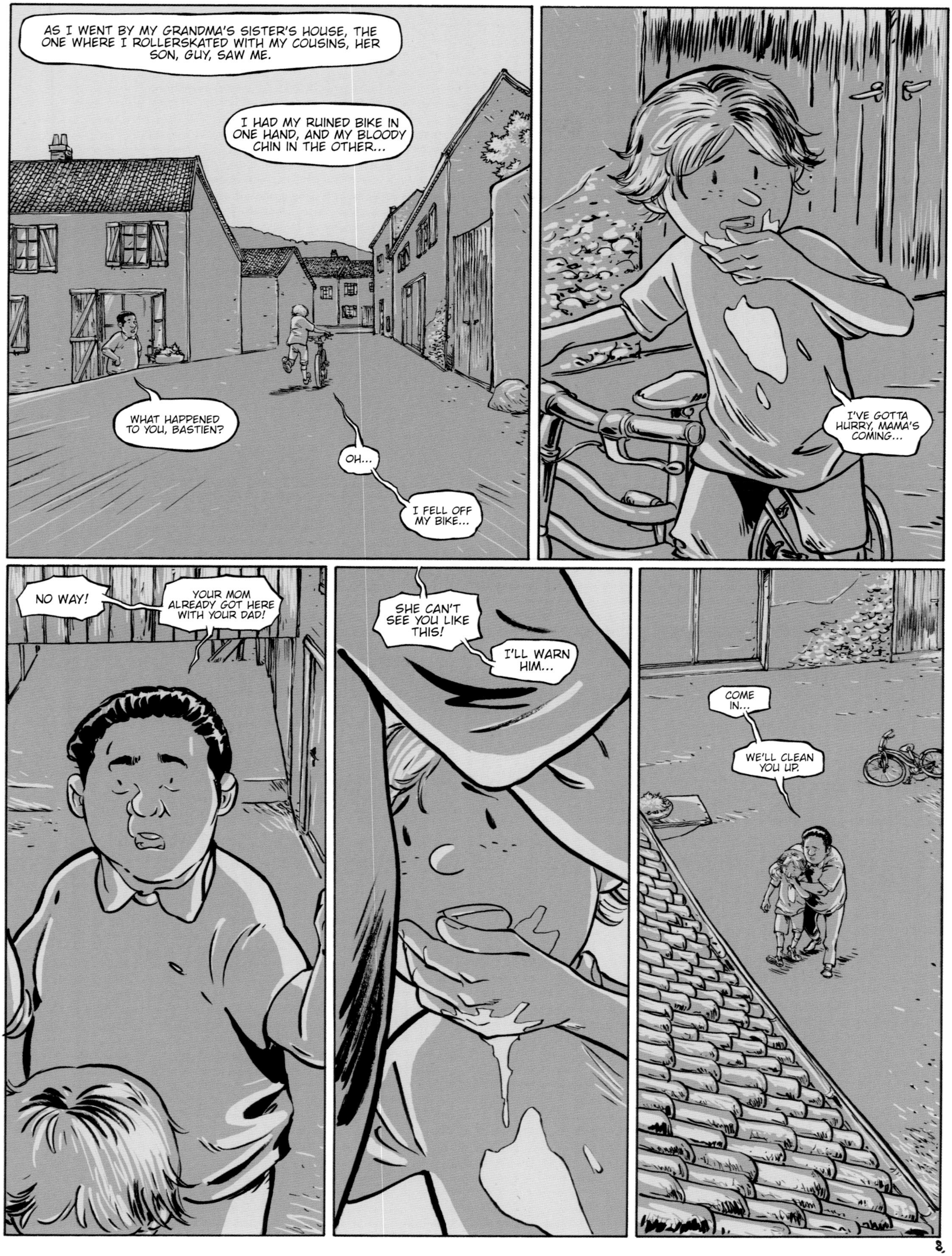
AS I WENT BY MY GRANDMA'S SISTER'S HOUSE, THE ONE WHERE I ROLLERSKATED WITH MY COUSINS, HER SON, GUY, SAW ME.
I HAD MY RUINED BIKE IN ONE HAND, AND MY BLOODY CHIN IN THE OTHER...
WHAT HAPPENED TO YOU, BASTIEN?
OH...
I FELL OFF MY BIKE...
I'VE GOTTA HURRY, MAMA'S COMING...
NO WAY!
YOUR MOM ALREADY GOT HERE WITH YOUR DAD!
SHE CAN'T SEE YOU LIKE THIS!
I'LL WARN HIM...
COME IN...
WE'LL CLEAN YOU UP.
8.

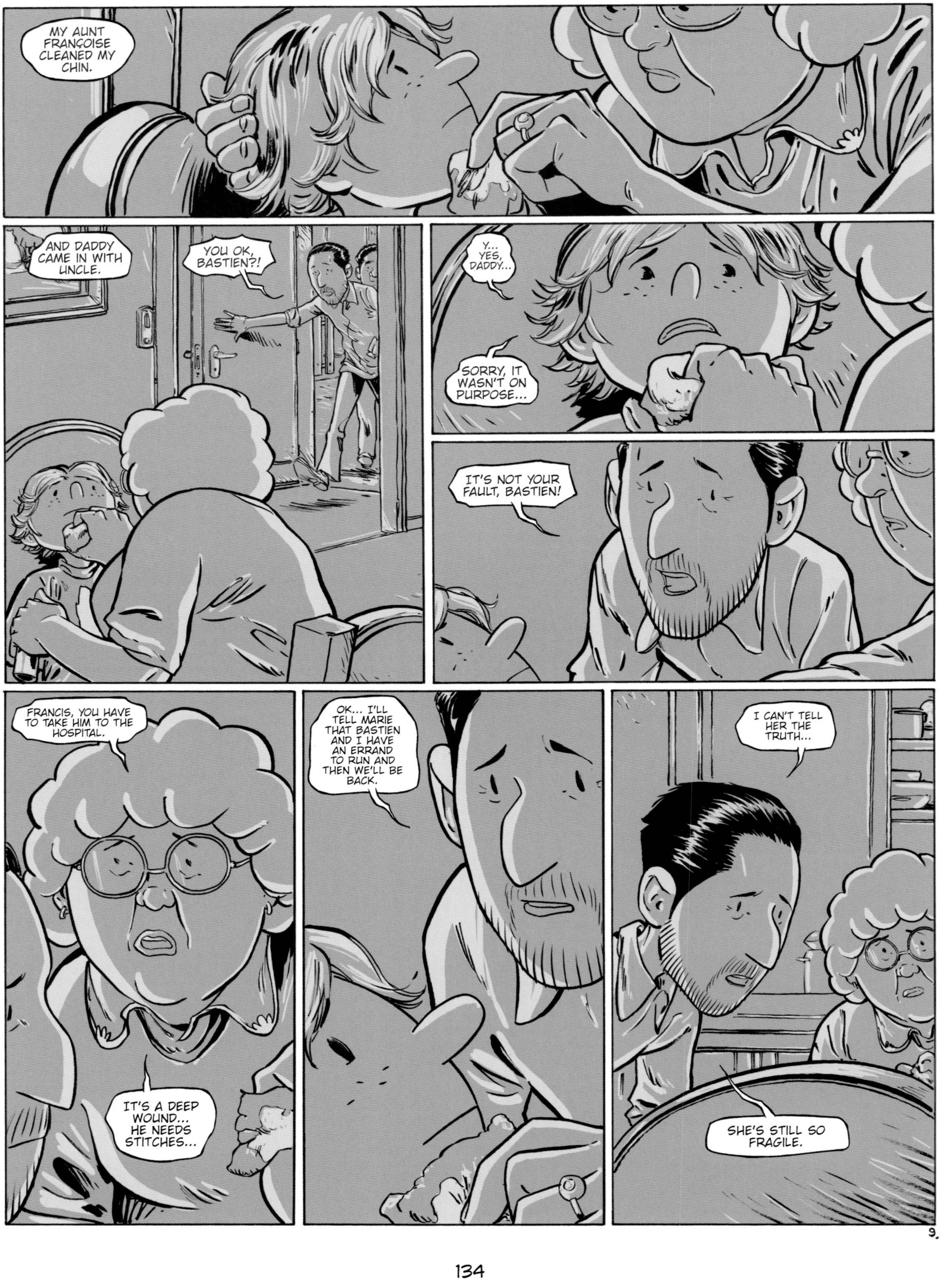
MY AUNT FRANÇOISE CLEANED MY CHIN.
AND DADDY CAME IN WITH UNCLE.
YOU OK, BASTIEN?!
Y... YES, DADDY...
SORRY, IT WASN'T ON PURPOSE...
IT'S NOT YOUR FAULT, BASTIEN!
FRANCIS, YOU HAVE TO TAKE HIM TO THE HOSPITAL.
IT'S A DEEP WOUND... HE NEEDS STITCHES...
OK... I'LL TELL MARIE THAT BASTIEN AND I HAVE AN ERRAND TO RUN AND THEN WE'LL BE BACK.
I CAN'T TELL HER THE TRUTH...
SHE'S STILL SO FRAGILE.
9.

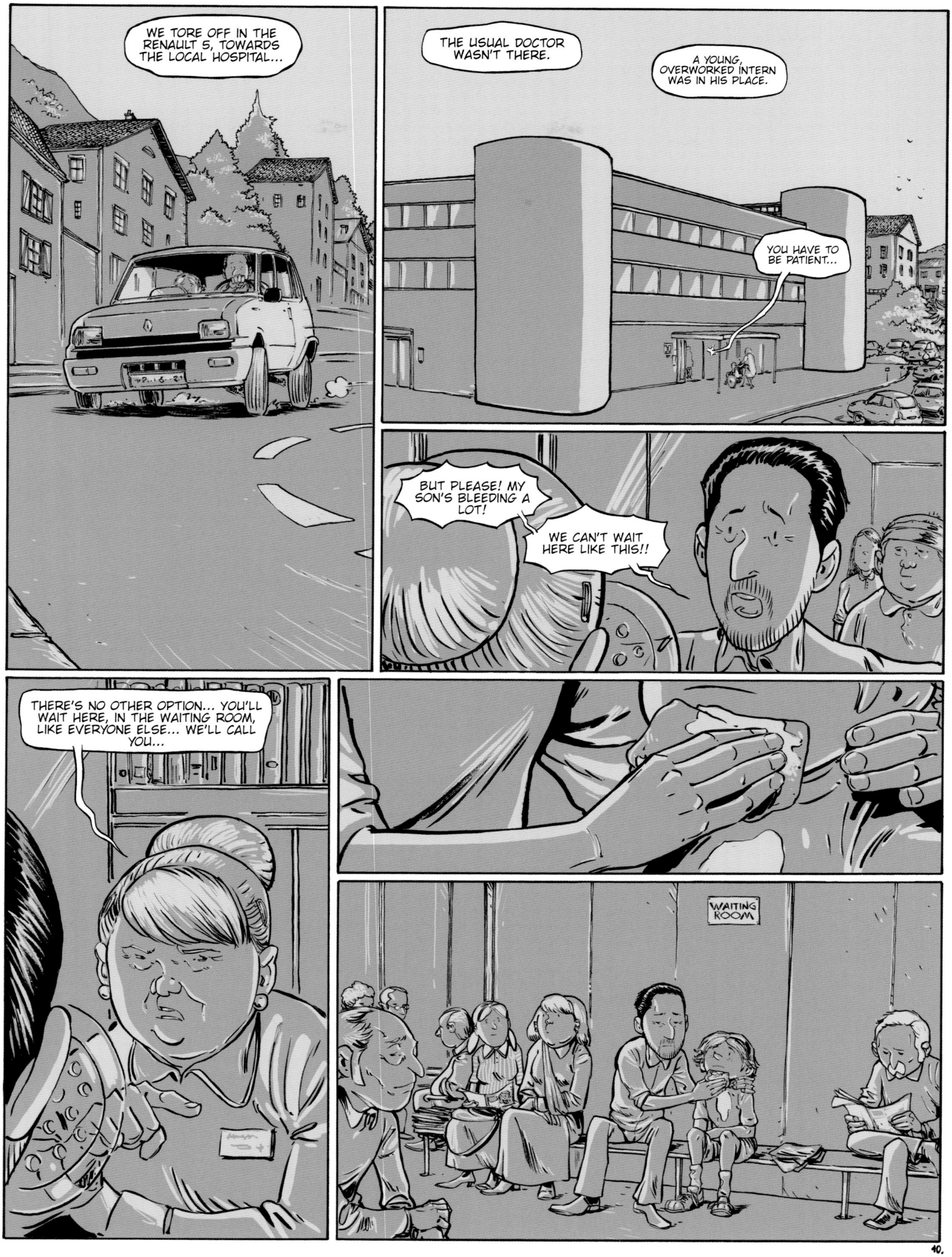
WE TORE OFF IN THE RENAULT 5, TOWARDS THE LOCAL HOSPITAL...
THE USUAL DOCTOR WASN'T THERE.
A YOUNG, OVERWORKED INTERN WAS IN HIS PLACE.
YOU HAVE TO BE PATIENT...
BUT PLEASE! MY SON'S BLEEDING A LOT!
WE CAN'T WAIT HERE LIKE THIS!!
THERE'S NO OTHER OPTION... YOU'LL WAIT HERE, IN THE WAITING ROOM, LIKE EVERYONE ELSE... WE'LL CALL YOU...
WAITING ROOM
40.

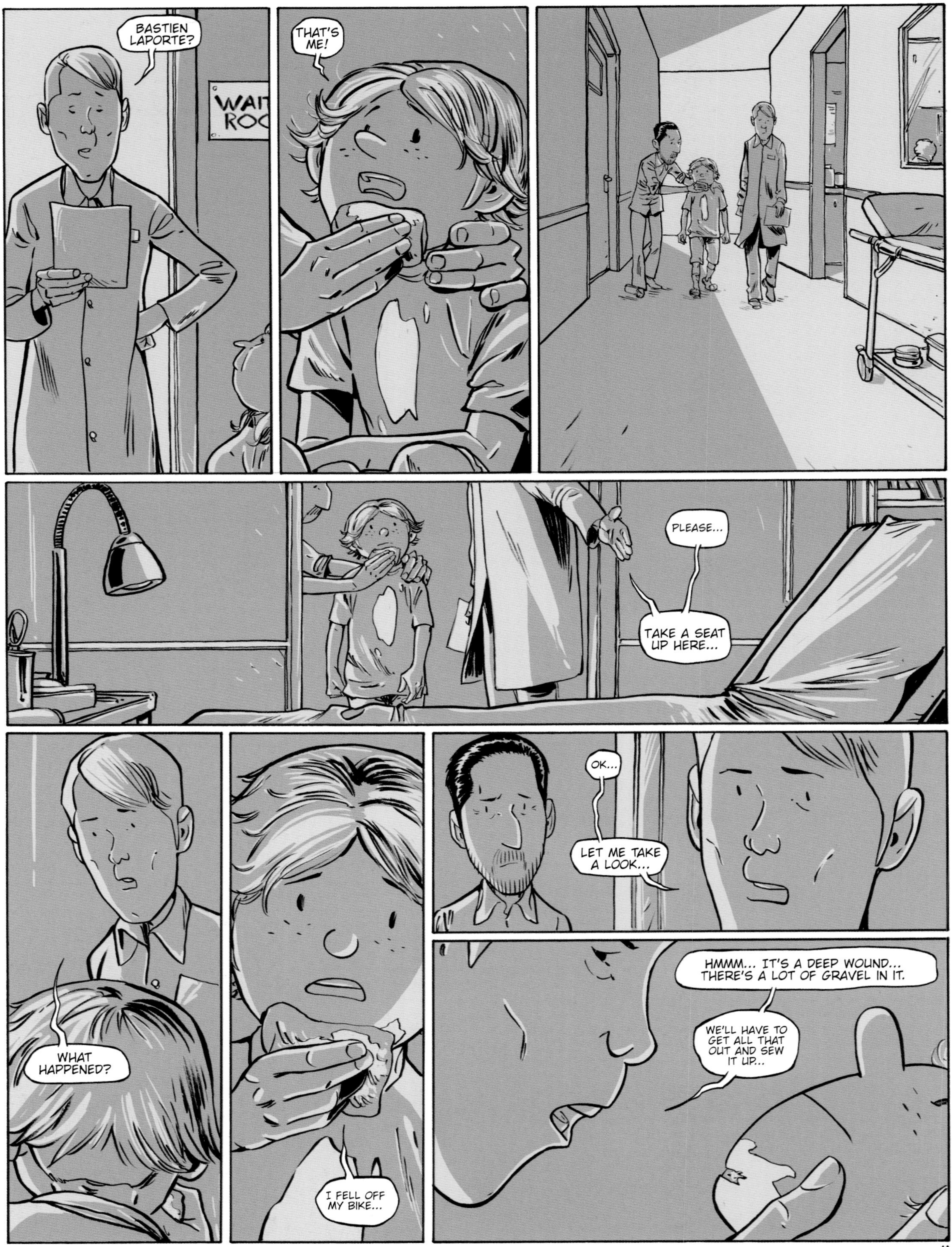
BASTIEN LAPORTE?
THAT'S ME!
PLEASE...
TAKE A SEAT UP HERE...
WHAT HAPPENED?
I FELL OFF MY BIKE...
OK...
LET ME TAKE A LOOK...
HMMM... IT'S A DEEP WOUND... THERE'S A LOT OF GRAVEL IN IT.
WE'LL HAVE TO GET ALL THAT OUT AND SEW IT UP...
11.

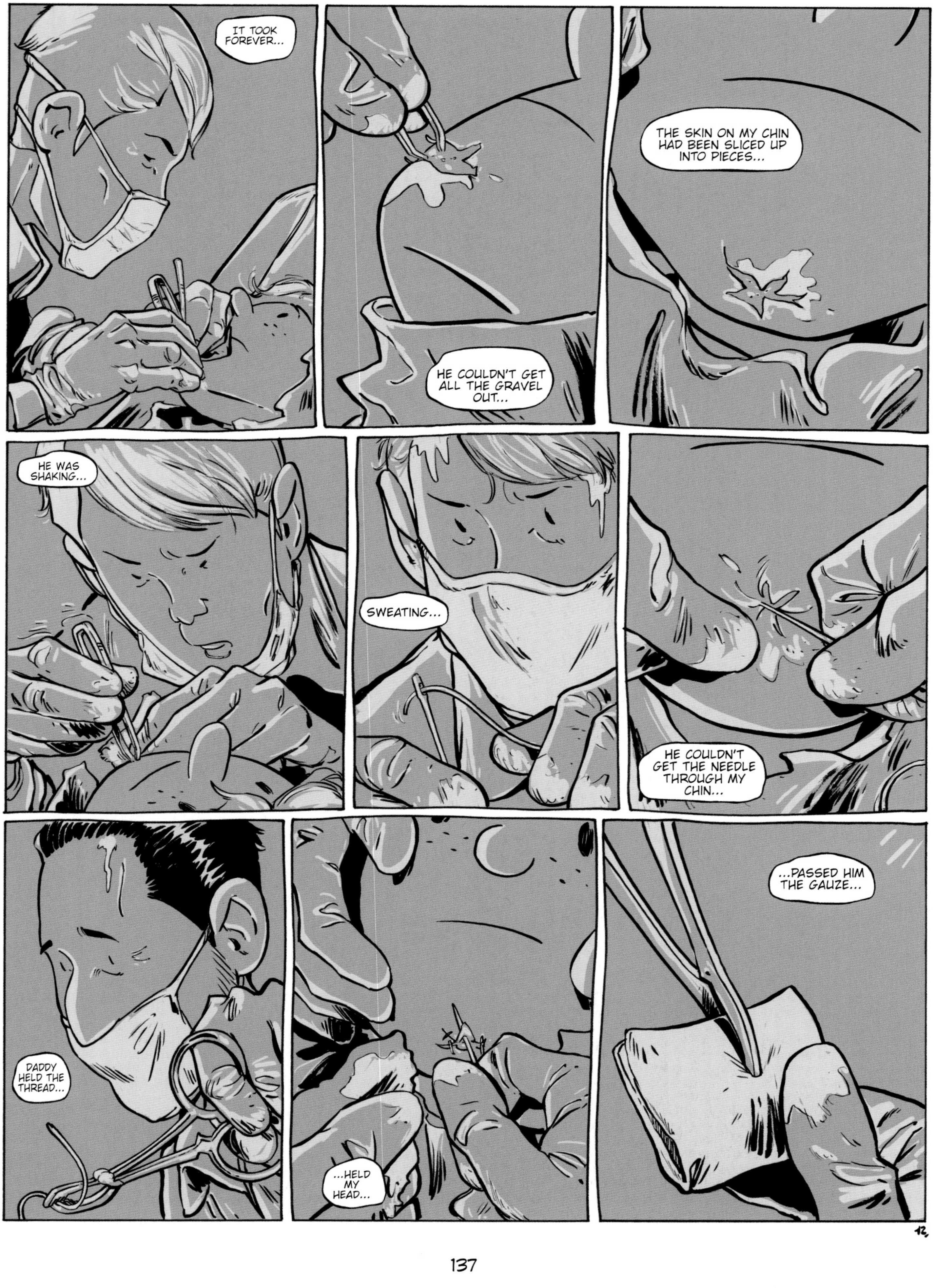
IT TOOK FOREVER...
THE SKIN ON MY CHIN HAD BEEN SLICED UP INTO PIECES...
HE COULDN'T GET ALL THE GRAVEL OUT...
HE WAS SHAKING...
SWEATING...
HE COULDN'T GET THE NEEDLE THROUGH MY CHIN...
DADDY HELD THE THREAD...
...HELD MY HEAD...
...PASSED HIM THE GAUZE...

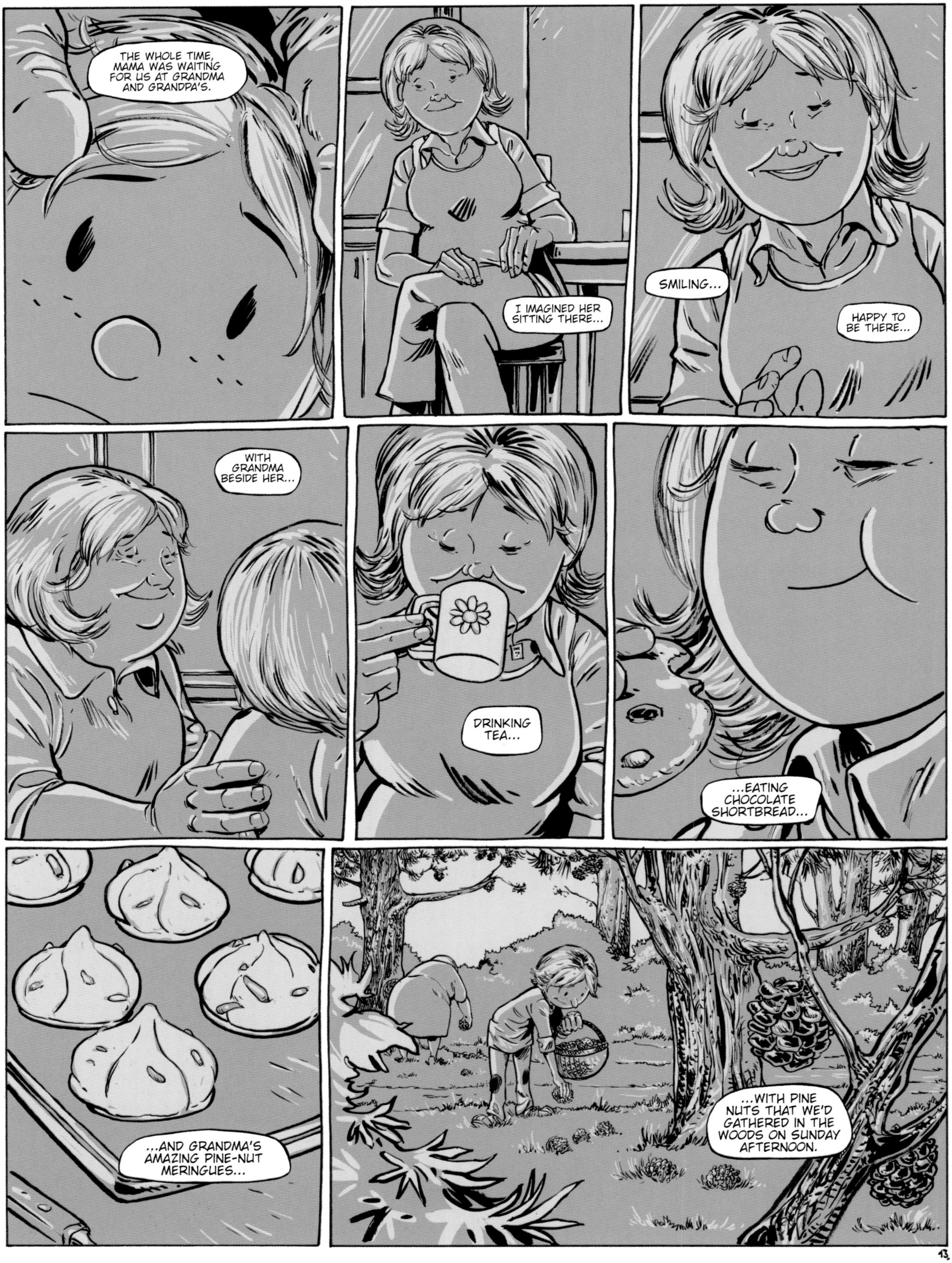
THE WHOLE TIME, MAMA WAS WAITING FOR US AT GRANDMA AND GRANDPA'S.
I IMAGINED HER SITTING THERE...
SMILING...
HAPPY TO BE THERE...
WITH GRANDMA BESIDE HER...
DRINKING TEA...
...EATING CHOCOLATE SHORTBREAD...
...AND GRANDMA'S AMAZING PINE-NUT MERINGUES...
...WITH PINE NUTS THAT WE'D GATHERED IN THE WOODS ON SUNDAY AFTERNOON.
13.

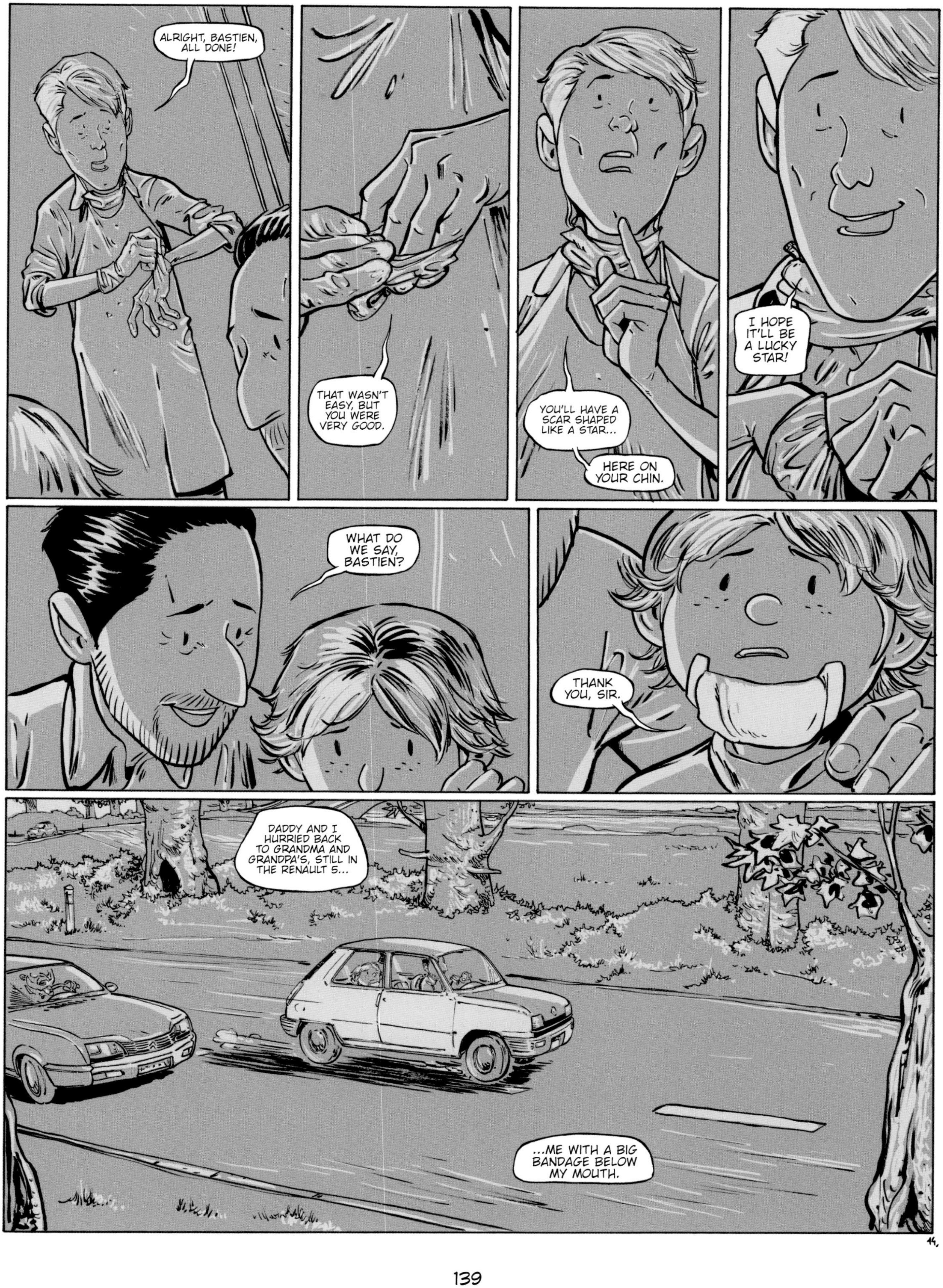
ALRIGHT, BASTIEN, ALL DONE!
THAT WASN'T EASY, BUT YOU WERE VERY GOOD.
YOU'LL HAVE A SCAR SHAPED LIKE A STAR...
HERE ON YOUR CHIN.
I HOPE IT'LL BE A LUCKY STAR!
WHAT DO WE SAY, BASTIEN?
THANK YOU, SIR.
DADDY AND I HURRIED BACK TO GRANDMA AND GRANDPA'S, STILL IN THE RENAULT 5...
...ME WITH A BIG BANDAGE BELOW MY MOUTH.

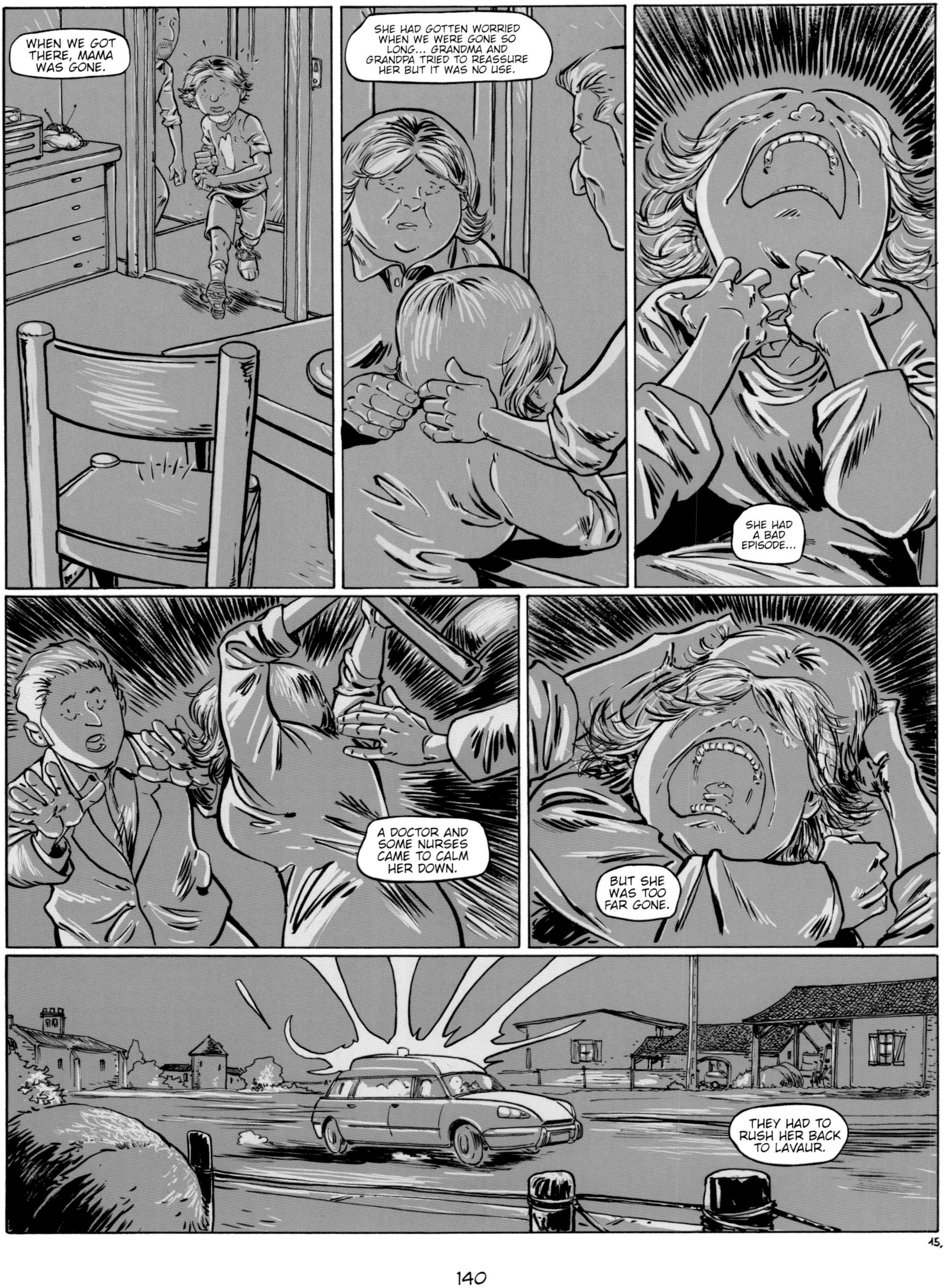
WHEN WE GOT THERE, MAMA WAS GONE.
SHE HAD GOTTEN WORRIED WHEN WE WERE GONE SO LONG... GRANDMA AND GRANDPA TRIED TO REASSURE HER BUT IT WAS NO USE.
SHE HAD A BAD EPISODE...
A DOCTOR AND SOME NURSES CAME TO CALM HER DOWN.
BUT SHE WAS TOO FAR GONE.
THEY HAD TO RUSH HER BACK TO LAVAUR.
15.

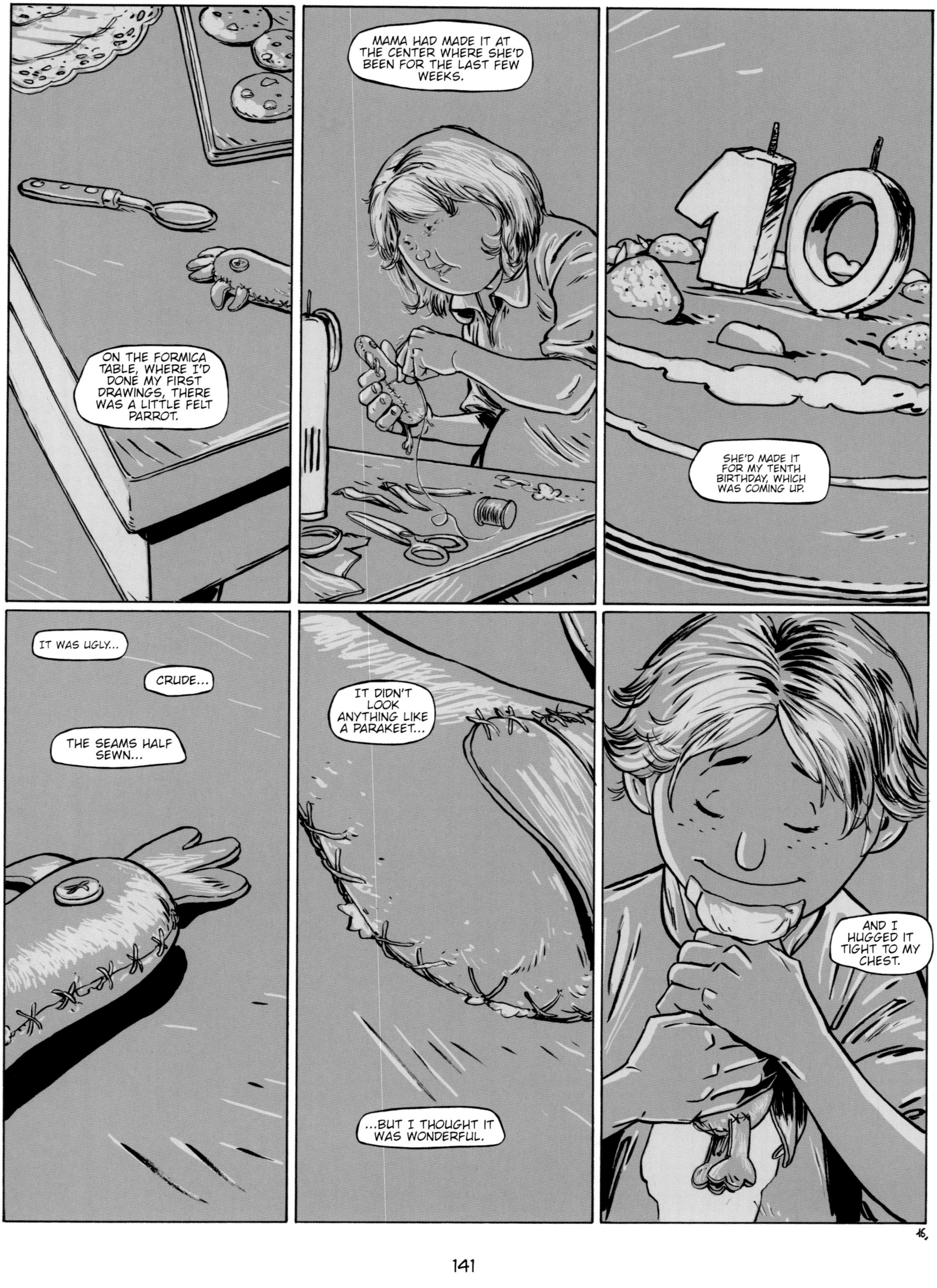
ON THE FORMICA TABLE, WHERE I'D DONE MY FIRST DRAWINGS, THERE WAS A LITTLE FELT PARROT.
MAMA HAD MADE IT AT THE CENTER WHERE SHE'D BEEN FOR THE LAST FEW WEEKS.
SHE'D MADE IT FOR MY TENTH BIRTHDAY, WHICH WAS COMING UP.
IT WAS UGLY...
CRUDE...
THE SEAMS HALF SEWN...
IT DIDN'T LOOK ANYTHING LIKE A PARAKEET...
...BUT I THOUGHT IT WAS WONDERFUL.
AND I HUGGED IT TIGHT TO MY CHEST.
16.

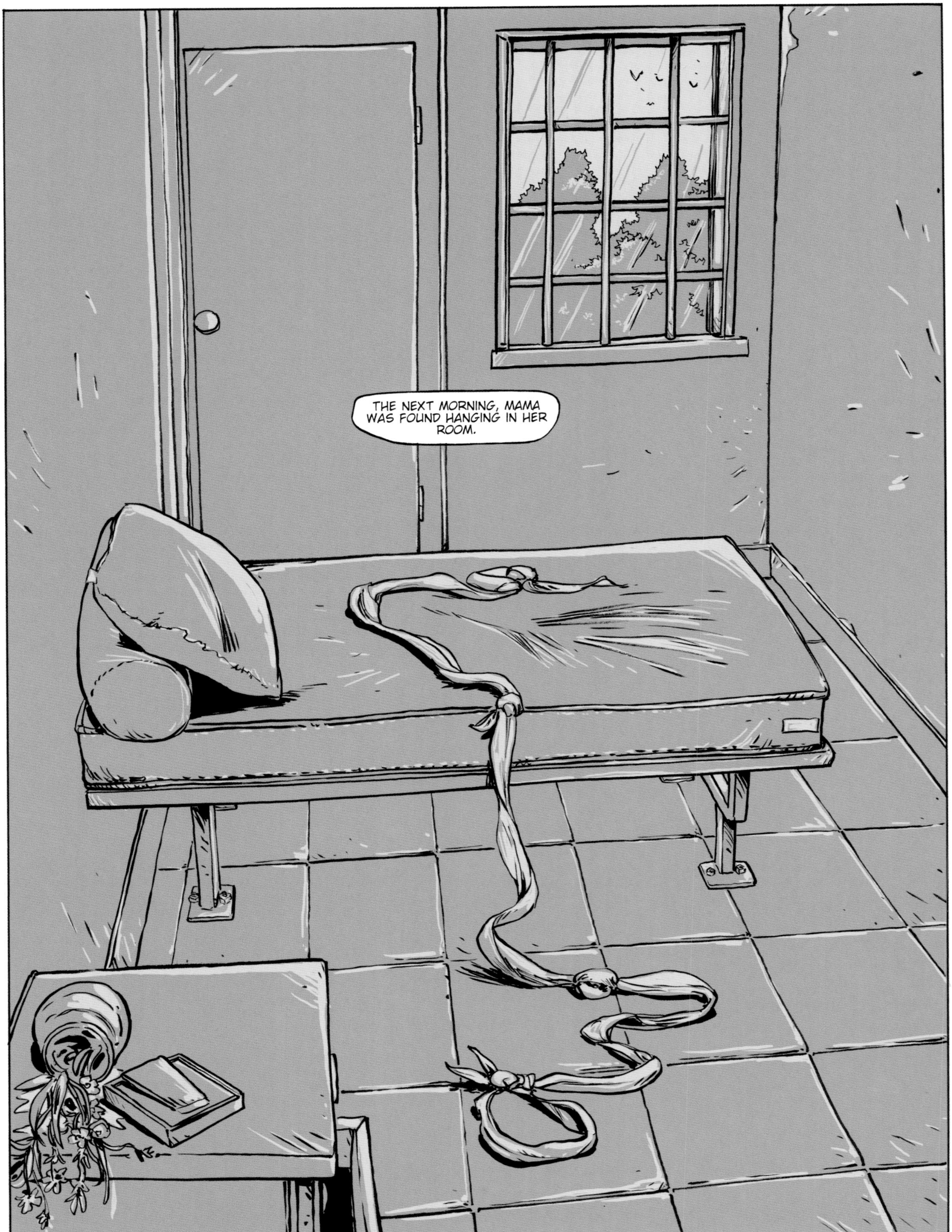
THE NEXT MORNING, MAMA WAS FOUND HANGING IN HER ROOM.

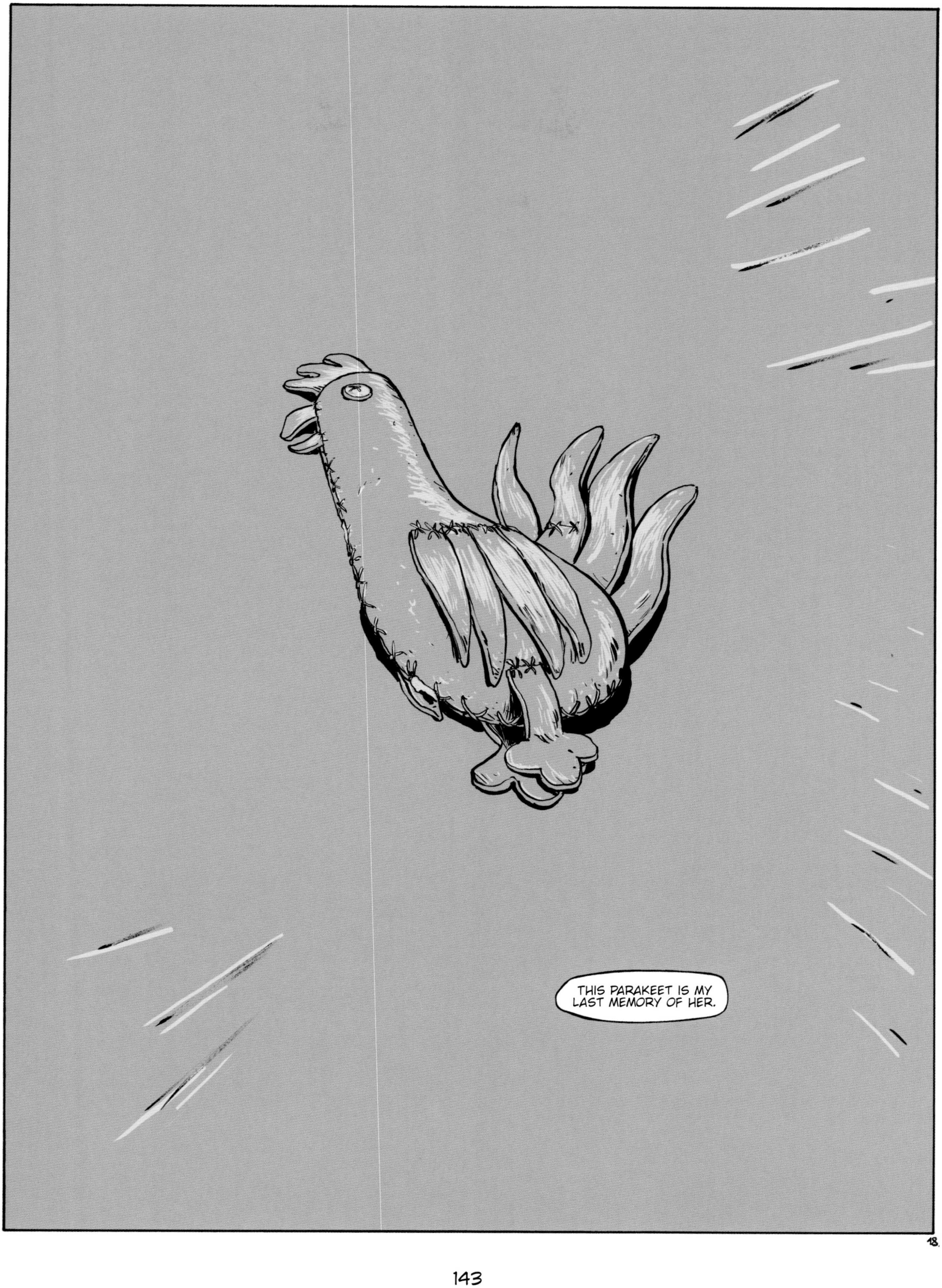
THIS PARAKEET IS MY LAST MEMORY OF HER.

18.

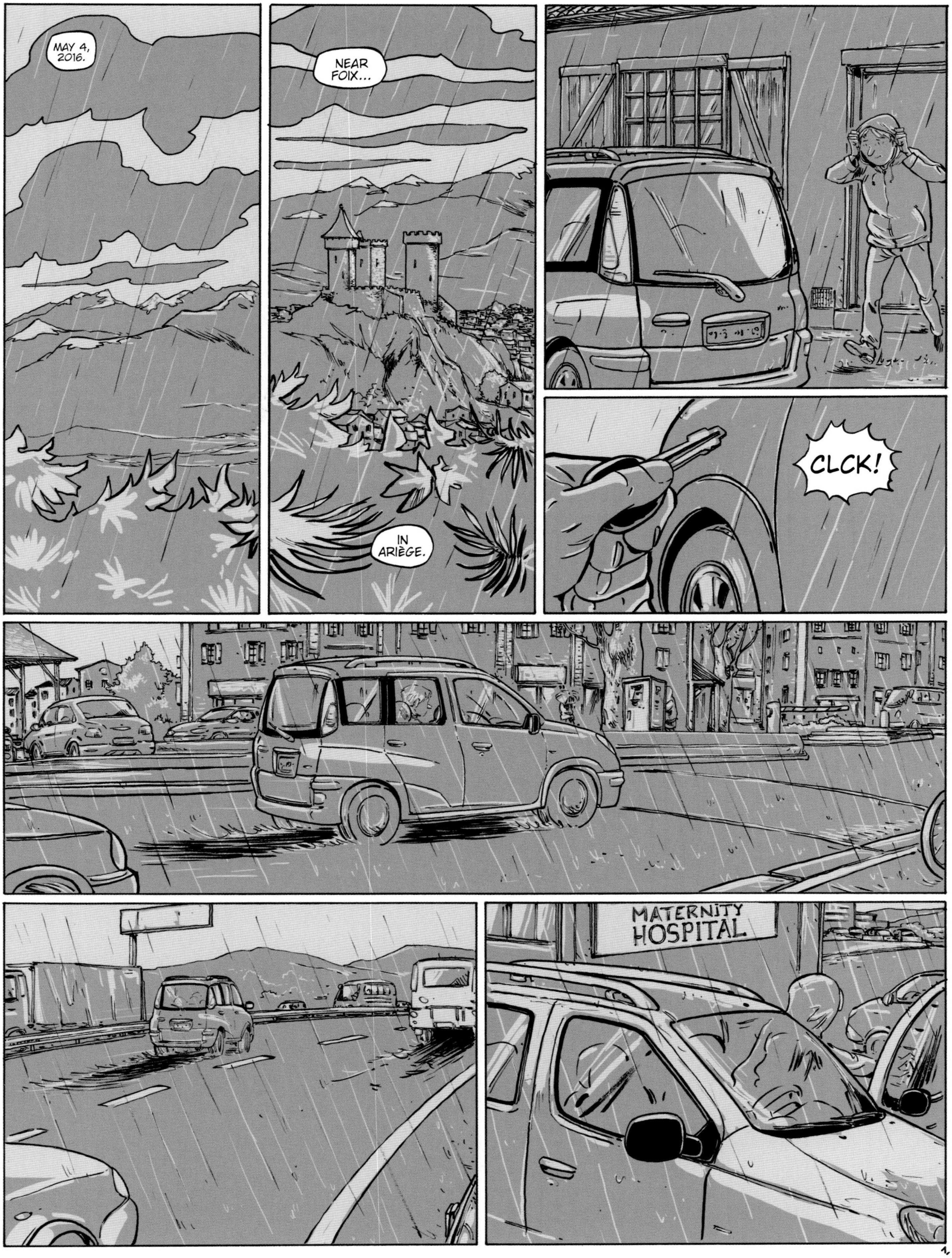
May 4, 2016.
Near Foix...
In Ariège.
CLCK!
Maternity Hospital
1

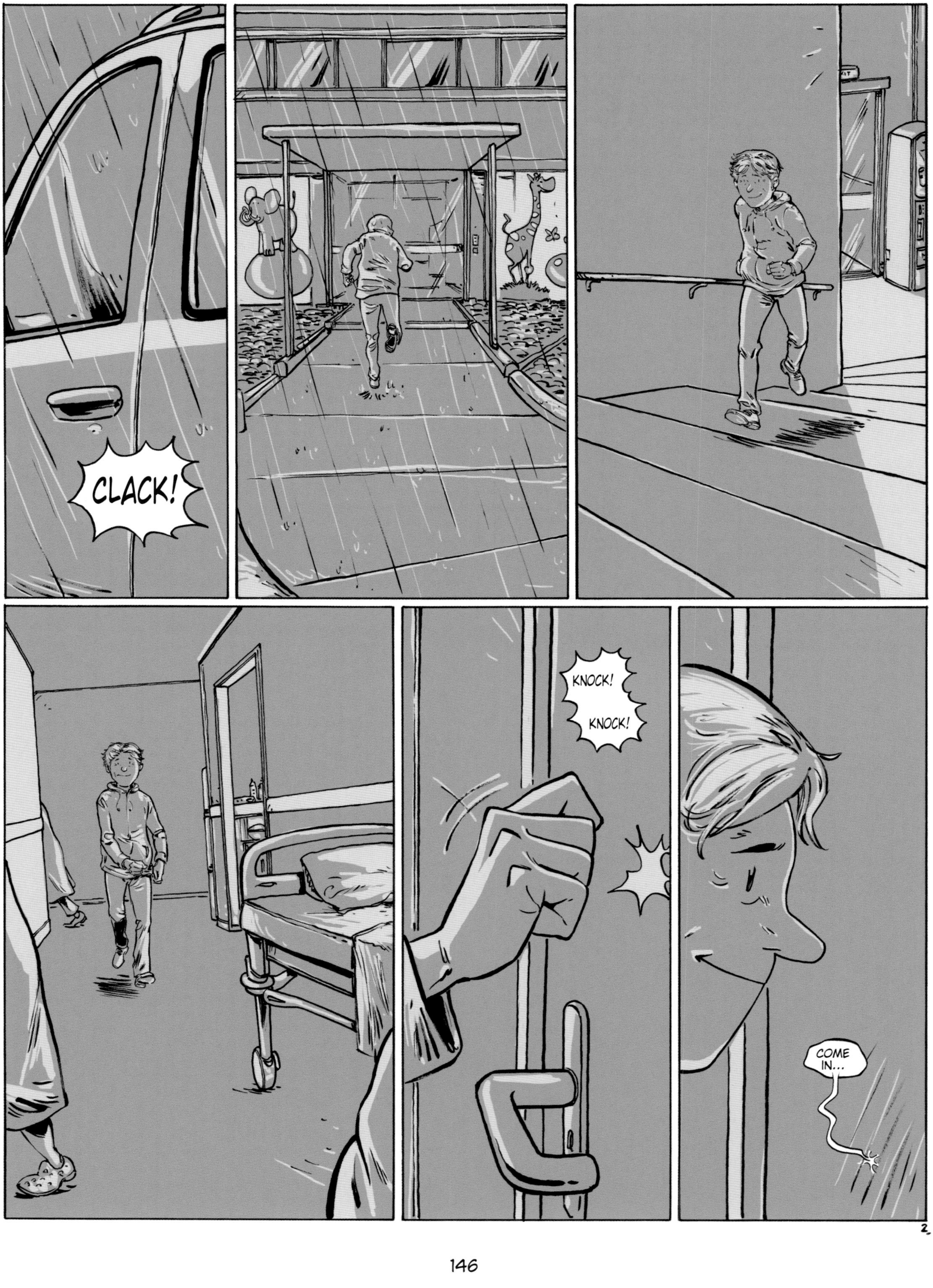
CLACK!
KNOCK!
KNOCK!
COME IN...

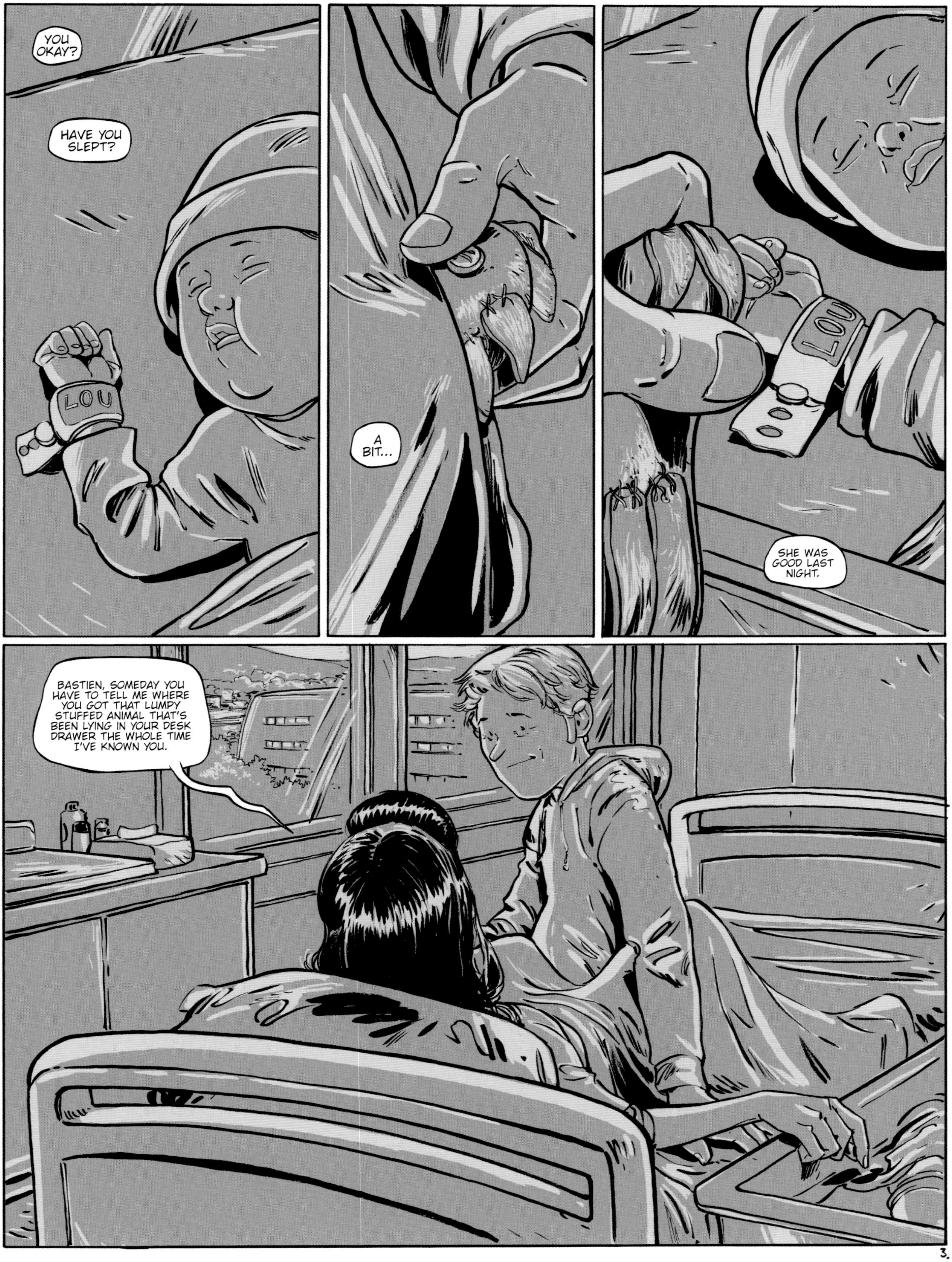
YOU OKAY?
HAVE YOU SLEPT?
A BIT...
SHE WAS GOOD LAST NIGHT.
BASTIEN, SOMEDAY YOU HAVE TO TELL ME WHERE YOU GOT THAT LUMPY STUFFED ANIMAL THAT'S BEEN LYING IN YOUR DESK DRAWER THE WHOLE TIME I'VE KNOWN YOU.
LOU
LOU
3.

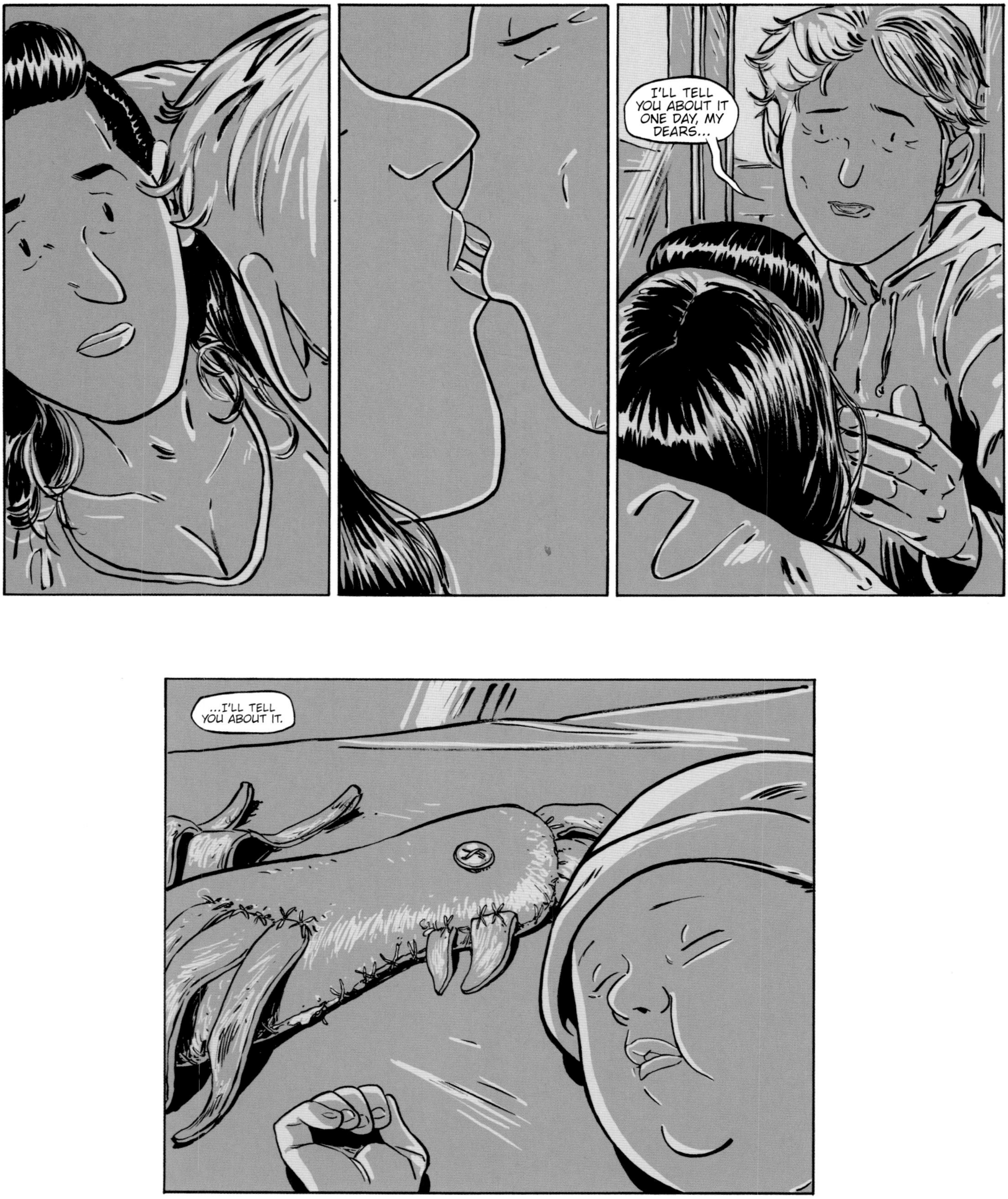
I'LL TELL YOU ABOUT IT ONE DAY, MY DEARS...
...I'LL TELL YOU ABOUT IT.

END